INTEGRATING THE ARTS IN THERAPY

ABOUT THE AUTHOR

Shaun McNiff is founder of the first integrated arts in therapy graduate program at Lesley University in Cambridge, Massachusetts. The discipline of expressive arts therapy emerged from the Lesley community and its international affiliates. McNiff's many books and writings have been translated into Chinese, Japanese, Korean, Spanish, Portuguese, Russian, German, and other languages. He is an exhibiting painter and an internationally recognized authority on the arts and healing, creativity enhancement, and art-based research which was first formulated by his writings. McNiff has received various honors and awards for his work and in 2002 Lesley appointed him as its first University Professor.

Pianofish [cover] by Shaun McNiff. Courtesy of Martha Barry McKenna.

ly read book, to document what I have learned from these difficulties and how the process of creation is informed by mistakes and uncertainties and requires the ability to stay with the discomfort they generate.

In my teaching, I discourage formulaic approaches to the work and ask students at every level to enter into their own firsthand experimentation with the material that we are studying. This goes counter to the desire for instruction that leads to the acquisition of established and predictable methods. A student recently told me with a smile how she had worked with both Paolo Knill and me and was taken aback by how two people who totally share core beliefs about expressive arts therapy can practice in such distinctly different ways. I replied that we are both artists who strive for this individuation of practice and I encouraged her to do the same.

What is constant in my teaching is an invitation to students to fully participate in the creative process and utilize their own resources of discovery and understanding. Even the most talented and adventurous students find it natural to resist the immersion in the unknown that accompanies creative expression and personal psychological inquiry. Thus the work has reliably generated tension.

I have learned that I need to stay with my beliefs and remember previous students who have successfully navigated this process of discovery. One of my former students, Stephanie Grenadier, who has become a leading expressive arts therapist and teacher, published what has become for me a landmark essay about her involvement with experiential learning. In writing about the need to abandon psychological formulas, she writes, "We are thrust into a perplexing tangle of unanswered questions and unclear destinations. We no longer lead; we follow and we don't really know where we are headed. But there is faith. Faith in Psyche's own predilection toward what needs to be or come into being" (1995, p. 401).

Therapists, teachers, and leaders need to persist through periods of creative disintegration during which others remake their worlds through the methods and materials that we introduce to them, realizing that we are figures within their inner dramas which will hopefully lead to a better understanding of experience.

Vivien Marcow Speiser who worked with me first as a student and then in founding The Arts Institute Project in Israel has committed her scholarship and practice to the role of conflict in creative transformation (Marcow Speiser & Speiser, 2005, 2007). She repeatedly says to me, "You taught me everything I know about conflict." As I predictably encounter the next instance of conflict in my own work together with the turmoil it evokes, I am buoyed by this affirmation. If I helped Marcow Speiser by demonstrating how to embrace conflict as an element of creation, she now returns the teaching when I need it. Conflict is unending, as W. B. Yeats said, and if we want to work closely with others and with the creative process, we must accept it and put it to use.

These conflicts and difficult moments with the work are formidable challenges for all of us, from the most inexperienced to the senior people in the field. When students ask: "How do you deal with it?"; I reply that I have learned how I need to open myself to the difficulty, take it in and hold it during a session, and then let it go. I describe how shamans practice "eating" pain and sickness as a way of healing another person, and they then need to discharge the toxins or allow them to pass through them. I cannot do the work if everything sticks to me. I have to let things go so I can open to what comes next.

As a leader, therapist, teacher, and artist, I allow the difficulties to act on me and then hold them in some way so that they help deliver me to a new understanding. After many years in various leadership positions within organizations, I can affirm the importance of empathy and being personally affected by the problems of groups. I value leaders who do not set themselves completely apart from the feelings of others, who do not profess to have easy resolutions, and who demonstrate how to creatively transform conflicts.

Those of us who stay with this work are strengthened by it and for me the challenge sustains involvement. Although there are many moments when transformations happen magically, the overall practice from my perspective is never easy, no matter how skilled and experienced we may become with the process. If it is easy; it is not the real thing. The work of healing and creative change tends to require a crucible, a certain alchemical cauldron, where elements can break in order to make anew. As I say in writing about my colleague Stephen K. Levine, we create with the shadow in expressive arts therapy (McNiff, 2008). Dark, fragmenting, uncertain, and troubling qualities are inevitably part of deep and major personal discoveries.

Perhaps the most reassuring and daunting message that I can offer to beginners based on my experience is the realization that self-doubt and crises of confidence are at the heart of the work. If I have been able to help others deal with these processes, it is because I have felt them so deeply myself. At this point in my career the dark and shadow elements of expressive arts therapy are more prominently part of my perspectives on practice. This is probably because I understand their necessary and formative roles better than I did in 1981 when writing *The Arts and Psychotherapy.*

I have also struggled throughout my career with the narrow thinking and prescription in professions. I keep discovering how professional groups, perhaps by necessity, are generally more concerned with self-preservation than with imagination and new creation. I have learned to accept this feature of life and also see the value of the more circumscribed positions regarding the arts and therapy and how they give me something provocative to engage and transform. My discontents have served as my most reliable and inspirational prompts for creation and inquiry.

There have been considerable challenges in advocating for integrated arts methods in a world that does take kindly to the blurring of boundaries. I have learned to accept these differences and embrace them as fuel in formulating my own vision of practice. I have also realized that it would be very boring without the push and pull of varied ideas, beliefs, and methods, as well as engagements with talented adversaries. However, all of us dealing with the arts and therapy, whether preferring narrow prescription or the full spectrum of creative expression in professional practice, share a common ground in relation to influencing health systems. I have always believed that every person trying to enhance the role of the arts in healthcare needs to give far more consideration to the shared commitment to healing through the creative process than to constructing barriers to collaboration.

A Comprehensive Focus on Practice

What distinguishes those of us who practice expressive arts therapy from more specialized creative arts therapists is the fact that we use multiple media. However, I must emphasize that the integration of media is not always a goal in my practice. My work is characterized by two distinct features, the integration of art forms and the use of different modes of expression. With regard to the latter approach, there are many occasions when we do not mix modalities. And even while integrating the arts, I like to say that when we paint we paint; when we sing we sing; and we always immerse ourselves in the distinct aspects of a particular medium. In this respect the arts are both separate and integrated in my work.

Frequently in my studios, I will introduce structures whereby we move from one mode of expression to another or simultaneously use different media, but I must emphasize in keeping with my original description in *The Arts and Psychotherapy* that the process of arts integration and the use of multiple modes of expression is a thoroughly natural and organic occurrence that happens on its own accord. This book strives to help readers become more sensitive to both the interplay of media as well as the distinguishing qualities of each mode of expression.

In addition to historical reflections on how expressive arts therapy has evolved since *The Arts and Psychotherapy* was published, this volume offers a more comprehensive focus on practice including suggestions for both arts integration and individual art forms. In keeping with what I said above, it is necessary to carefully examine the distinct properties of the arts; knowing more about their individual qualities furthers an understanding of their commonalities and how art modalities can relate to one another during an expressive arts therapy session. This appreciation of the particular healing qualities of different art forms underscores the respect that myself and others within expressive arts therapy have for those who chose to work exclusively with one medium.

When discussing a particular art mode, I will often mention how it relates to other art forms and sustains the more general process of integration. Also, each modality tends to contain the others within its expressions. For example, language has its kinesthetic, aural, visual, and theatrical dimensions. In this respect one form of sensory communication generally cannot exist without the others.

Since my discussion of practice suggestions deals almost exclusively with the dynamics of artistic expressions, one might ask: Where is the therapy? How is this different from arts education or a more generic approach to fostering creative expression?

These are important questions relating to the fundamental nature of professional expressive arts therapy practice and training. In my opinion the therapeutic and healing qualities of arts experiences are determined by the intentions and sense of purpose that participants, therapists, and institutions bring to the specific engagements.

Context and attitudes are thus major determinants as to whether or not making a dance, vocal improvisation, poem, painting, or the dramatic integration of these activities is determined to be therapeutic. Art is always art, and in my studios we strive to make the most creative and satisfying expressions possible; a factor that I also see as a determinant of therapeutic efficacy. As an expressive arts therapist, I am committed to the primacy of the art experience in every aspect of my practice and I have always found that the melding of artistic and therapeutic dimensions happens naturally.

Therapy is a point of view as well as a profession. For example, a retiree describes how he writes poetry because he enjoys it and it is therapeutic. In this respect, the pure experience of an art form unto itself can be profoundly therapeutic and healing outside the context of professional therapeutic practice (McNiff, 1992, 2004). I greatly value this self-help and public health dimension of expressive arts therapy and I hope that this book empowers readers who wish to understand more about how the arts heal and I urge more comprehensive personal practice and participation in schools, health and cultural centers, community programs, and every kind of institution that attempts in some way to serve people. I am especially committed to the encouragement of closer collaboration with arts educators, artists, and volunteers who have not always been welcomed as colleagues by creative arts therapy disciplines.

The professional practice of expressive arts therapy occurs within situations where trained and qualified therapists pursue these same healing objectives with people. The nature and purpose of the particular therapeutic setting whether it is a mental health clinic, a cancer treatment center, a hospice, a school for emotionally troubled children, a physical rehabilitation center, or other context, will inform the nature and purpose of the therapeutic activity. In this respect, the artistic practice suggestions that I provide are to be adapted to the particular mission of the therapeutic milieu as well as individual treatment goals provided by expressive arts therapists who serve as professionals within these varied settings.

Although I have learned that the core elements of what I do with people in the arts are relatively constant, the goals are always adapted to the needs of individual people and environments. As I say to my students, the applications of artistic practice in therapy are incessantly variable and something that we explore within the supervision of the work that they are doing with others. Even in the most purely artistic settings, expressive arts therapy is a clinical practice which is keenly sensitive to how the arts further both the overall well-being of people and the treatment of particular problems and needs.

The arts heal and further all forms of therapeutic practice by giving the psyche opportunities to treat itself through creative expression. This ability is unique to the arts and it accounts for the way in which C.G. Jung, James Hillman, D. W. Winnicott, J. L. Moreno, and others have embraced creative expression as the primary process of psychotherapy. In all of these approaches to therapeutic practice creative expression is given the freedom to move according to the immediate and infinitely variable conditions of a person's life. As we immerse ourselves in different arts experiences, they take us where we need to go and generate the medicines which heal in the ways I attempt to describe in this book–transforming tensions and conflicts into affirmations of life, enriching our appreciation of experience, and infusing creativity into our daily lives.

Like the dream, spontaneous artistic expressions give form to sensibilities, concerns, thoughts, and possibilities that lie outside our present awareness. Unlike the dream, creative expressions integrate the conscious and nonconscious workings of the psyche and give them tangible expression within the present moment. This special quality of the arts enables us to move between realms of consciousness in ways that are not possible in therapies based exclusively on verbal communication. Similarly, the use of all of the arts can further possibilities for expression and understanding beyond the limits of what can be done with a single medium.

These powers and intelligences of the arts and creative imagination have over the years taken my practice from the mental hospital and elementary schools where my career began to the realm of depth psychology and the lives of people in all sectors of society. Engaging the complexities of emotional experience through the arts has in turn reinforced the principles of simplicity, repetition, and immersion in the present moment that permeate this book. My work with groups throughout the United States, Canada, Israel, and many countries of Europe keeps taking me back to my point of beginning, back to the most basic things that I did at Danvers State Hospital, back to the place from which all the streams flow and ultimately return to "run again."

II. ESTABLISHING EXPRESSIVE ARTS THERAPY

A DISCIPLINE OF ARTS INTEGRATION

I am often asked by students to describe how I started my own work in expressive arts therapy and how the discipline grew and took shape over the past four decades. Since so much of the formal organization of the expressive arts therapy discipline grew from initiatives at Lesley University during the 1970s and 1980s, I will attempt in this section to give an account of how this context was established and the way it opened to other historic and archetypal aspects of integrated arts practice.[1]

Creating an Expressive Arts Therapy Studio at Danvers State Hospital, 1970–1974

When I first set up an expressive arts therapy studio at Danvers State Hospital in early 1970, I tried to create a place charged with artistic energies that would act upon all of the people involved. Having been trained to paint in the abstract expressionist tradition while a college student in New York City during the mid 1960s my natural inclination was to foster an environment where people could express themselves freely and spontaneously.

At Danvers, a large state hospital offering a psychiatric residency program in cooperation with the Massachusetts General Hospital, I had the opportunity at the age of 23 to participate in group therapy training programs and supervision that introduced me to the therapeutic community movement initiated by Maxwell Jones. I later established a relationship with Jones whose therapeutic community studies (1968, 1982) resonated with my values. He introduced me to the social psychiatry community and supported a focus on

---

1 In the Netherlands where there is a long tradition of viewing creativity as a core therapeutic process underlying all media, the government supports undergraduate schools training students to practice what is call *kreative therapie*. These Dutch programs predate the emergence of expressive arts therapy. Throughout most of Europe and the world, specialized work in a single modality was prevalent when we began our work at Lesley.

15

Figure 1. Danvers State Hospital (photograph by Don Snyder-courtesy of J.M. Snyder, Addison Gallery of American Art).

the arts and the creative process. In Jones, I discovered a mentor whose democratic values regarding therapeutic treatment, both in terms of empowering patients and leveling the hierarchies in mental health professions, affirmed the vision that I held for the new expressive arts therapy discipline.

In the hospital studio I explored how group experiences and a creative community spirit could influence people. The studio became an artistic sanctuary within an often harsh and bleak institutional setting. From these first experiences I developed a sustained and lifelong commitment to making creative spaces and communities as the principal goal of my practice. I repeatedly witnessed how the studio environment, viewed as a therapeutic milieu, will act upon people in different ways and that each of us can receive what we need from the overall circulation of creative energy. My primary job, then and now, was to lead and cultivate the creative space that people made together. This approach to practice has been equally relevant to my work outside therapy in schools and organizational leadership.

Soon after I began to work as an expressive arts therapist, Rudolf Arnheim agreed to supervise my studies in a field-based graduate program at Goddard College. Arnheim, the world's leading figure in the psychology of art and then at Harvard University, was the only person who responded to a letter I sent to a number of professors at institutions in the greater Boston area in search of field faculty advisor. My relationship with him was the single-most influential factor in solidifying a commitment to expressive arts therapy in the 1970s. In Arnheim, I discovered a role model for integrating my artistic, psychological, therapeutic, and educational interests (McNiff, 1975, 1994, 2007).

Within the art and mental health literature, I was attracted to Hans Prinzhorn's presentation of art made by emotionally troubled people and his reflections on how these expressions responded to universal human urges (1972). The life-affirming tendencies that Prinzhorn described were consistent with Arnheim's beliefs and what I was experiencing in the expressive arts therapy studio where the creative process had a generally helpful impact on participants. In addition to the benefits received through expression, art making was a source of personal individuation that brought a sense of dignity to people living on the hospital wards. Prinzhorn's studies focused on the positive and objective qualities of artworks as contrasted to the negative and highly speculative psychiatric approaches to art analysis that characterized the mental health field at the time.

With the more handicapped and disturbed hospital residents, who had difficulty with self-motivated creative expression, I used the arts to further relationships with others and the environment. Inspired by Arnheim's writings I explored how the process of making art objects and then reflecting upon them with the assistance of spoken language furthered perceptual and more general behavioral awareness. I also researched the application of these methods with children (McNiff, 1974, 1976).

In keeping with the research of Gestalt psychologists in the area of visual perception (Köhler, 1970), we discovered that if people could perceive balance, movement, beauty, and other aspects when looking at an art object, there was a parallel effect on consciousness. The same principles were applied to my use of music, movement, and the other arts (McNiff, 1973).

During my second year at Danvers, Arnheim sent me a student from the Harvard Divinity School and then another from Harvard College and a third MFA student from the School of the Museum of Fine Arts in Boston. Students from other local colleges joined us and with this team I began my lifework in expressive arts therapy education and training.

In later years as my studios connected the arts with depth psychology as a result of the needs of the people with whom I worked, Arnheim's influence remained constant. His studies of the autonomous way structural configurations in artworks in every medium conveyed expression established the basis for my lifelong commitment to engaging them as partners within expressive arts therapy (McNiff, 1994; 2007).

Varied forms of artistic expression have emerged naturally in my practice with others. When I first began to work with the visual arts at Danvers State Hospital, poems, music, dance, and drama happened spontaneously. The same thing occurred in my early work with young children.

My interest in using all of the arts was primarily driven by a pragmatic attempt to engage the whole person and the expressive potential that people brought to the studio. The emergence of integrated arts practice as a deliberate method of engaging adults and children was informed by collaboration with Karen Gallas (1994). While I was beginning to work at Danvers State Hospital, Gallas was starting her career as an educator of young children. She introduced me to informal and integrative education practices that corresponded closely to my experiences in therapy.

Karen Gallas had studied integrated arts methods in an open education graduate program at Lesley University from 1971–1972. These progressive educators were attuned to how creative expression affects learning and change at a time when mental health systems focused almost exclusively on the so-called psychopathology of art. The educators were also more open to how the creative process works, how individuals and groups make use of the complete spectrum of cognitive and emotional faculties, and like Maxwell Jones, they were keenly sensitive to community and environmental dynamics.

These experiences with young children and teachers informed my first theoretical investigations into the process of arts integration. Educators at that time were seriously involved in examining how learning is enhanced by varied sensory activities and media of expression. Their methods emphasized the flow from one mode of inquiry to another and how access to a spectrum of creative possibilities furthers understanding. Gallas describes how "children do not *naturally* limit the forms their expressions take" (1994, p. xv). It is the inflexibility of institutions and, especially in my opinion, professions, that restrict innate communications. Gallas asks what education might become if opportunities are given for children to "expand, rather than narrow" their expressions through every form of artistic expression (p. xvi).

The poems, dances, songs, rhythms, enactments, and stories that people created in the expressive arts therapy studio established an overall creative environment where the different forms of expression enhanced one another. My discipline became the whole landscape of artistic expression and media. Within the hospital there were no formal or departmental divisions between the arts that often create the separations that exist in schools, universities, and the creative arts therapies. I was encouraged to work with all art forms.

In addition to feeling that I needed to respect and support all forms of artistic expression in the expressive arts therapy studio, I discovered that I was more stimulated and challenged when all of the arts were all present. I observed how people will often gravitate toward particular forms of expression and I also learned how the media that we may avoid and/or fear sometimes bring the most striking therapeutic outcomes. I saw how the arts reinforced and informed one another, and how expression in one medium can flow naturally into another.

We studied how shifting media can help us as Jung said, to "imagine further," go deeper into a situation, experience it differently, clarify a feeling, intensify or diminish an emotion, or simply sustain the energy and benefits of creative expression.

The engagement of all of the senses was important in itself, but I also learned how creative movement and dance might inform painting; how poetic language emerged from reflections on artistic expressions in other media; how everything we did in the arts demonstrated qualities of dramatic enactment. In keeping with the classical definition of creative imagination as a gathering and synthesis of all expressive faculties, including reason (Richter, 1973), I observed how our studio became a more stimulating and creative environment when all of the arts were welcomed.

Through every phase of my practice of expressive arts therapy I have worked with groups of people, sometimes engaging entire communities in the arts. Within this context, where the goal is typically the release and appreciation of creative expression, it has always been natural to welcome all art forms.

When engaging groups and communities the inclusion of varied forms of creativity corresponds to the different interests and abilities that exist within every group. I apply this same line of thought to the individual person, emphasizing how we have a range of expressive resources and possibilities within us; how the person is analogous to the group where we want to affirm the spectrum of expressive potential and how different modes of creative activity reinforce one another and build a dynamic whole.

The group environment, especially when fostered in an open and receptive way, naturally elicits varied forms of expression. In this sense, the spontaneous creations of participants in the expressive therapy studio formed the basis for establishing an integrated arts approach to practice.

Cooperation with the Addison Gallery of American Art, 1972–1978

During the third year of the Danvers expressive arts therapy program, the Addison Gallery of American Art at Phillips Academy in nearby Andover organized a major exhibit of the patients' art. We were awarded a grant by the Massachusetts Council for Arts and Humanities which enabled the exhibition to travel to university galleries and museums throughout the Northeast (McNiff, 1974). The public response to the exhibit was enthusiastic and the Addison Gallery committed itself to becoming actively involved in the Danvers expressive arts therapy studio. Christopher Cook, the museum director, joined our studio team and brought students from the academy to sessions over a two-year period.

Cook, a conceptual artist, was immersed in the new portable video technology as an art form and he wanted to explore its therapeutic applications with me. When group participants were given the opportunity to express themselves on camera, all of the arts emerged spontaneously—dance, song,

Figure 2. Video Session inside Danvers Studio.

instrumental music, performance art, drama, storytelling, the reading of poetry, and other forms of expression with a common emphasis on improvisation (McNiff & Cook, 1975).

After two years of successful use of video in the Danvers studio, Cook established an expressive arts therapy program at the Addison Gallery and reached out to people within the cities and towns surrounding the academy. We created expressive arts therapy studios in two of the most prominent spaces of the museum, hired an expressive arts therapy staff, and invited the entire spectrum of child and adult mental health programs within the surrounding communities to become involved in the museum program. It was a bold and radical initiative to bring truly hard core expressive arts therapy programs into an eminent art museum. Sherman Lee, the esteemed Director of The Cleveland Museum of Art, reflected the antipathy in some quarters to what we were doing when he said, "Art is not therapy . . . or social uplift and a museum is not a community center" (Temin, 1991).

As might be expected, the permanent museum staff of curators, administrators, maintenance workers, and guards did not know what to make of our expressive arts therapy program at first. But within a short time, as they established relationships with patients and children who visited the museum, they all made their unique contributions to the overall therapeutic atmosphere by approaching what we were doing as thoroughly natural and valuable. In keeping with the operation of therapeutic communities described by Maxwell Jones (1968, 1982), the staff took pride in the program and became major contributors to its positive energy and creative spirit.

The Addison was one of the first museums to dedicate itself to American art and we worked every day in expressive arts therapy studios constructed in galleries adjoining the permanent collection of leading American artists that included Homer, Cassatt, Hopper, Dove, Hartley, O'Keefe, Pollock, Stella, and many more. We often held our sessions in the company of these masterpieces and my first work with image dialogue involved patients in playful videotaped conversations with paintings by Whistler and Eakins that had become familiar figures to them.

The entire museum became a therapeutic milieu. It was an unusual program, described in the 1977 volume *The Art Museum as Educator* (Newsome & Silver), which grew from the social change values of the 1970s and attracted considerable public attention and a talented staff. I worked with a team of Lesley graduate students and drove patients from Danvers for weekly sessions at the Addison Gallery which served as a bridge to living outside the hospital. Many of the adult artists discussed in the following section created works within the Addison program.

We used the permanent collection frequently in our expressive arts therapy activities, encouraging participants to establish relationships with individual works of art, but there is no doubt that the entirety of the museum's physical and human environment had the most lasting impact of every person involved. Participants in the program as well as expressive arts therapy staff members described how they were affected by the overall space of the museum and I believe that this mutuality of influence and inspiration was the most influential feature of the program. Participants spoke consistently about how they were inspired and personally elevated by the environment, how they were influenced by particular exhibits and artworks, and how proud they were to be part of Addison Gallery community.

The Addison Gallery experiences solidified my lifelong commitment to the use of new media and the work revealed how video inspires and supports expression in every art form. Making a video encouraged us to gather together all of the arts and in this respect the medium was a major factor in generating expressive arts therapy practice and the process of total expression with all of the senses. The camera elicited expressions in the most comprehensive media which in turn responded to the need for video content. The video sessions provided consistent opportunities for the creation of methods that furthered integrated arts practice. When the benefits of complete expressive arts therapy experiences became clear to me, I continued to work in this way "off camera."

Figure 3. Danvers Group inside Addison Gallery.

Figure 4. Danvers Group outside the Addison Gallery.

Adoption of the Term Expressive Therapy, 1972–1974

In 1972, two years before establishing the Lesley University graduate program, William Goldman, MD, the Commissioner of Mental Health for the Commonwealth of Massachusetts, appointed me to represent "expressive therapy" on his advisory committee for professional training and staff development within the state's Department of Mental Health. This was my first official involvement with all of the arts in therapy. Goldman introduced the term expressive therapy in Massachusetts and defined it as a joining of all of the creative arts therapies. In addition to representing art therapy on the committee, I spoke for music therapy, dance therapy, drama therapy, psychodrama, poetry therapy, and bibliotherapy.

The experience of sitting at the table with all of the major mental health professions underscored the importance of joining the creative arts therapies as a single unit with profound similarities. Even as a combined arts therapy discipline we were tiny when compared to the larger mental health professions. I have never deviated from this practical realization and continue to hope that someday the creative arts therapy community will unite in common interest.

Goldman was promoting multidisciplinary training and collaboration in all sectors of the Department of Mental Health. If expressive arts therapists were being urged to train with psychiatrists, nurses, social workers, psychologist, and other professionals, it made little sense to emphasize the separation of the different arts therapies. The Department of Mental Health was striving to ease the barriers between disciplines rather than increase the number of professions. Although different domains of practice were recognized and affirmed, our work was focused on what they shared and how effective treatment requires teamwork.

I resonated deeply with these values and when given the opportunity to start a graduate program at Lesley University, I chose to call our discipline expressive therapy and to organize the first completely integrated arts approach to training. The University of Louisville art therapy graduate program predated Lesley and used the term expressive therapy, but their focus was on visual art therapy.

Through my work with the Department of Mental Health, we were able to secure a grant for Lesley to create a multidisciplinary clinical training program that enabled expressive arts therapy students to train together with psychologists, social workers, and other mental health disciplines. The values of integration and cross-disciplinary cooperation permeated every aspect of our Lesley programs.

Lesley Beginnings, 1973 and 1974

Through contacts established by Karen Gallas, I offered my first art therapy graduate course at Lesley in January of 1973, an intensive month-long session primarily involving students in special education. Other well-enrolled evening courses followed in 1973 while I was working at Danvers, and in early 1974, I left the hospital and started the expressive therapy and integrated arts in education graduate programs at Lesley.

I had just turned 27 and in addition to directing and developing graduate programs at Lesley, I was also coordinating the Addison Gallery project. The responsibilities at the Addison complemented my Lesley courses and I worked with a team of graduate students in offering comprehensive expressive arts therapy experiences to various groups of children, adolescents, and adults at the museum.

Both the therapy and education programs at Lesley were committed to integrating the arts and other disciplines. We espoused progressive ideals within a period that supported more creative ways of working with others and relaxing boundaries between professional domains. In a guest editorial entitled "Strategies for Unification" that I wrote in 1975 for the Newsletter of the Educational Arts Association, I emphasize how art must be open to all forms of expression if it is to relate to the whole person. Like so many other innovative organizations, the Educational Arts Association was short-lived and it is striking that the Lesley programs have been sustained with considerable vitality over four decades. Lesley became the institutional anchor for the work that we did with others.

The vision informing our work at Lesley was a desire to establish a community and ways of working with people that gathered together all of arts. The two master's degree programs were offered by the Institute for the Arts and Human Development that I established in Lesley's expanding graduate school.

We created courses and concentrations in the particular modalities of visual art, dance, drama, poetry, psychodrama, creative writing, and storytelling. Students were encouraged to explore all of these areas, as well as courses focused on the integration of the arts, and then create individual ways of combining media according to their interests, expressive styles, and the needs of the people with whom they worked. I described what we were doing as a liberal arts approach to training; we offered a breadth of studies that supported endless combinations and variations of the integrative process. Rather than creating a particular method for integrating the arts, I was more interested, then and now, in how the creative process will work most effectively and find new directions for practice when it has access to varied resources.

The Expressive Therapy masters program was organized in a way that allowed students to select different core groups where they worked together over the course of the academic year. In addition to core groups focused on arts integration we offered choices in single modalities–art therapy, dance therapy, music therapy, and psychodrama–largely in response to the interest that some students had in focusing on a particular art form. These specialized groups were also created because a number of faculty members, the majority even within our interdisciplinary community, were more comfortable when they concentrated their teaching on one modality.

In my own case, the visual arts have always been what I call "the trunk of my integration tree." I work with all of the arts but visual expression, and especially painting, serve as my primary discipline both in my work with others and in my personal artistic expression. Yet in my studios, movement, performance, voice, and poetic expression tend to play a role equal in importance to the visual arts. Paolo Knill who was my principle partner at Lesley in developing expressive arts therapy is primarily a musician and he reached out to integrate all of the arts from his history with that discipline.

In the first years of our Lesley program, we discovered how students explored the integrative process in many different ways, affirming our approach to offering a variety of options for study. A number of students, following a more conservative path, continued with familiar tracts in a particular artistic discipline. However, the Lesley program at that time required them to study other media in keeping with the purpose of integrative expressive arts therapy. These requirements were welcomed by the students and they chose Lesley because of them.

I was especially intrigued by the common pattern of a professional dancer deciding to join the visual art therapy group, or a painter with an MFA degree selecting dance or psychodrama as a focus. The frequency of these choices and student satisfaction with the outcomes bolstered our approach to integrating the arts.

These artists not only learned new ways of expression in different media but they found that the expansion of their expressive repertoires strengthened work with their original artistic disciplines. But most importantly, everyone was striving to use the enlargement of personal expression as a way of helping others express themselves in the widest range of artistic modalities. The primary goal of the Lesley program was training expressive arts therapists to further creative expression in whatever forms met the individual needs of the people and groups with whom they worked. We learned how there can be considerable educational advantages in focusing studies on areas of expression where a person perceives deficits. This approach not only helped to enlarge our range of expression, but it furthered a deeper understanding of the dynamics of different media and empathy with others who may feel inadequate with certain art forms.

Over the first 20 years of our work at Lesley, the majority of students selected the integrated arts approach to expressive arts therapy. They pursued a core course of studies that explored relationships amongst the arts and then augmented their education with individual courses in dance therapy, art therapy, and other disciplines.

Two Wings of One Flight: Co-creation with Paolo Knill

Paolo Knill was my longstanding colleague in the first two decades of developing the new discipline of integrated expressive arts therapy. He was a visiting professor in music and child development at Tufts University when I met him soon after opening the Lesley program. Norma Canner, the prominent dance therapist who was the first faculty member that I brought to Lesley, was working together with Knill, Mariagnese Cattaneo, Iris Fanger, and Elizabeth McKim as a creative arts team at the Eliot-Pearson Department of Child Development and the Summer Institute of the Department of Education at Tufts. I recruited him to teach, first as an adjunct since he was still committed to positions in his native Switzerland. When it became clear that the Lesley program would continue, he joined us full time in 1976.

My first major goal in establishing the Lesley program was appointing Norma Canner to the faculty, feeling that her presence would give credibility to the program and help attract students and other talented faculty. All of her colleagues at Tufts, including Knill, ultimately joined us. Canner, the eldest member of the faculty group, was an anchor of community during our first 15 years, helping to resolve differences and sustaining a common purpose. She had a formative impact on my practice as my core orientations to simplicity, the movement and bodily basis of all expression, the creative potential of groups, the ability of untrained people to make significant artistic expressions, the use of natural sounds with no recorded music, and letting creative forms emanate from spontaneous gestures, were all reinforced by collaboration with her.

Beginning her career as an actor directly from high school, Canner later studied creative movement with Barbara Mettler whose work reinforced the natural and essential expression that we both cultivated. Although masterful at integrating the arts and inspiring all of our students, Canner became increasingly focused on the dance therapy community and body-oriented psychotherapy, working closely with Myron Sharaf, an authority on Wilhelm Reich who also joined our faculty.

Knill and I sustained the focus on integrating the arts. He engaged all of the arts in his courses, led the first core group in "expressive therapy," and formed his own method called "intermodal expressive therapy" (Knill, 1978,

1995). Originally trained as both a musician and as an engineer Knill had a natural inclination toward establishing an infrastructure and systems for arts integration. I affectionately called him the "engineer" of expressive arts therapy as I continued with my commitment to a liberal arts approach to training within our Institute, encouraging these different ways of achieving common goals.

I was committed in the first years of our program to close collaboration with psychologists and psychiatrists. But over time, we discovered that few were dedicated to reciprocal learning in the arts. As we began to experience bifurcation rather than integration with required courses in the general areas of psychotherapy and diagnostic methods, Knill took on the task of teaching and developing an arts-centric curriculum for these fundamental courses based on what we called "theory indigenous to art" (McNiff, 1986). His assessment course engaged the *Diagnostic and Statistical Manual of Mental Disorders*, the most essential of medical model texts, from an arts perspective.

In developing courses that explored methods for working with all of the arts Knill coined technical terms such as "intermodal transfer" [moving directly from one modality to another] and "low skill-high sensitivity" [facilitating competence in artistic expression regardless of the person's formal art training] (Knill, Barba, & Fuchs, 1995, pp. 147–153).

Paolo Knill's teaching was so successful that many had a tendency to define the integrated arts approach to expressive arts therapy as "intermodal." I have not personally used this term to describe the whole context of what we did at Lesley and the discipline of expressive arts therapy that grew from our work in Cambridge, but I recognize it as an important thread of expressive arts therapy initiated by Knill and adopted by many of his students. In recent years, Knill also describes our all-encompassing discipline as expressive arts therapy which involves intermodal theory and methods together with other approaches, including my own.

The early growth of expressive arts therapy was closely tied to my collaboration with Paolo Knill. Amongst the original faculty, we maintained a complete commitment to arts integration. At the very start of the Lesley program, I served as the director and dean. When Knill joined us full time, he began to expand his teaching in music to focus more on perfecting the discipline of expressive arts therapy. He took my art therapy class and also attended Norma Canner's dance therapy classes, poetry with Elizabeth McKim, and psychodrama sessions with Joseph Powers. Knill probably spent as much time in other people's classes as he did teaching, and this mode of learning and research was consistent with more general liberal approach to training. I was similarly involved in closely studying how Knill used music and how other colleagues worked with the different forms of artistic expression. In 1975, we wrote our first article together describing our experimentation with the integration of the visual arts and music.

During this period, Knill wrote his doctoral dissertation on *Intermodal Learning in Education and Therapy* (1978) and I served on his committee. As I reflect on my career and lifework, I see how important Paolo Knill was in sustaining my involvement with integrated arts practice in therapy. I founded the Lesley graduate program on the basis of an idea and he was the faculty member who responded to it most completely and ultimately dedicated his life and considerable genius to it. This pattern continued in my collaboration with Knill. I would typically introduce an idea or new direction for the work in a conversation or in an essay draft that he would read, and he would immediately begin to work it, connect to other ideas, enlarge it, and help establish its presence in the world. He read everything I wrote in draft form and became an invaluable source of support and affirmation as I explored new ways of perceiving expressive arts therapy practice. Knill also arranged for the translation of a number of my early writings into German and initiated his own considerable record of publications in Germany and Switzerland (1979, 1983).

Our work together was itself a gathering of expressions and ideas that corresponded to integrated arts practice. Where Emily Dickinson described how her purpose was "to sing what matters if no one listens," I needed the kind of listening, responding, igniting, and transformative action that Paolo Knill provided. He was my closest colleague and we experimented on a daily basis until he left Lesley in 1994. We researched integrated arts practices, connections between expressive arts therapy and shamanism, arts-based research, and many other strains of practice that grew from the Lesley community.

I began to refer to my philosophical orientation to practice as *Gesamtkunstwerk*, literally meaning total artwork, but we expanded the notion to total expression. This nod to Knill's language and to the history of integrated arts practice in German artistic history pleased him greatly.

The term *Gesamtkunstwerk* grew from a tradition of German and English scholars who viewed the creative imagination as an intelligence that integrates all of a person's expressive faculties. In mid seventeenth century England, Thomas Hobbes viewed imagination as a connecting and integrating power which functions organically as contrasted to mechanistic and linear chains of thought. Similarly, imagination was described by Mark Akenside as a mediating intelligence, a "middle place" between perception and reason (1744), and by Samuel Taylor Coleridge as an "intermediate faculty" and "esemplastic power" capable of making new syntheses from varied sources (Coleridge, 1817). Corresponding initiatives took place within the German-speaking world where Jean-Paul Richter, in his classic *Vorschule der Aesthetik* (1804), extolled imagination as the "faculty of faculties" which collected all of the other forms of knowing into a holistic and transcendent intelligence.

Figure 5. Paolo Knill and Shaun McNiff in Israel.

I like to imagine Paolo Knill and myself as sustaining this tradition of imagination in thought and practice. In a 2002 essay about my work with Knill, I described our interactions as an ongoing "conversation" and how the process of these exchanges is a "transformative environment" that parallels the integration of the arts. New ideas and expressions spring from the "communal conversation" of creativity that offers much more than an individual mind working alone.

The Creation of International Training Sites, 1980–1994

Paolo Knill was also a close partner in furthering the international development of expressive arts therapy. Throughout his time at Lesley, he stayed closely connected to Switzerland and Germany. Beginning in the late 1970s, he established collaborations with Hans-Helmut Decker-Voigt, the well-known German music therapist, that continue to this day. He recruited many gifted German-speaking students to Lesley, and this infusion of international talent greatly enhanced our overall community.

In addition to my work with Knill, partnerships with two Lesley graduates were the basis for the widespread international development of expressive arts therapy in the 1980s. In the late 1970s, Vivien Marcow Speiser, a 1977 Lesley graduate who was living in Israel, made me aware of the great interest in the arts in therapy within that country. I worked with her and other Israeli colleagues in establishing the Arts Institute Project in Israel. This program grew in a dramatic way, becoming a major focus for all of us. The Israeli project ultimately became larger than the Cambridge program and it has had a major influence both in Israel and the world. The international partnership continues to this day.

Shortly after establishing the affiliate programs in Israel, Phillip Speiser, a 1978 graduate, invited me to Sweden where he was establishing The Scandinaviska Institutet for Uttrykande Konst (Scandinavian Institute for Expressive Arts) in Gothenburg in 1980. Speiser shared my commitment to arts integration in both therapy and education. He organized an annual Nordic Conference on Expressive Arts which promoted these methods, and I gave the keynote at the first conference in 1982 and worked closely with him in developing the institute which grew to include affiliates in Denmark, Norway, and Finland as well as Sweden.

Beginning with the Israeli program, affiliation agreements where established where students traveled to Lesley during the summer and worked toward a master degree combining studies in their home country and Cambridge. The model was successful and the international summer school was expanded to include students from the Scandinavian institute and an affiliate that we established with Paolo Knill in Germany and Switzerland, the Lesley Institut für Medien und Ausdruckstherapie (The Lesley Institute for Media and Expressive Therapy, LIMA).

In 1985, LIMA changed its name to ISIS, the International School for Interdisciplinary Studies, and in 1991, Stephen K. Levine and Ellen Levine established ISIS Canada in Toronto which also cooperated with Lesley. Stephen Levine had spent the 1985–1986 year as a post-doctoral fellow at Lesley and became a significant figure in the development of expressive arts therapy in Canada and then on an international scale. He was a social science professor at York University and began teaching courses in expressive arts therapy at York upon returning from Lesley.

In the 1980s, American affiliations were established with Bruce Moon's graduate-level art therapy clinical training program at Harding Hospital in Ohio and Mount Mary College's art therapy training program in Milwaukee, led by Lynn Kapitan. Students from all of the affiliates studied together each summer in Cambridge. The mix of international and Midwestern students created a unique atmosphere for training and creative expression with Moon and Kapitan, who are now prominent leaders within the art therapy community, being introduced to expressive arts therapy methods and the worldwide practice of the work.

During this period of internationalizing expressive arts therapy, I taught frequently in Europe as well as Israel. I met Annette Brederode through Phillip Speiser in 1983 and worked closely with her in the Netherlands and Finland.

In 1994, Knill left Lesley and cofounded the European Graduate School (EGS) in Switzerland which together with the Arts Institute Project in Israel have sustained the international character of the expressive arts therapy community. I have stayed closely connected to both of these prominent international programs where many of my closest colleagues teach and it is my hope that the EGS and Lesley communities will be fully reunited.

Expressive Arts Therapy and Building a Professional Community

In our work during the 1970s and 1980s, the term "expressive arts therapy" emerged organically from the original expressive therapy title. When people asked, "What is expressive therapy?" I would answer, "It is the use of all of the arts in therapy." We discussed how the expressive therapist often worked with more than one art form and might integrate these media in sessions. In time, the term "expressive arts therapy" began to be used in place of expressive therapy in conversations as a fuller and more complete designation.

There were a small number of people within our community who were not strongly committed to the arts, but who identified with "expressive" therapy. Psychodrama was an important part of the Lesley training program during the formative years and this discipline attracted some people who were more interested in expression and action-oriented therapy than the art of drama and J. L. Moreno's original conception of *The Theatre of Spontaneity* (1973). But over time, the overwhelming majority of people at Lesley studying expressive therapy aligned themselves with the arts. Peter Rowan, our senior psychodrama faculty member became one of the programs leading advocates for the integration of all art forms. He led the program when I stepped down as Dean in 1989 to focus on teaching and assured the continuation of arts integration values and methods with future generations of Lesley students with the support of Margot Fuchs-Knill, Laury Rappaport, Karen Estrella, and Mitchell Kossak.

Phillip Speiser describes how he heard Paolo Knill and I use the term expressive arts therapy interchangeably with expressive therapy at Lesley during the 1970s and he also confirms that it was not widely adopted by others at that time (personal communication, October 14, 2007). In keeping with Speiser's observation, I mentioned both names throughout *The Arts and Psychotherapy* and explicitly used expressive arts therapy to define the integrated arts process–"Rather than refer to individual dance, drama, music, poetry, and visual art therapies, I will conceptualize them generically with the term 'expressive arts therapy'" (McNiff, 1981, p. vii). In 1981, a book was published by Elaine and Bernard Feder entitled *The Expressive Arts Therapies.* Feder and Feder were not known to those of us practicing within the discipline before or after the appearance of the book, which contributed to the growing appreciation of how the arts in therapy belong together.

The naming and branding of the integrated and multi arts discipline was an emergent process over two decades after we began to formally train people to work with all of the arts in therapy. Although "expressive therapy" was the name of the Lesley program, I never referred to myself during the formative years as an expressive therapist. In contrast, most of our students did adopt the professional identification. My tendency was to emphasize expressive arts therapy, underscoring the "arts." I described myself as an artist working with all of the arts in therapy and my definition of art has always included all media which accounts for my comfort with the idea of art therapy. I have also been consistently involved with the American Art Therapy Association serving on the Board for two terms in the late 1970s and later as President. All of us teaching at Lesley belonged to the various creative arts therapy associations.

As stated earlier, the term creative arts therapy has generally been used to signify the collection of the specialized arts therapy disciplines. Within our community of progressives committed to the relaxation of boundaries between these entities, the creation of a yet another organizational structure was not a high priority. I hoped that the different creative arts therapy organizations would see their common identity and join together as one grouping in keeping with my liberal orientation toward integration. *The Arts and Psychotherapy* (1981) was written in this spirit as contrasted to trying to create yet another arts therapy field. However, experience has revealed that there are many factors that reinforce modality-based professional separations; and more importantly, students who graduated from our expressive therapy tract with an equal commitment to every art form and the process of arts integration were not represented by a professional association.

In 1980, Steve Ross, an early leader in the American Art Therapy Association and former President of the New York Art Therapy Association, left AATA because he felt that therapy was an art practiced by artists and that the discipline should not to be limited by particular media. He established an association called the American Association of Artist-Therapists. Ross and I shared an admiration for Otto Rank (*Art and Artists*, 1968), who originated the "therapy as art" idea. I supported Steve Ross's vision and his conceptual art focus and gave the first AAAT conference keynote address in 1981 in New York City.

Ross, who was significantly involved with credentialing within the American Art Therapy Association in the 1970s, initially focused on registering "artist-therapists." He responded to the needs that expressive arts therapists had in relation to professional identification and since many of his members had connections to Lesley and its various affiliate programs, he moved to copyright the expressive therapy term and changed the name of his organization to the National Expressive Therapy Association (NETA).

Steve Ross helped to gather together the first expressive arts therapy professional community. In addition to people connected to Lesley, Jack Weller and others from California joined the group and prominent figures such as Rudolf Arnheim became fellows. But when Ross chose to maintain NETA as a for-profit organization, this spurred the creation of a new, not-for-profit, member governed association.

When Phillip Speiser, an adept organizer, returned to the United States from Sweden in 1990, conversations developed between him, Stephen Levine, and Jack Weller about forming a new integrated arts professional association. I was also involved in these discussions where we deliberated on what the discipline should be called.

Jack Weller, who founded the Expressive Arts Therapy certificate program at the California Institute of Integral Studies in 1988, was an important force in the development of expressive arts therapy in that he organized a large network of people on the West Coast to join with Lesley's East Coast, European, and Israeli communities.

Upon returning to Toronto after his year at Lesley, Stephen Levine introduced expressive arts therapy in Canada as mentioned earlier. When we were discussing the name for the integrated arts discipline in 1990, Levine established *CREATE: Journal of the Creative and Expressive Arts Therapy Exchange* in Toronto. The first annual issue was published in 1991.

Both Speiser and Levine had thus already made formal use of the term expressive arts therapy in their work; Speiser's dating back to 1980 with the creation of his Scandinavian Institute for Expressive Arts. In the conversations that I had with Levine, Speiser, and Weller about naming our discipline, we determined that the copyrighting of the established Lesley term, expressive therapy, by NETA actually furthered our decision making. The term expressive arts therapy was adopted and we felt that the addition of the "arts," in keeping with my experience over the years with defining the work, would actually make for a stronger and more descriptive title.

Three years later, the International Expressive Arts Therapy Association (IEATA) was established in 1994 with Speiser, Levine, Weller, and Anin Utigaard serving as co-chairs of the organization.

Together with Weller and Utigaard, Wendy Miller and Natalie Rogers, all Californians, were principal contributors to the founding of IEATA. Rogers established and directed a training program, The Person-Centered Expressive Therapy Institute in Northern California, which furthered the growth of expressive arts therapy.

Important recent contributions have been made to the IEATA community by Sally Atkins and Appalachian State University in Boone, North Carolina. Atkins and colleagues began offering expressive arts therapy courses at the university in the mid 1980s and ASU established a specialization in Expressive Arts Therapy within the Master of Arts degree in Community Counseling in 1999. In 2007, Atkins organized an international IEATA conference at ASU that highlighted the growth and appeal of the discipline. Another successful and creative new graduate program was established in 2002 at Prescott College in Arizona by Cappi Lang Comba. Prescott offers an Expressive Arts Therapy concentration within a Counseling Psychology masters program and combines studies in an annual Summer Institute with distance learning.

Where many graduate programs in the creative arts therapies had a tendency to compete with one another during the early years of their development, often on the basis of different theoretical constructs, the expressive arts therapy community has been more prone to establish collaborative networks reinforcing commitments to shared values such as arts integration and art-based approaches to practice, training, and research. I believe that these tendencies toward the creation of a unified community have emerged from the many decades through which expressive arts therapy lacked a supportive organizational structure. A certain sense of marginalization within the creative arts therapies, a collection of disciplines which ironically continue to aspire to mainstream recognition, has engendered a strong community spirit and to my delight expressive arts therapy has maintained progressive values and openness to others who want to become involved in the work.

Stephen Levine has furthered a shared sense of theory and practice within the discipline through his contributions as an editor of journals and edited volumes (1999, 2002, & 2005). In 1999, he established the annual *POIESIS: A Journal of the Arts and Communication* in place of *CREATE*. *POIESIS* has flourished as a community forum of ideas, art, and therapeutic practice. It is the first periodical within the creative arts therapy field that is thoroughly art-based, presenting an overall design of form and content that looks and feels like what we do with the arts in therapy.

An Ongoing Creative Tension

Although there are many forces working against the use of all of the arts and arts integration within the creative arts therapies community, I have witnessed an increased openness in recent years.

Bruce Moon and Lynn Kapitan (2003), now working together at Mount Mary College, have been amongst my closest collaborators over the past two decades. Since 1983, I have led the opening colloquium for the Mount Mary Graduate Programs where the faculty and students have welcomed other art forms in relation to their work in art therapy. A similar receptivity has developed within the American Art Therapy Association due to the influence of Bruce Moon, Cathy Moon, Lynn Kapitan, and Lori Vance who also worked with us at Mount Mary. Arthur Robbins has also made consistent and important contributions to both opening therapy to the whole range of artistic expressions and reinforcing the artistic identity of art therapists (1976, 1980, 1987). In addition to the work of Robbins at the Pratt Institute in Brooklyn other art therapy programs, including Ursuline College in Ohio, led first by Sr. Kathleen Burke and now by Gail Rule-Hoffman; Marywood University in Scranton; and the Naropa Institute program in Boulder, Colorado, directed by Michael Franklin; and Suzanne Lovell's longstanding course of studies at Sonoma State University, have been open to this larger sense of creation while meeting their commitments to art therapy training.

Within all of the creative arts therapies, there is an ongoing tension between entry-level professional training in the mental health field and making the arts available to as many professionals as possible. In 2000, Cathy Malchiodi edited a special section of *Art Therapy: Journal of the American Art Therapy Association* focused on whether art therapy is a profession or an idea. In her introduction, she wrote: "The idea of art therapy is endlessly resilient and will go on with or without art therapists" (p. 243).

At Lesley, the Integrated Arts in Education program that I started has become one of the largest in the university over the past two decades, engaging many thousands of professionals in cohort groups across the United States. My vision of integration was in some respects realized more completely in this education program where teachers in many disciplines and administrators come together to explore how the arts and the creative process can inform their work. Since the program does not deal with licensure, it is free to more completely engage the creativity of participants. Ironically, it was an expressive arts therapist, Vivien Marcow Speiser, who incited the major growth in this program when she served as my Assistant Dean in the late 1980s and infused the curriculum with expressive arts therapy methods focused on helping the participants realize their personal creative potential in courses dealing with all of the arts.

When I served as the President of the American Art Therapy Association, we carried on an extended discussion about whether or not art therapy is a profession or a modality. In spite of my best efforts, the former position prevailed. In keeping with a core commitment to bringing creative expression to as many people as possible, I have always felt that art therapy and expressive arts therapy can be both professions and modes of expression which can be available to all therapists, healthcare professionals, and educators (McNiff, 2000). But this openness does not fit well with the way in which professions draw clear and certifiable boundaries in order to grow and preserve themselves, often in response to external regulations.

Throughout my career, I have continued to advocate for this inclusive approach. I support the profession and the need to train qualified and skilled professionals who can lead and train others. However, I also believe that art is a healing experience, an enduring form of public health that needs to be accessible to everyone (McNiff, 2004). Within this broad spectrum of activities, we can have professional expressive arts therapists working as psychotherapists as well as high school students helping elders with dementia in an art room. Every degree and variety of creative expression carries medicines. The professional licensure requirements of different disciplines must in this respect be distinguished from the many settings where art heals.

This embrace of the widest range of partnerships and creative possibilities has in some ways made it challenging for the expressive arts therapy community to define itself as contrasted to more circumscribed groups. In recent years, IEATA is succeeding in clearly articulating the unique benefits of integrated arts practice and how these methods complement other approaches to the arts in therapy.

Expressive arts therapy respects and promotes an understanding of the distinct dynamics of individual arts modalities. In my own experience, I shift constantly between references to the integrated arts work that I do within expressive arts therapy and my official service to the art therapy and poetry therapy communities and my personal artistic penchants for movement, percussion, voice-work, and performance. I see no contradiction in being committed to more than one thing and the expressive arts therapy discipline encourages this multiplicity of engagements.

Expressive arts therapy is inseparable from the history and practice of the various creative arts therapies of art, dance, drama, psychodrama, and poetry. Like many other expressive arts therapists, I maintain in-depth relationships with individual arts therapy media and communities of practice. Paolo Knill pursued and received certifications in a number of these disciplines to underscore the importance of careful study of the unique qualities of each modality as well as their combined effects.

Art therapy is the largest of the individual creative arts therapy disciplines. Music therapy, which is unique in giving professional status to bachelor degree graduates, is also a relatively large discipline, followed in size by dance therapy and the smaller disciplines of drama therapy, psychodrama, and poetry therapy.

Within expressive arts therapy, as contrasted to the specialized arts areas, we focus on the comparative analysis of art forms examining both unique and common elements of artistic expressions in varied media; why a particular medium might be effective in a situation and another medium less useful; how shifting from one art form to another can augment or clarify expression; and so forth. We are also committed to studying how vital connections amongst art forms further the expressive process. The history of art communities in different parts of the world underscores the positive way in which the gathering together of the arts and artists from varied disciplines not only enhances expression within the individual art forms but stirs a larger and transcendent quality of imagination.

David Read Johnson brought early promise to the National Coalition of Creative Arts Therapies Associations (NCCATA) and he has consistently emphasized qualities that are shared by the arts in therapy (1984, 1985, 1999), but in spite of his leadership and that of Kenneth Bruscia, a serious integration of the creative arts therapy associations has not happened. A similar pattern has occurred in Israel where organizational separation of the arts persists even though leaders like Avi Goren-Bar, who wrote what I consider one of the best journal articles dealing with integrated arts practice (1997), have worked tirelessly to develop the discipline.

In observing how expressive arts therapy has established itself and grown, it is intriguing how my original vision of arts integration has unfolded. I was wrong, to date at least, in idealistically thinking that it was possible for the arts specializations to celebrate their common identity within one community strengthened by a greater range of resources. Bob Fleshman and Jerry Fryrear who assert in their 1981 book *The Arts in Therapy* that "there is an overall field of arts therapies," similarly discovered in their research how people committed to one modality "objected" to this idea (p. 9). Yet, perhaps the persistence of these communities of specialization also furthers my deeply held beliefs in the importance of variety and as emphasized throughout this book, I thoroughly appreciate the value of studying and maintaining the distinct qualities of individual media. The separation of the arts requires people committed to "the one and the many" to navigate amongst different groups and guilds and maybe we are the better for it.

However, those of us who saw the need for a community that embraces all of the arts in therapy were also correct. Expressive arts therapy has developed separate from but parallel to the other creative arts therapies as a distinct discipline with many areas of mutual interest and overlap; and as Paolo Knill has emphasized, this approach has historical roots just like the specialized modalities. I see clearly now how the solidification of a distinct professional disciple, even though this might go counter to my liberal ideals, is necessary for the survival of the work.

Although my communal inclinations still push against the human tendency to separate domains that share so many things, the creative tension may ultimately enhance expressive arts therapist. I have never been more convinced of how all of the arts work together to maximize their healing powers, and based on my experience, I trust that the professional discipline of expressive arts therapy will continue to find its way to the most complete realization in the world.

EXPRESSIONS OF A UNIVERSAL STREAM

Archetypal Foundations

Although I have written extensively about the shamanic dimensions of expressive arts therapy practice (McNiff, 1979, 1981, 1988, 1989, 1990, 1992, 2004), it is important to do so once again here in order to connect this account of the contemporary establishment of expressive arts therapy with the larger continuities of human experience.

When I began to explore connections between expressive art therapy and shamanism in the late 1970s, I never imagined that this idea would have such appeal. The response has been so strong that some have exclusively identified my work in expressive arts therapy as shamanic where I see myself being more fundamentally attached to integrated arts and art-based methods of practice and psychological understanding. However, I have always been keenly interested in the archetypal dimensions of these ways of engaging the arts.

I had read Eliade's classic book *Shamanism: Archaic Techniques of Ecstasy* (1964) as a student and I was familiar with the practices of indigenous healers when I started my work as an art therapist. A key turning point toward shamanism in my practice occurred during a Union Institute doctoral seminar that I attended together with Robin Larsen, the wife of Stephen Larsen, author of *The Shaman's Doorway* (1976), who was initiating her doctoral research in this area. Stephen Larsen had recently completed his studies at Union and was closely associated with Joseph Campbell.

After the seminar, I reread Eliade's *Shamanism*, realizing that most of things that he described about classic shamanic healing practices corresponded to what we were doing with the arts in therapy. In shamanism, I discovered a way to identify expressive arts therapy with a world tradition of healing through creative expression in all of the arts, dreams, ritual, and sacred experience.

In the 1970s, there was a prevailing tendency to view the arts in therapy as adjunctive mental health professions. I was not interested in committing my lifework to being an adjunct and I was convinced that expressive arts therapy was linked to essential and profound human experiences persisting through the ages.

As I have emphasized in previous publications, I have always approached the shaman as an archetypal figure who has different names in various traditions. I have never tried to be a shaman in the literal sense and have no interest in appropriating or exploiting the traditions of indigenous communities. My interest has always been the "idea" of the shaman and the universal phenomena associated with it.

I am fascinated by the way core practices and beliefs manifest themselves across human history and culture. I try to identify likenesses and characteristics which unite all people in this current era where the emphasis on differences often obfuscates the appreciation of the common pulse of creation and identity. As I reported in an early essay on cross-cultural psychotherapy and art (McNiff, 1984), the examination of the unique cultural features of different therapeutic practices and beliefs needs to be combined with an examination of similarities in human aspirations and ways of responding to afflictions through creative transformation.

The most striking of the universal themes within indigenous healing traditions is the definition of illness as a loss of soul and the shaman as one who helps restore soul to the person in need. Shamanic practices throughout the world are similarly characterized by imagination, mythic patterns, and creative expression. The shaman travels, assisted by helping spirits, to retrieve the soul which is frequently perceived as being abducted by malevolent forces. The drum and its rhythms are imagined as the shaman's horse and source of power. Through ritual enactments and ceremonies, the shaman acting on behalf of the community, strives to bring back the souls of sick and troubled persons. These ways of viewing and treating illness and disturbance correspond completely to what we do in expressive arts therapy.

In stressing the archetypal aspects of shamanism, I have encouraged people to discover the shaman within themselves (1988), to appreciate the shamanic aspects of art and artists (1990), and to view images and artistic expressions as shamanic helpers who are able to assist us in restoring soul to our lives (2004).

My own research into these processes was originally informed by work that Paolo Knill and I did with a group of graduate students and other faculty colleagues in the late 1970s and early 1980s. We created the "Healing Lab" and experimented with completely spontaneous and unplanned expressions involving percussion, rhythm, trance, sustained improvisational dance, sound, and ritual.

During this period, I established a core commitment to the use of percussion and rhythm in my studios that has been sustained over the past three decades. The drum and other percussive instruments help us let go and express ourselves from the body and in sync with our most natural gestures and urges. The work in the Healing Lab also reinforced the importance of repetition, group energy, vocal improvisation, spontaneous performance, and many other practices that permeate my work today.

Rather than traveling to distant places to learn about shamanic archetypes, we found them in the most intimate recesses of our expression and community.

Enactment and J. L. Moreno (1889–1974)

When first studying the connections between shamanism and expressive arts therapy I observed how J. L. Moreno's use of enactment was perhaps the most complete manifestation of the shamanic archetype within the formative era of twentieth century psychotherapy. Moreno's emphasis on how therapeutic transformations occur through spontaneous creations in group situations had a significant impact on our early work at Lesley. Although I was never comfortable with the degree of control maintained by the psychodrama "director" working in the Moreno tradition, I was intrigued by the method's consistent focus on creativity and spontaneity as a basis of therapeutic treatment (Moreno, 1973).

I was impressed by the intense degree of the protagonist's catharsis in psychodrama as well the empathy demonstrated by audience members. Moreno described the energy that connected people within these group experiences as "tele," a Greek word that he used to suggest feeling that is passed from one person to another. The concentration of emotion in psychodramatic enactments was palpable and I connected it to the universal shamanic patterns that were activated by a person's complete and spontaneous expression in the present moment while being witnessed and supported by others. There was a distinct sense of soul being aroused and restored to a person in keeping with the process of soul retrieval in shamanic practices.

I was attracted to Moreno's vision of therapeutic enactment returning to the origins of theater as a way of engaging conflict. In contrast to Freud, he viewed creativity as a positive life force that cannot be bifurcated into conscious and unconscious acts (1973, p. 42). He reinvigorated theater as well as therapy by demonstrating how people can replay their lives, embrace wounds, and move the past "out of its coffin" into a spontaneous enactment, what he called a "*true* second time" that becomes "liberation from the first" (p. 91).

Moreno, like all of the other figures described in this book as manifesting the universal stream of art healing across historical periods, embraced discontents and difficulties as sources of creative transformation. He described how "the love for its own demons" account for art's healing power (p. 91). I personally trace all of these alchemical positions to Friedrich Nietzsche (1844–1900) who articulates how creativity and healing are united in their common focus on transforming our deepest pain and afflictions into affirmations of life (Nietzsche, 1967).

James Hillman's Influence

Howard McConeghey first introduced me to James Hillman's work in 1984 when I was a visiting professor at the University of New Mexico's summer program. McConeghey's focus on archetypal art therapy was informed by Hillman's Post-Jungian Archetypal Psychology. I devoured Hillman's books and essays on images (1975, 1977, 1978, 1979, 1983, 1984), sent him my book *The Arts and Psychotherapy* (1981), and he invited me to meet at his home in Connecticut. After decades of living in Europe and many years as the director of training at the C. G. Jung Center in Zurich, he had returned to the United States, first to the University of Dallas, and then to New England where he continues to live today.

When Hillman opened the front door of his house to greet me, he stretched out his hand and said, "I have been reading your book and I see that we are both dedicated to the destruction of psychotherapy."

I learned to be wary of literal interpretations from Hillman. At the time of our first meeting, I had been training therapists for over ten years and he had been involved for a much longer period. I believe that he was responding to my critique of the highly speculative diagnostic art practices that were prevalent at the time. He affirmed my primary emphasis on artistic expression and imagination as ways of therapeutic transformation. But Hillman does believe that conventional psychotherapy has largely proven to be ineffective (Hillman & Ventura, 1993) and feels that the soul is better served through an education of imagination.

Over the next decade, Hillman was closely connected to our Lesley community. He was a frequent guest lecturer and introduced me to Thomas Moore (1989, 1990, 1992) who taught in our program and also became a close colleague. From these relationships with Hillman and Thomas Moore I became more deeply immersed in Imaginal Psychology which was fully in sync with all of my previous work on art-based psychological theory and practice.

The influence of James Hillman is shown in my book *Art as Medicine: Creating a Therapy of Imagination* (1992). Through our collaboration, I developed a deeper understanding of the need to establish the autonomy of images; how personifying images helps us to engage them in more creative and complete ways; how images, as particular phenomena, are distinct from symbols; that psychological experience is characterized by multiplicity; how literalism is a great flaw when interpreting artistic expressions and dreams; and most importantly, how creative imagination is the intelligence informing everything we do in expressive arts therapy.

Hillman had a significant influence on my teaching and practice of expressive arts therapy. He reinforced my tendency to keep the work based in the arts and the creative process. He emphasized "sticking to the image"; withholding judgment; "keeping" the image through sustained concentration and observation; making ongoing analogies to other aspects of experience; restating in many different ways what we see in an image; personifying and letting the image speak for itself; and viewing our discipline as a practice of imagination where there are few and perhaps no absolute meanings or explanations when interacting with the things of the world. Healing occurs through an infusion of imagination and its creative vitality into our lives, by refashioning our tired stories, and changing our relationships to the things that afflict us.

Perhaps the most transformative impact Hillman had on my practice relates to the phenomena of pathology. He emphasizes how "pathologizing" is part of the soul's expression and that wounds are openings to our deepest emotions. From this vantage point, we need to show restraint in quickly analyzing and labeling pathological figures in artistic expressions and dreams and make more of an effort to welcome them, get to know them better, and learn from what they have to say about themselves. I realized how my problems with psychopathological approaches to art diagnosis were concerned with the literal and reductive modes of interpretation. Hillman helped me approach artistic expression with more empathy for the pathos of soul.

I discovered how pain and suffering in artistic expressions are not necessarily things to be fixed—we might be better off creating with our disturbances, changing our relationships with them, moving out of the victim role, and using the energy of afflictions as a source of expression. As Hillman says, when we focus exclusively on curing our wounds we may "cure away soul" and disregard their pleas for engagement and "love." His psychology focuses on giving closer and more imaginative attention to our symptoms and soul wounds with a belief that they have important contributions to offer human understanding.

Hillman shows us how to look more creatively at disturbing images in art and dreams, and to appreciate how the difficult expressions often take on a malevolent guise in order to communicate, catch our awareness, and immerse us more deeply in the ways of soul. I learned how the most troubling dreams and images are the ones that may have the most to offer, and how they help us engage the things that we repress and avoid. They increase their pressure to gain our attention. All of these ideas and approaches to images are in keeping with how nature operates and the role of physical symptoms in helping the body deal with maladies and restore a healthy circulation of energy and vitality.

Like Jung, Hillman appreciates the significance of repressed and dark perspectives, the shadow side of a person or situation, and he is committed to understanding how the disparaged point of view might be the most helpful way of looking at a situation. In our work together, he would take a problem, such as his recent book on war (*A Terrible Love of War*, 2004), and pragmatically ask what is really going on here? Why are we continually fascinated with this phenomenon?

These experiences with James Hillman gave me the opportunity to watch "how" he worked with others. He has a special ability to help people see the attitudes and assumptions that are contained in the language they use. He is especially critical of stereotypic clinical language, still all too common in our world as discussed in a later section of this book. In *The Myth of Analysis* (1978), he writes of how "Once depth psychology spoke with a living tongue," with imagination, and in a way whereby the manner of speaking, the ways of expression, can change our relationships to experience (p. 121).

I observed how Hillman was carefully attuned to how well-meaning people are prone to moralize about social problems in stereotypic ways, often imbedded in ego judgments. I was taken aback by his ability to confront people with the goal of revealing how psychological assumptions hindered their ability to engage problems and life situations in new and more imaginative ways. He challenged people to let go of their psychological jargon and look at life from the perspective of the varied things that people do in the world, which, of course, includes the arts.

James Hillman and his writings have also had a major impact on Paolo Knill, Stephen Levine, Margot Fuchs, and Bruce Moon and others who have exerted an increasing influence on the theory and practice of expressive arts therapy. He has created a compelling and practical psychology of the imagination which supports the use of every possible form of creative and artistic expression in therapy, healing, problem solving, and learning.

C. G. Jung (1875–1961) and Active Imagination

Through my association with Hillman, Moore, and McConeghey, I revisited my relationship with C. G. Jung, which had been largely suspended since I studied his thought as a college student. Archetypal and Imaginal psychology demanded an immersion in the Jungian tradition.

I moved away from Jung while working with Rudolf Arnheim, who had difficulties with his mystical aspects and the idea of the collective unconscious as a motivating force for particular forms of art making. I was not attracted to Jung's way of attributing a person's artistic expressions to particular mythic themes, a practice which grew into dogmatic approaches to archetypal labeling in many sectors of Jungian psychology. His psychological types (introvert and extrovert, and so forth) were equally unsettling because of the way people used these concepts in perfunctory ways. However, I was intrigued in the early 1980s with how Jung and Arnheim were thoroughly dovetailed within the work of my colleague Howard McConeghey (1994, 2003). As an admirer of McConeghey, I concluded that I must revisit Jung.

Hillman speaks about how "there are many Jungs" and I discovered that the Jung who promulgated the mythic tagging of expressions is quite different from the Jung who strove to understand, in the most objective and intelligent way, how the creative process operates. As I deepened my studies of Jung, it became clear that he anticipated the full spectrum of expressive arts therapy activity in his practice of active imagination originating in the early twentieth century (Chodorow, 1997; McNiff, 2004). In addition to Jung's own seminal research, many of what I consider to be the best writings on how to work with artistic expressions and images in therapy are linked to the Jungian tradition of active imagination. These include James Hillman's Inquiry into Images essays of the late 1970s; Patricia Berry's essay, An Approach to the Dream (1974); and a book by Mary Watkins on imaginal dialogue (1986).

Jung worked with all of the arts in his practice of active imagination and he has received very little acknowledgment for being the first psychotherapist to fully integrate the arts into everything he did. This absence of attribution is largely due to the silos of separation that permeate professions and the forces described earlier that keep arts therapy specialization separate from one another. I often say to art therapy colleagues that Jung would not meet today's narrow standards for practice. He called his methods "active imagination" and not art therapy, dance therapy, drama therapy, expressive arts therapy, and so forth. Yet in my opinion he used all of the arts with a depth and sophistication that stands as a model for all of us practicing today. Another reason for the lack of credit given to Jung is the fact that his methods integrated all of the arts and these modes of practice, as we know as expressive arts therapists, have not been adopted by many within the professional domains committed to the use of a single artistic medium.

It is likely that Jung also helped to distance himself from the ensuing growth of the arts in therapy by his reluctance to adopt artistic perspectives on his work. He spoke of the negative effects of a "merely aesthetic attitude" and actually said that creative expressions should be approached as "worthless, otherwise my patients might imagine themselves to be artists" (Chodorow, p. 93). I believe that he was approaching art from a narrow perspective as a realm of practice restricted to recognized artists.

Within Jung's language, the aesthetic consciousness is perceived as superficial as contrasted to his commitment to expression having a "living effect" on a person. In contrast, Hillman and other post-Jungian Archetypal psychologists have embraced aesthetic perception and the arts as primary modes of depth psychology which welcome the contemplation of beauty and pathos. The problem here may be largely a matter of language, translation, and changing conceptions of art. Jung also felt that aesthetic analysis assumes a lack of psychological depth. Perhaps he perceived the aesthetic perspective to be purely formal and disconnected from the authentic expression of a person.

In my practice, I share Jung's dedication to the "living effect" in a person's expression. There is a palpable and distinct difference between this kind of experience and the superficial phenomena that he tried to avoid. However, I find that the arts and aesthetic perception provide the most reliable ways of accessing the vital expressions and the authentic contents of the psyche.

No matter how one feels about Jung and his psychology, which can sometimes alienate as much as inspire, what he actually did with the varied media of artistic expression is in complete sync with today's expressive arts therapy practices and ideals. Creative expressions are the core of Jung's practice of active imagination, not only as modes of communication, but they also serve as the media through which the psyche heals itself.

Jung made use of drawings, paintings, dance, drama, and other creative expressions as ways of "perceiving and giving shape" to the contents of the psyche that were not accessible through reason and analytic inquiry (p. 173). He first discovered these powers during a personal crisis in 1912–1913 following the dissolution of his relationship with Sigmund Freud when he himself used the arts to heal. He witnessed and followed the lead of the creative imagination while staying attuned to particular images. Through these experiences, Jung realized how a person can "clarify a vague content by giving it a visible form" through the arts and how the physical actions of expression can resolve problems that elude the mind (p. 57).

He concludes that the quality of therapeutic outcomes depends on "how we look" at an image. "Give it your special attention," he said. "Concentrate on it, and observe its alterations objectively. Spare no effort to devote yourself to this task, follow the subsequent transformations of the spontaneous fantasy attentively and carefully. Above all, don't let anything from outside, that does not belong, get into it, for the fantasy-image has 'everything it needs'" (p. 170).

I view Jung's practice of active imagination as a therapy of integration using different media to embody the varied contents of the psyche which are transformed and shaped into affirmations of life. One expression flows from another allowing the psyche to express its multiplicity and achieve natural and unplanned states of wholeness. Rather than producing fixed solutions, the process for me is dynamic and ongoing within each instance of creation ultimately receding and leaving an empty space for those that follow. Also as stated earlier in relation to the place of disintegration with expressive arts therapy, creative transformation may demand a breaking apart in order to generate expressive vitality and a healthy circulation of creative energy.

Jung made comprehensive and skilled use of the most complete practice of what we now call expressive arts therapy, urging people to use whatever medium supports spontaneous expression. He anticipated all of our current methods of practice encouraging shifts from one medium to another in therapy—responding to a painting with a dance; personifying and giving voices to drawings and dream images and letting them enact a drama or tell a story. Jung affirms the endless variations in expressive styles and how people integrate experience in different ways—"dramatic, dialectic, visual, acoustic, or in the form of dancing, painting, drawing, or modelling" (p. 159). These explorations repeatedly underscore how the arts offer insights that cannot be accessed through reason alone.

But perhaps most importantly, Jung came to realize how the overall activation and circulation of creative energy was a primary source of healing and well-being. In this sense he grasped how the psyche will heal itself when given the proper support and environmental resources. Thus, the core focus of therapeutic practice becomes one of sustaining creative energy with the realization that it will find its ways to the transformation of difficulties.

Within this perspective, we focus less on the linear task of trying to determine causes and attempting to fix them. We are more concerned with cultivating the flow of creative expression with a belief that the essential conditions of our lives, positive and negative, will feed the circulation of creativity and be transformed by it. These methods are effective because most emotional and life problems cannot be reduced to singular causes. The serious problem is typically a *complex*, a gathering of forces that are often elusive, but yet fully accessible to be channeled into creative expressions which can alter the overall conditions of our lives.

My experience affirms how the deepest and most transformative expressive arts therapy experiences occur when, as Jung said, we imagine the creative expression further. He grasped how the practice of healing through the creative process depends upon giving people the most complete freedom of expression—"We must be able to let things happen in the psyche" (p. 74). He is particularly helpful in showing how the difficult and disturbing situations and expressions, the shadow aspects of our lives, hold the greatest resources for expression and learning.

The modern practice of comprehensive expressive arts therapy was thus anticipated by Jung. As training programs continue to flourish and many thousands of students throughout the world explore the practice and history of healing through the arts, far more attention and credit needs to be given to C. G. Jung's seminal vision.

Creative Expression as a Primary Medicine

In addition to its embrace of all art forms, the expressive arts therapy community is distinguished by the core position that healing occurs through immersion in the creative process as contrasted to more analytic and verbally oriented approaches that have permeated many other historical threads within the creative arts therapies. The various formative influences that I have described within this chapter affirm creative expression as a primary medicine in every aspect of practice.

The Freudian and Jungian strains of depth psychology offered two distinct approaches to therapeutic treatment with the former striving to solve problems through rational analysis and the latter trusting the transformative intelligence of creative imagination. The classic analytic approach used the arts as subject matter and communication tools within a context governed by reason whereas therapies of the imagination view artistic processes as primary ways of knowing and problem solving that cooperate with the reasoning mind.

Through my studies of the various strands of the arts in psychotherapy that pre-dated our work in the early 1970s, I see how they tend to fall into one group or the other. In art therapy, for example, Margaret Naumburg (1947, 1950, 1966, 1973) and Edith Kramer (1958, 1971, 1979, 2001) identified themselves with Freudian methods, although the later has always placed significance emphasis on the healing process of expression and her own commitment to art-making. Naumburg by contrast viewed the making of art as a "supplemental" mode of communication and a dynamic activator of unconscious contents within the psychotherapeutic relationship. As art therapy and other creative arts therapy specializations began to develop in the United States, the analytic orientation to practice prevailed.

The historic achievements of Hans Prinzhorn in early twentieth century Europe (1972), unappreciated for so many years in the United States, had close affinities to the writings of C. G. Jung. They both affirm the presence of a universal urge within the psyche to express and heal itself and make meaningful contact with others through creative expression.

It is noteworthy that I am completing this account of the formation of the contemporary expressive arts therapy discipline with reflections on the contributions of Prinzhorn, whose *Bildnerei der Geisteskranken* [*Artistry of the Mentally Ill*] (1922) was the first text to capture my imagination at the start of my career and which Rudolf Arnheim summarized for me in meetings before it was available in English (1972). Other than Arnheim, there were few sharing my passion for Prinzhorn who had been so thoroughly overlooked.

The study by Prinzhorn, a psychiatrist and art historian, featured a collection of remarkable paintings and drawings produced by people living in mental hospitals throughout Europe from 1890 to 1920. Although Prinzhorn's research had an impact on European expressionism and other artistic developments seeking to restore innate and authentic methods of expression, it did not significantly influence the art therapy field. His clear and convincing descriptions of how painting and drawing answer universal human needs for expression were not widely adopted by therapists.

In keeping with the writings of Friedriche Nietzsche and D. H. Lawrence, who he translated into German, Prinzhorn likened creative expression to instinctual life, passion, and play. He believed that creative art is an organic and life affirming "urge" that can be a source of health and vitality. This view is totally in sync with the contemporary view of creativity as an "immune system of the mind" as stated by John Holt in England (2005) and my own efforts to describe how art heals. However, Prinzhorn's support for the intelligence and healing powers of natural urges contradicted the primary tenets of early psychotherapeutic systems striving to replace instincts with reason.

Oskar Pfister, a prominent Freudian felt that Prinzhorn failed to explore the underlying psychodynamics of the artworks in his research (1923). Prinzhorn, more attuned to the principles of phenomenology and Gestalt psychology, would not entertain reductive and speculative psychological explanations which attributed art motivation to unconscious conflicts and this no doubt distanced him from the rising tide of psychoanalytic therapies.

Prinzhorn's approach to expression was much closer to Jung's focus on letting the psyche care for itself through natural creative expression. He wrote, "All expressive gestures as such are subordinated to one purpose: to actualize the psyche and thereby to build a bridge from the self to others. That they do this freely and completely clearly gives them their value" (1972, p. 13). In this passage, Prinzhorn attributes the motivation of creative expression to life-affirming instincts and he goes on to say: "we speak of a tendency, a compulsion, a need for the expression of the psyche, and thereby denote those compulsive vital processes which are not subordinated to any outside purpose but directed solely and self-sufficiently toward their own realization" (p. 13).

The influence of Jung's archetypal theory is suggested by Prinzhorn's assertion that the expressive urge is an inborn drive which enables the person to "escape" from the restrictions of individual life conditions and to experience "the expanse of common life" together with others (p. 13). This view is consistent with Jung's emphasis on encouraging spontaneous expression in the psyche. He believed that the work of healing through the arts was an organic process, an essential function of nature.

Prinzhorn's ideas are affirmed in the work of Edward Adamson who established an art therapy studio within an English mental hospital in 1946 and anticipated the importance of studio-based practice. Like Prinzhorn, Adamson's focus on the inherent healing qualities of the art experience has not been fully appreciated and known within the United States.

Adamson may have created the first recognized and ongoing art therapy studio where the qualities of "the creative space" treated the soul (Adamson, 1990). He describes how he served as a facilitator of the therapeutic environment and how the atmosphere of the studio and the positive energy of creative expression acted on people. The studio became an "oasis" where individuals were "accorded the dignity of helping to cure themselves" by choosing to come on a regular basis (p. 2).

Art therapy was particularly reluctant in its formative phases to be associated with activity and occupational therapies and this was no doubt a factor in keeping art-oriented methods at bay. However, from the perspective of Jung's depth psychology, Adamson and Prinzhorn were engaging the bedrock and mainstream of the psyche. As Adamson states, the arts "are more than a palliative—under the right guidance, they can be a vital form of self-help which allows Nature's healing powers to restore balance and harmony to the troubled mind" (p. 5).

Prinzhorn and Adamson, both of whom predate the creation of the expressive arts therapy discipline, reinforce the archetypal nature of our work. The fundamental ideas and practices that form the basis of expressive arts therapy are not new. There are many other figures who contributed to this vein of practice that I have not included here. Similarly, positions taken by C. G. Jung were informed by ideas that were already established within artistic, philosophical, and psychological discourse. Jung is in this respect a master synthesizer of archetypal forces.

What can be considered new, and a distinct historical phenomenon, is the way these ideas and methods were gathered together by a particular group of people and ultimately influenced the creation of the discipline of expressive arts therapy which gives people throughout the world opportunities to experience healing through creative expression.

I have learned, however, that the practice of expressive arts therapy is largely concerned with helping and guiding people who lack self-confidence in opening to the innate forces of creative expression. As I have described earlier, the great majority of participants at first resist, fear, or even disparage the work, and these adversities, to be addressed in detail in the following pages, are as universal as the healing powers of art. My goal in this book is to assure present and future expressive arts therapists that they are not alone in the challenges they face in offering people access to the medicines of the arts and that the most vexing problems in helping others express themselves are inextricably connected to how the arts heal.

PART III. FORMATIVE EXPERIENCES

HEALING THROUGH IMAGINATION WITH YOUNG CHILDREN

Childhood Imagination as a Foundation of Expressive Arts Therapy

Children were my first teachers in relation to the process of interpreting and responding to art with more art. They showed me how one creation stimulates another and that what tends to matter most in expressive arts therapy is sustaining the process of total expression, supporting and augmenting the circulation of creative energy with the realization that understanding and well-being are not planned and calculated outcomes. The boundaries of artistic disciplines are constructs that we adults impose, sometimes to the detriment of a more complete process of expression. In childhood, the natural integration of the arts in creative expression often occurs in spite of our intentions and we need to decide whether or not we are going to fully embrace what happens spontaneously in our sessions.

When I first met with children to make drawings and paintings, I was surprised to see how they innately responded to their pictures with stories and dramatic enactments. I would ask simple questions such as, "would you like to say something about the painting," and very often the child began to tell a story or play out the contents of a composition with full bodied gestures, sounds, and dramatic improvisations that expressed the flights of planes or birds, explosions, the movements of animals, and other aspects of imagination. It was in these early sessions with children that I began to see how everything we do within expressive arts therapy is part of an all-encompassing creative enactment. The different art media give form to the ongoing dramas of imagination in which children are immersed.

Experiences with image dialogue happened spontaneously in this early work with children when they spoke directly as figures or things within a picture rather than as themselves in a first-person voice. They let the pictures and characters within them tell their own stories and introduced me to role of imagination in expressive arts therapy.

51

I discovered that my primary role in helping children express themselves was one of offering open-ended invitations and then supporting the boys and girls as they explored artistic media. With some children, I might need to give more encouragement and coaching, but overall I found that if I am relaxed, playful, and open to the broadest range of expressions, this will help the more resistive and cautious children.

From my first experiences in expressive arts therapy, I sensed that my primary objective was the establishment of safe, supportive, and stimulating environments and art spaces that help children and adults realize their natural creative expressions. I learned that an atmosphere that kindles imagination will result in much deeper expression and insight and that the most effective expressive arts therapy practices emerge naturally from the creative expressions of participants. Where more conventional psychotherapeutic theories focused on transferences between therapists and patients, I was more concerned with how the environment of the studio acted upon the person.

D. W. Winnicott affirmed this emphasis on the therapeutic agency of the creative space and viewed imaginary play as the bedrock of healing in psychotherapy. He described how therapeutic relationships involve therapists and children in mutual play that needs to be spontaneous as contrasted to a directive process that places the child in a more submissive role. He concludes that the play must be genuine "if psychotherapy is to be done" (1971, p. 51).

My experiences with children have affirmed the need for clear and strong structure in situations where they are unable to play freely and with a sense of confidence. But I will introduce direction only to the extent that it is needed to provide the kind of environment that supports a child in taking personal initiative in creative expression. Determining the extent to which we give direction to another's expression is always a principle focus within expressive arts therapy training programs. As an advocate of free expression, I paradoxically find that clear structures and limits are fundamental to realizing our goals.

In the early years of our expressive therapies program at Lesley University, Paolo Knill taught a play therapy course by helping the adult therapists play as well as they could while simultaneously perfecting their abilities to help others play. Although not directly influenced by the writings of Winnicott during the 1970s at Lesley, our values and methods were in sync with his emphasis on creating a space for the imagination in which "psychotherapy may begin" (p. 54).

If psychotherapy with children is to be viewed as play, then everything that children make and the responses to artistic expressions by both therapists and children are part of an ongoing improvisational drama and process of communication. Artistic expression is an innate way of knowing and healing in childhood. We need to do everything we can to support this process and examine how children can teach adults how to reconnect with the most fundamental ways of art healing.

Karen Gallas was my closest collaborator in the early 1970s when I sought to complement my Danvers experiences with adults by researching expressive arts therapy methods with children. In addition to engaging boys and girls in clinical settings, I worked with Gallas in public school classrooms where we explored how multiple modes of artistic and sensory expression shape a child's understanding of the world. We observed that if supported by their environment, young children will make natural use of different media to further their overall expression in contrast to adults and older children who have generally constricted their communications to spoken language. Even with the strongest support and environmental encouragement, adults tend to resist expressing themselves outside the limits of verbal conversation.

Two decades after we worked in public school classrooms, Karen Gallas published *The Languages of Learning: How Children Talk, Write, Dance, Draw, and Sing Their Understanding of the World* (1994), a seminal book dealing with how children express their deepest concerns through the many modes of communication. Gallas defines childhood language as a trans-verbal medium that innately uses all of the arts to create "stories" expressing inner and outer experiences. She urges everyone working with children "to offer expansive opportunities for expression of those stories" (p. 162) in different media and then concentrate on what the children communicate about their worlds.

Susanne Langer similarly draws attention to how we overlook the whole spectrum of symbolic media and ways of understanding experience (1951, 1953). The continued absence of this complete process of knowing and communication in many sectors of education and therapy is troubling. There is a one-sided expectation placed on children to speak in the language of adults and not enough realization that they are thinking and speaking to us in ways that we neither appreciate nor understand. "What if," Gallas asks, "we were to assume that children came to school more, rather than less, able to communicate their thinking about the world?" (p. xv).

Childhood disturbances often result from the inability to exercise and sustain this natural expressive process in relating to others. The vignettes of my work with children presented in this chapter offer examples of how if given the opportunity and support, children will activate these innate ways of making meaning and healing. They can also show adults how to connect to these powers.

Edith Cobb's classic book *The Ecology of Imagination in Childhood* (1993) supports how creativity in adults is tied to the ability to sustain the foundations of childhood imagination. Cobb presents childhood imagination as a wellspring to which we return throughout our lives for sustenance. This return to childhood as a source of imagination and renewal is distinctly different from the conventional psychoanalytic view of creativity as regression. So much of the psychodynamic theory of the past century traced adult problems to childhood trauma and pathology, almost exclusively emphasizing what went wrong in the past.

Wounds abound in childhood, but the exclusive focus on past trauma misses the opportunity to appreciate how these difficult experiences, as demonstrated by the children described in the chapter, generate creative transformation. As Cobb, Gallas, Winnicott, and many offers have discovered, creative imagination is the realm where inner and outer experiences can meet and create together. The imagination welcomes good and bad, joy and fear, and all the other ingredients of experience and uses them as sources of its life enhancing expression.

Viewing childhood imagination as a regressive state is an avoidance of its intelligence and wisdom. The imagination of childhood is the lost soul that we strive to regain in order to heal and live more complete lives. The integration of inner musing and the demands and opportunities of the external world is the perpetual objective of the creative and healthy person in childhood and during every ensuing phase of life.

Art Objects Evoking Story and Drama

From the very beginning of my work with children, I observed how the visual images in paintings, drawings, sculptures, and other artworks consistently elicit imaginative and insightful responses. In responding to pictures, children taught me how to naturally move from one medium to another within the context of creative expression. The art object offers a concrete and direct invitation to tell a story or enact a feeling. In keeping with what jazz musicians say when describing the dynamics of improvisation, the visual image gives the child something to "bounce off." I encourage readers to view the pictures in this section as participants and catalysts within a larger ecology of expression.

Perhaps the presence of the image keeps us attached to concrete experience and avoids the emptiness, anxiety, and lack of direction that we often feel with totally open-ended invitations for expression in a particular medium. Structure paradoxically liberates expression so long as it also provides the freedom and support to respond in different ways. This improvisational movement from one expression to another is an essential feature of expressive arts therapy practice. Providing access to varied artistic modalities, as illustrated by the children responding to pictures with stories, movement, and dramatic enactments, augments the possibilities for communication and discovery and gives a more complete range to the play of psychotherapy.

Artworks can be especially helpful in stimulating nonverbal children to speak and express themselves with imagination when describing their pictures. A six-year-old girl in a small group that I led spent months doing drawings that divided her paper in quarters with diagonal lines going from one corner to the other. She then randomly inserted colors and lines within the four areas. She rarely spoke and attempts at speech consisted largely of mumbled words. The other children in the group tended to speak for her as proxies and do whatever they could to compensate for her inability to respond to questions and participate in conversation.

Her older brother, whose name was Buddy, was a member of our group and he would often speak for her and the other children intervened in much the same way. They were aware of her difficulties with communication and there was a general tone of kindness and concern for her when they acted as surrogates.

While making pictures, I noticed how this young girl was more actively engaged with the environment and responsive to tasks and directions. In each of our weekly sessions, she made her albeit repetitious pictures in a forceful style with bold gestures. She seemed to enjoy making drawings and using colors and she worked with intensity every time we met. In comparison to the other children, I felt that her gestures were more passionate, but she could not move beyond the template that was repeated every time she made a picture.

I sensed that perhaps the repetition of the same configuration week after week was part of her overall reluctance to initiate communications with other people or respond to statements addressed to her. Yet I was intrigued by the energetic way that she made pictures and the vitality of her more general bodily expression. The life force was alive in her, manifesting itself in these oblique ways, but yet she was consistently reluctant to be part of direct verbal communications within our group meetings.

After our group had met for a number of months, her brother Buddy was hit by a car and hospitalized. In the first session after the accident she completely broke her past pattern and produced a graphically clear and expressive picture (Fig. 6). She drew her brother in the center of the composition and then surrounded him by a visual dramatization of the accident.

In the bottom right corner, she showed the impact of the accident and with swirling lines represented her brother flying through the air. This picture affirmed the power and bold directness that I sensed in her graphic expression. I was fascinated by the change in her art and the way she moved outside the rigid frame of her previous compositions. I was particularly intrigued by the movement in the picture and the forceful portrayal of action using the entire surface of the paper.

Figure 6.

After making the picture, she looked at me and clearly said, "This is a picture of Buddy gettin' hit by a car and flyin' through the air."

She had never spoken directly to me before.

The other children in the group were clearly distressed by the accident and when they heard her speak, they began to repeat what she said. Their expression grew into a collective chant. They repeated it over and over again and with enthusiasm—"Buddy got hit by a car and is flyin' through the air."

I affirmed the vocal expression and encouraged the children to keep repeating it. They were sitting and I asked them to stand and express flying "through the air" with arm movements. The movements built to a forceful catharsis and we initiated a gradual denouement, chanting the statement more softly as we moved in a circular configuration, and bringing ourselves to a resting place.

I told the children how moved I was by what they did and how supportive they were to both Buddy and his sister. I felt that the chant and the physical enactment of the accident gave an outlet for the tension and fear that they were feeling.

The creation of the dynamic picture and the words of the chant by this previously nonverbal child made the process appear magical and this perhaps intensified the cathartic aspects of the group's spontaneous expression. The power of the enactment felt like an archaic community response to forces beyond its control. The vocalization and drama struck me as an affirmation of the group's strength and resolve. The children expressed themselves like shamans intent upon retrieving the lost soul of an afflicted person.

This sequence of expressions emerged from the young girl's artistic response to a traumatic incident. She repeated the event but shaped it into a new creative expression which ignited the imagination of the other children who responded with yet another transformation and amplification of her expression.

Stephen Levine feels that the expressive arts therapies can help us deal more effectively with trauma by replaying the experience in a different way rather than staying "trapped in a repetition of the event" (2002, p. 88). J. L. Moreno similarly emphasized how we can relive upsetting situations through artistic expression and have a second chance to deal with them (1973, p. 101). The difficult experience or memory is made into a new creation rather than being repeated in the same way.

In this particular instance, the young girl unexpectedly enacted the traumatic experience in her painting and her verbal response to it. The other children in the small group seemed to instinctively appreciate the significance of what she had done and they reinforced and augmented her expression with their collective creation. All of these responses to the accident used the unsettling experience as a source of spirited expressions which replayed and transformed the event within the imagination. I sensed that it was helpful for everyone involved, including me, to move beyond passive fixation and do something creative in response to the trauma. We were not able to directly support Buddy at that moment, but the expressions of the group helped everyone deal with the situation, feel compassion for him and his sister, and affirm the power of the children's group.

Emergence of Creative Expression from Elemental Movements

An experience that I had working with a five-year-old boy offers an illustration of how movement-based expressive arts therapy can be done in collaboration with another art form, in this case painting. The child was so threatened by the school environment after starting kindergarten that he did not speak and stood alone in a corner of the classroom, sucking his thumb. Whenever the teachers tried to engage him in some form of activity, he began to cry. When I first met with the teachers, we noticed that the boy tended to look toward the art activity area in the classroom and I began to take him there to explore the space.

In the early stages of our work together, I tried to encourage him to move with and relate to physical materials. In our first two sessions, he spent virtually all of the 45 minutes stirring various jars of paint. He seemed to take pleasure in the rhythmic motions and appeared to be stimulated by the movement configurations and kinesthetic swirling designs that he made with the paint in jars.

I noted that the actions were purposeful and, even through he did not make a picture, I thought that his manipulation of the objects and materials was significant. I was buoyed by thoughts about Piaget's emphasis on the importance of sensorimotor exploration as a prelude to other cognitive and emotional functions. It also seemed natural to explore the properties of the art materials as a prelude to painting, albeit the boy's persistence in the act of stirring was unusual in comparison to how the other children immediately began to paint pictures whenever they had the opportunity to work freely.

As a way of building on what the child did naturally and in an effort to orient our work together toward something that he did well, I shifted my attention from painting to movement. This change of direction in relation to goals and purpose helped me appreciate the significance of what he was already doing in a more complete and positive way. As described earlier, I felt that we should build a basis for expression on what the boy would accept as a starting point. In addition to the significance of his movement, I felt that it was helpful for him to establish a certain degree of control and confidence in the tools and materials that he was using.

The repetitious and trance-like stirring motion was rhythmic and sustained. It may have helped the child to move beyond fears and inhibitions. If nothing else, it did seem pleasurable for him. Rather than be distracted by thoughts or concerns about obsessive-compulsive disorders and pathological perseveration, I chose to look at what he was doing in a constructive way and embrace it, thinking that the stirring motions might ultimately transform themselves into other kinds of expression.

I was pleased to hear from the teachers that after these first sessions, the boy developed an interest in water play and he seemed to enjoy repetitious pouring motions. His engagements with paint and brushes could be perceived as foundations for more expansive movement explorations, as a way of literally "stirring" other forms of expression.

In time, he began to lose interest in the stirring movement. In later sessions, there were longer and longer intervals between his movements with the paint. Soon I realized that these moments of inactivity or pauses were significant transitions in the overall progression of his movement.

After a number of weekly sessions, the boy took the brushes out of the jars and began to paint randomly on the paper while standing at the easel. His art evolved to a form of expressive painting that resembled a dance in which he changed the brush from hand to hand, used both hands, and developed a wide variety of imaginative gestures. His movements were forceful and dramatic.

The pictures made during this period were primarily kinetic, a form of early childhood action painting, and he appeared to have little interest in representing visual subject matter. He was engrossed with the sensory act of moving the paint on the paper with his body and the brushes. The flow, texture, and colors of the paint seemed to be his primary focus. He struck me as returning to the first stages of graphic expression in childhood, like a two-year-old who was exploring movement for its own sake in a preschematic act of painting. But in contrast to younger children, this child was able to combine the pure act of moving with paint with the conscious direction of gestures and then reflect upon the resulting expressions.

I felt that he not only released energy and emotion through these movements, but there was an accompanying process of learning how to control the effects of the brushes and the paint. He was able to repeat these essential movements from session to session and experience a degree of predictability in relation to his ability to direct the process and achieve a satisfactory outcome. I saw the paintings as partners in his movement. They affirmed his expression and left tangible records of forceful gestures.

Another significant aspect of this expressive movement was the way the boy concentrated on what he was doing through every phase of the process. He was gaining confidence in his ability to move with materials. He appeared to lose himself within the texture and flow of the paint and I felt that his movements grew more relaxed and fluid, almost as though he was incorporating the qualities of the paint medium into his expressive style. In keeping with the homeopathic principle of correspondence, the immersion in painting stimulated a reciprocal influence on the boy's overall behavior. Life was imitating art.

The classroom teachers appreciated the significance of the boy's interest in painting and they encouraged him to sustain this activity in the time between our sessions. After a few months of working together, it became clear that the activity with movement and painting served as a bridge and transitional step to broader areas of movement within the classroom. The time spent at the easel allowed him to gradually separate from his previous pattern of immobility and withdrawal and he became involved with the more general movement flow of the classroom.

In later sessions, we shifted from painting to the more forceful movement activities of hammering and sawing in the carpentry area of the classroom, all the while keeping our attention focused on moving with objects. He greatly enjoyed the carpentry and began to make complicated wooden structures exploring principles of balance.

With sculpting activities and the process of arranging wooden materials, he moved with his whole body and with other people. The scope of his wooden block constructions grew larger as he created enclosed environments. He viewed the creations as houses, ships on the ocean, and spaceships within which he enacted imaginative dramas.

The boy's expression shows how dance and movement can evolve in response to the physical environment and grow from activities which might appear to have no apparent relationship to the art of dance. In these later sessions, the child essentially constructed environments for his movement. These physical spaces aroused his imagination and his earlier focus on manipulative and repetitious movements evolved into dramatic enactments where he creatively played out feelings, tensions, and fantasies through movement alone and without the use of words.

Over the course of our work together, the boy's movement in the classroom with other children became more independent and expressive. By the midpoint of the school year, he was participating in all aspects of the school experience. He grew increasingly confident in his ability to move about the classroom, and when engaged in communal dance experiences, he was one of the most energetic and expressive of the children.

This experience illustrates how expressive arts therapy can take direction from an interest that a child shows and build upon it in supportive ways. A comprehensive focus on movement was sparked by an interest in the qualities of paint and the act of stirring. One art form flowed from another without a design or plan. Together with the classroom teachers, I worked with what the child was willing to do and we used his interests as a means of furthering expressiveness and sense of mastery. Over time, these achievements within more solitary forms of expression led to his integration into the general activity of the classroom as a productive member of the group who had unique things to offer others.

Chaos and Control

There will always be instances in expressive arts therapy groups where the process of expression threatens control and order, where I am challenged as a leader, or where I have to intervene to help people stabilize themselves, catch their breath, establish a sense of balance, or regain their sense of purpose and focus. However, I have learned to avoid inviting expressions from outside a person's natural and internal process of managing and controlling expression.

The media of voice, instrumental sounds, and body movement are uniquely capable of conveying primal and very direct expressions of emotion which can create difficulties. Sound, and especially vocal expression, have the ability to shatter a person's and group's sense of control because they are able to penetrate defenses, personal space, and the overall sense of order.

One of my most formative therapeutic experiences happened in a group where I encouraged a child to make expressions that were beyond his ability to control himself and my power to support him. I was conducting a sound improvisation session with a group of emotionally troubled eight- and nine-year-olds in a relatively open and public place. One of the boys was consistently interrupting the group process with angry gestures. I thought that it might be helpful to give him the space to enact his feelings rather than have him continuously interfere with the group activities in order to receive attention. We would give him the attention that he seemed to want, encourage him to express himself in a solo, and make this part of the overall group experience.

After randomly banging on a series of objects with long sticks, he released a number of tumultuous screams and began to lose control. The screams were extremely loud. They not only frightened the other children but threw me and the other therapist working with me off balance. This type of unexpected and uncontrolled expression tends to be as threatening to therapists as to the clients in that our personal feelings of order and control are seriously jeopardized. I instinctively picked up the child and held him, all the while speaking to him in a gentle voice. The firm holding brought calm and it affirmed the need to figuratively hold groups in terms of safety and a clear sense of purpose within an expressive arts therapy studio.

In many of my studios, the group is able to hold and support people expressing feelings of rage, chaos, and despair. However, with this young boy, the environment was incapable of supporting his expression and it was questionable whether the discharge of rage could serve any positive or creative purpose. I do not think he was capable of "purging" himself of his angry feelings. His wrath was so all-encompassing that he completely lost control when he expressed it. The child's fury seemed endless and the screams were not only futile in venting his feelings, but furthered his agitation.

From this mistake, I learned that emotionally troubled children need very close limits and controls when expressing feelings, and especially with media such as the voice and body movement. In listening to the boy's screaming, I encountered the depth and power of his pain over which he had no control. Anger and aggressive conflicts need to be channeled and transformed by expressive activities that will not overwhelm the child.

This experience of losing control with the young boy has influenced everything I do in the expressive arts therapy studio. I approach each artistic experience, and particularly free vocal improvisation, with a keen sense for structure, purpose, and environmental safety. I try to be as attuned as possible to the expressions of the people with whom I work, doing my best to provide a clear sense of purpose. As I emphasize in other sections of this book, structure tends to enhance rather than restrict spontaneous and free expression.

Responding to Traumatic Loss through Mythic Enactment

As mentioned earlier, the integration of all modes of expression tends to occur naturally and nearly effortlessly when working with children. The child's expressive faculties have yet to go through the socialization process, which separates and isolates them from one another. My philosophical and practical orientation to expressive arts has in many ways been an outgrowth of my experience with children. The innate spontaneity and expressiveness of most children has given me the opportunity to follow their lead with art media and learn how the movements of imagination shift, expand, and focus in relation to the inspirations received from different kinds of expression.

Adults and adolescents generally need a more structured approach to artistic activity and support for free expression. Some demonstrate the openness, flexibility, and self-initiative that is more common with young children, but these tend to be an exception to the more general state of inhibition that begins to emerge during adolescence.

One of my most instructive and inspirational experiences with children involved work that I did as a beginning expressive arts therapist with a six-year-old boy. This child was not considered emotionally disturbed, but he experienced considerable conflict and anger in relation to the death of his father in Vietnam when he was four months old. In his drawings, storytelling, movement expressions, and fantasy enactments, the boy consistently dealt with themes of war and death. He taught me how children enact archetypal themes in their most personal expressions. He was a bright child with a vivid imagination. I was able to meet periodically with his mother throughout our work together, and our mutual assessment was that the loss of his father confronted the child with emotional and existential realities that most young children do not face. At the beginning of the first grade when all of the other children were expressing how they wanted to learn more about dinosaurs and how to read, he told the teachers that he would like to know more about "God and war."

In my first visit to the boy's classroom, he walked right up to me and introduced himself. As it turned out, the teachers considered referring him for expressive arts therapy because they felt he could benefit from a relationship with a man and that he needed an ongoing expressive outlet for his feelings. Although he was doing well in school from an academic standpoint, he attracted attention to himself by physically pushing other children and interrupting discussions. He consistently tried to control group activities through disruptive expressions. The teachers felt that making art with me would allow him to vent aggressive feelings and provide focused attention that he seemed to need.

For the first two months, we worked alone within the informal environment of an open classroom. Since there were many different activities taking place simultaneously within the space, we were able to blend into the more general flow of classroom activity. He initiated discussions about his feelings concerning his father's death and it was clear that he immediately developed a trust toward me. I decided in consultation with the teachers that it would be helpful to him if we could start to work within a small group setting where attention might be focused on the social interactions that caused his problems in the classroom.

We invited two other six-year-old boys to join the weekly group sessions. One of the children was also fatherless, and the other's father was absent from the home. When the two boys joined us, we held our meetings in a room adjoining the classroom, where we could freely express ourselves with musical instruments and engage the whole body in dramatic enactments and movement experiences.

I continued to work with the child whose father died in Vietnam throughout the year within both individual and group sessions. Although the intent in forming the group was to bring together three boys who were perhaps all feeling similar feelings of loss in relation to their fathers and who the female teachers felt could benefit from an ongoing relationship with a man, he was the only one of the three who directly expressed feelings about his father, and this was done largely in our one-to-one sessions. Within the group sessions, I believe that he was continuously dealing with his father's death and absence through mythological and fantasized enactments ranging from *Star Wars* and outer space battle pictures to personal dream imagery and heroic adventure stories.

Over the course of the year, the expressive arts therapy process did not precipitate dramatic changes in his behavior, but it did provide him with a regular means of communicating feelings. Through integrated arts expressions he was able to experience and share the intensities of his emotions.

In our first session together in the classroom, he drew a picture of his family, without any direction from me, and as he worked with felt-tip markers he said, "I like markers, but I like you best . . . because you're a man. I never saw a man before, except when I was a baby." He then described the figure that he was drawing as his father and told me that he wanted me to get to know his friends so that they could come and ask me to play with them. I was struck by his directness, candor, and ability to talk about emotional themes without being prompted in any way.

He spoke in our next meeting of how he dreamed of marriage and how people get married "because they want to see their baby so much. They want to see how he looks, how cute he's going to be. They want to see him because they think he's important to them. At night parents fear that their children will die."

In our third session, he once again articulated feelings about the death of children and loved ones. "I'm going to worry about if a baby is sick and dies . . . if there is someone you love the most. Sometimes I like someone and they die and then those people who are killed don't feel so well . . . people who are dead are dead and can't do anything about it." I asked him a few minutes later that if he could change anything what it would be. He replied, "I would be God so I could be anything."

He continued to draw pictures and tell stories about death and "killing" in subsequent sessions saying, "Nobody wants to be dead, nobody wants to be dead, nobody will be dead . . . I don't want to be dead, but I am dead. Webs will come on my grave. Nothing makes any sense."

In these first meetings with me, he was not only dealing with the loss of his father, but as is commonly the case with the death of a parent, he was experiencing his own mortality. It seemed that he was role reversing with his father in trying to understand what it feels like to be dead and to miss children and family. I think that he affirmed his own existence by fantasizing how his parents would miss him if he were to die. In these sessions and throughout our year of work together, he also tried to understand the significance of death, its meaning, and why people kill each other. He not only played his father during battle enactments, but he took on the role of the person, or people, who killed him.

Although he demonstrated great strength in sharing these feelings, his fear was persistent from week to week, and there were few meetings when he did not deal with death in his art. At times his imagery was quite ominous. For example, in one of our earlier sessions he began to draw a picture of a box and said, "The box is going to get my brother and me. Everything will be different. We will have to live in it. It is dark."

Our first two months of meetings seemed to be a period of catharsis for him. In addition to revealing his fears of death, he was able to describe why he gets into trouble in the classroom. "I didn't get enough attention. I really want it when I do not get it. I get angry and hurt kids because they don't give me attention . . . so I trip them. Fathers get attention, sons don't. Babies always get attention."

It appeared that at times he almost resented the attention that his father got, while he is left without having a relationship with him. The reference to babies getting attention may relate to the immature, baby-like behavior that he often exhibited at school and at home.

Figure 7.

Figure 8.

Figure 7 is one of the first pictures that he drew with me and it demonstrates how all of his creations during this period ultimately related to the theme of death. He began the picture as a tree house and went on to draw vines growing all over it. He said, "The vines are bad for wood. They kill it." And continued, "It was a perfect day when we met. I have fun with a man like you. It's all new." He then turned his tree house into "a candy house with a witch in it at midnight."

With the picture serving as a stimulus he initiated a dramatic enactment and described how "The biggest star is a magic star. It makes every wish come true. It makes you rich and kills the witch." After this statement, he drew a "witch helicopter" on the left side of the picture and told me that his father flew jets and helicopters when he was in the war.

While I was tying his sneaker at the end of the session, he kept saying, "Killing is terrible."

The boy's more diffuse feelings and expressions about war and death were most focused in a series of pictures that he drew during a session after we had been working together for a month. His first picture during this session, Figure 8, was one of his *Star Wars* images.

From this meeting and others that followed, I discovered how what might first appear to be stereotypic imagery in children's art often has significant personal meaning. When working with artistic expressions, it is important to do our best to withhold the tendency to make judgments of any kind. The therapeutic discipline applies sustained and open attention in a way that empowers the creative process to unfold in ways that lie outside our preconceptions.

The *Star Wars* mythology of life and death, war and peace, good and evil, heroes and villains, perhaps helped the child deal with his loss. My work with him in turn enabled me to see the personal value of images and enactments that we often quickly dismiss as stereotypic manifestations of popular culture. The sequence of pictures and the dramatic enactments that he initiated in this session seemed to help him clarify and articulate the feelings that he had about his father's death. In response to Figure 8, he described how "the ships are fighting. They're getting killed. I feel scared. My dad went on a battle cruiser, something stupid, he got killed. There was this bad guy in front who wanted to kill my father. He said, 'Go forward,' and my father got killed by the spaceship."

In his picture and the accompanying stories and enactments, the child seems to imaginatively integrate *Star Wars* mythology with his father's death. He described his feelings about the picture: "I'm in a fight because I do not know anything about my dad. I love spears because they're tough. I want to know more about him. I want to be a hero."

As the session progressed, he did two fantasized pictures of his father as an elevator man at a shopping center. He created a drawing (Fig. 9) which

Figure 9.

started out as a picture of dinosaurs. At first, I thought this might be a stereo-typic covering of the feelings that he started to express about his father, but as he verbally dramatized what the picture represented, I again realized how important it is to reserve hasty conclusions about apparent stereotypes.

"This is a picture of dinosaurs and my father. My father is getting all the dinosaurs. They have hearts. [All of the picture was drawn with blue except for the hearts, which were colored red.] He's getting the bones for dogs. The big dinosaur is going to chomp him. He's going to get killed. He's picking up his body. My father was holding a book, but he dropped it. He just ate my dad. The dinosaur says that tastes cool, but should I have eaten him or not? My father opened the dinosaur's jaw and got his parachute, and got free, and jumped down. He hollered help. That's his pants, shirt—his pants are slipping off. Now he's getting so close to the other dinosaur."

This was a truly remarkable enactment of his father's plight. He utilizes the mythological structure of a hero being overwhelmed by forces beyond his control. The battle can be likened to Ahab and the white whale in Melville's *Moby Dick* and other archetypal themes of protagonists confronting powers beyond the human sphere. Like Jonah being freed from the belly of the whale, his father escapes, but this resurrection is only temporary, as he affirms the finality of death by falling toward yet another dinosaur. In this

Figure 10.

picture, he also attributes feelings of ambivalence to the dinosaur after eating his father.

Figure 10 is typical of a series of subsequent pictures, not shown here, in which the boy acts out frantic battle scenes without directly speaking about his father.

"It's a rocket ship getting ready to blast off. It's in trouble because it's going to explode and there's a mini-ship on the nose that they'll get into. The bad ship (on the left) is going to kill them because bad guys hate good guys. They're going to laser them. The bad guys are going to win. They always do. They have more stuff. The bad guys ruined the whole ship because they just wanted the gold door. People fight for babies, bad stuff, and everything. People kill each other."

In Figure 11, he drew a series of graves and introduced Jesus as the victim who lives on in personal memory.

"I'm making graves all bent over. It is very interesting for you to learn about. I'm going to add Jesus. He's got arrows pointing into him. These little men, little ants [note mythological parallel to Swift's *Gulliver's Travels*] are trying to kill him and put him into the biggest of the graves. I am thinking all the way back in time. They stabbed him with a knife in the heart. He's dead, but he's in your mind all of the time."

Figure 11.

I asked if there was a reason for his death, and he answered, "Yes, he was trying to kill them, so they killed him . . . If people want to make war, they can. The spaceship [left side of picture] is trying to kill the ants, but they're too small, and it got Jesus, the God, by mistake."

In this picture and the accompanying dramatization, he is beginning to come to grips with the realization that his protagonist was an equal partner in the life-death struggle and that both sides were perhaps trying just as hard to kill each other. He also introduces the possibility that the figure may have been killed by mistake.

He dealt with this theme again in our next session and created the following story from a drawing: "A captain from long, long ago, like my dad. He sometimes wrecked his life himself. He used bombs to wreck other ships, and they bombed his ship. The iron face killed my dad. It's a metal ball type ship, and everything bounces off it. But this isn't my dad. Here's his grave. I'm going to make his grave. He's dead. The man who killed my dad is floating away."

In a later session focused on movement and dramatic enactment to the theme of "under," he began his movement expression with yet another enactment of death themes embodying the evil force in the form of a snake.

After the enactment he made Figure 12 and responded to it with a story. "The bad guys threw a ball down into the sea and put a snake and tarantu-

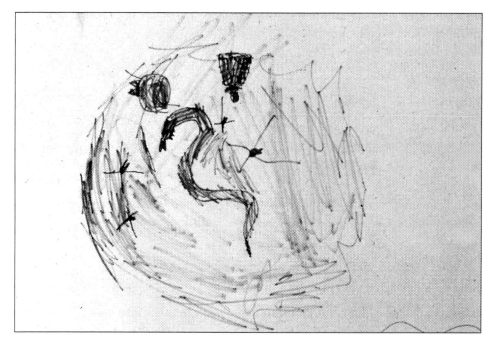

Figure 12.

Figure 13.

las into it. They wanted to kill people who went diving and would eat the poison by mistake. That's my uncle swimming. If he was Superman he could see what was inside the ball. He's going to die, not in real life but in the picture. It's interesting to me. Everybody likes to know about dead people. They go to the graveyard and pray and draw pictures of how they died. I like it when they were alive, but they are dead now. The people who are left alive hurt themselves because they're so angry. They want to be with those dead people."

In the final sequence of pictures he becomes more closely identified with the protagonist. In Figure 13, he is the one who kills the snake who is about to kill the queen.

His most forceful, aggressive, and violent enactment came in the following session where we began by letting the children take me along with them in their movement dramatizations. He had me play the role of the evil monsters that he constantly confronts in his pictures, and the physical contact with me intensified his emotion.

He drew Figure 14 afterwards and described it to me. "In my picture, you're deadly, a giant. I have wires connecting your brain to mine. I am taking your memory to know what you were back in time, to know who you killed. I want to take all of your brain. The army is shooting at you because you're deadly. You're wicked angry because we are attacking you. You picked up the general and chewed him up and spit him out with his guts and all. I got hold of all the cannons and pressed all the buttons. They went mad. I knew everything you do. I knew everything you do. The best way to kill him is to pull down his pants in front of a firing squad. I know everything you do."

In Figures 14 and 15 that he drew in our final session, he is assuming control and power over a variety of malevolent forces. He said that he was drawing monsters over and over again "because I have to get it out of my mind. Then I don't think of it anymore."

In Figure 15, he is completely victorious over the evil characters and portrays himself in a massive representation of muscles and blood. "The grizzly wants to kill people and Godzilla comes along and all the people cheered for him and raised a flag. They shouted for him, and he made trees fall down on the grizzly. He breathed fire on him."

The violent fantasies that this boy experienced are universal aspects of the human psyche and not necessarily wrong. Serious problems occur when children and adults can no longer distinguish between having dark thoughts within the imaginal realm and acting them out in the world in ways that harm themselves and other people. In our sessions, the boy gained confidence in his ability to control emotions of anger, fear, and loss while channeling them into creative expressions.

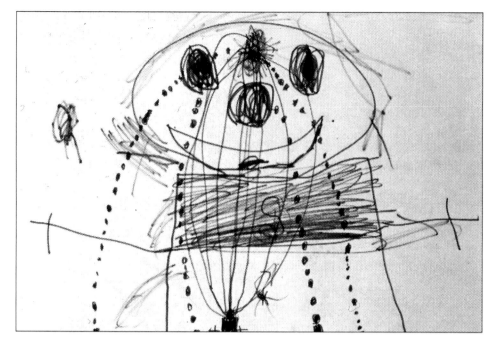

Figure 14.

Figure 15.

Two months after we completed our work at the end of the school year, I received a phone call from the boy's mother and she asked if I could see him again because he appeared to need the regular outlet for his feelings that was provided during our sessions. She said that while making art with me he was able to express emotions with her. From time to time, he would have uncontrollable outbursts and she sensed that this was perhaps a necessary release of feelings that he had previously repressed. His dialogue in our sessions also confirms how drawing enactments and narrative were used to express and perhaps understand a deep complex of emotions about tragic and traumatic life events and losses.

We met again and he said that he missed me, and I said the same to him. At the end of our meeting, he summed up our work together in a statement that I cannot improve upon with regard to the purpose of expressive arts therapy—"It's good to get your feelings out. You tell people how much you feel so they'll understand and share their feelings with you. You're supposed to let feelings out so other people will know how you feel. Life doesn't just belong to you but to other people too."

An Improvisation Group

Over the course of a year-long period, I worked with three six-year-old boys and girls in a weekly creative improvisation group. All of the children had difficulty listening, controlling impulses, and expressing themselves clearly with others. In our group, we used musical and dramatic dialogues to address these problems and help the children practice being attentive and sensitive to the expressions of their peers.

After first demonstrating how the simple manipulation of objects in our environment could become sources of expressive sound (tapping pencils on books, drinking glasses, and so forth), I gradually introduced a variety of percussion, wind, and string instruments suggesting that they explore different kinds of sounds that the instruments make. The process resembled the tuning up period of a band or orchestra. We often did this one by one with individual children experimenting with sounds while the others listened.

The children would settle into working with an instrument that interested them on a particular day. As we began to play together and search for a common rhythm, the children's playing was at times chaotic. I would intervene and attempt to create a supportive and orderly structure. If the sounds were random and quite loud, I might ask them to play as softly as they could and from this transition some form of cohesion would usually develop. I often played an instrument myself and helped the children listen and find common rhythms through sounds that I made rather than giving them verbal directions.

I find that musical disarray is often due to confusion, a lack of self-confidence, and the inability to listen. I try to deal with the problem by sensitizing participants to sound and helping them listen more carefully to their own playing and to the sounds that others are making. I stress how complete beginners can make musical sounds in unison with others if they listen carefully and stay with a common rhythm. I might focus the group on sounds that a child is making and then have them make the sounds together.

In our group, I asked one child to begin a rhythm and invited others to join the expression on a one-by-one basis and at other times the whole group would respond. The interactive rhythms produced a sense of excitement as variations and new sounds grew out of a constant pulse in which everyone was immersed. The children had to listen closely to one another if they were to make sounds in an organized and rhythmic fashion. They also developed a sense of timing, order, and an aesthetic sensitivity to appropriate and effective ways of expressing themselves in relation to others. There was a negative value placed on impulsive and egocentric expressions in group musical improvisations. The children were able to determine how unrelated and dissonant sounds affected the overall rhythm.

Within a musical improvisation, interruptions and impulsive actions tend to generate an immediate sense of incongruity and irritation. I observed how the children in our group were keenly aware when they were out of sync with their sounds, whereas this type of sensitivity was not present in their more general behavior. I believe the differences can be attributed to how the musical improvisations held their attention.

Although I generally let improvisations develop naturally, I would sometimes "conduct" the music by encouraging the children to speed up their playing and then slow the process down; build progressively from soft and gentle sounds to more forceful expressions and vice versa; gradually come to a stop and a period of silence; intersperse rhythms with intervals of silence; and so forth.

The children enjoyed the feelings of order that accompanied their working together in unison and they liked having their sounds conducted by another person. They took turns conducting and controlling the group musical process.

We also engaged in improvisational dialogues where one child expressed sounds to another who listened and played them back again, sometimes adding a new dimension. The children would switch roles and the exchange might be repeated three to five times.

These one-on-one improvisational interactions were often extended to include the third child in the group and myself. When working together as a group, individuals took turns responding and adding to the improvisation, and we repeated each new response together before moving on to another person. We would sometimes go through three or more sequences involving each of us. Playing together in this way reinforces the common pulse and builds group momentum and support for each child. And again the children had to listen carefully to rhythms and threads of communication in order to express themselves in ways that contributed to the mutual composition.

When I began to work with the children in this group, I did not have a script to follow. The direction unfolded from my engagement with them, the improvisational expressions, and my emerging sense of what they needed. The artistic medium in many ways informed our overall purpose and my therapeutic strategy. In this way, the core dynamics of artistic expression and the demands of a medium guide us toward optimum cooperation, the elimination of dissonance, and the realization of the most effective expression possible.

In other sessions, we would use the same improvisational structures as a basis for dramatic enactments, storytelling, group poems, and dances. The children would give and receive movements and words; repeat them; slow the expression down or speed it up; arrange the elements into new combinations; take pauses; and sustain the overall improvisation in varied ways, sometimes staying with a single medium or integrating more than one. These experiences with children keep reinforcing how whatever we do with a particular artistic modality can be applied to others with the goal of generating new cycles of expression which act upon us in different ways, stimulate various contents, and invigorate the overall creative process.

Battles within the Imagination

The work that I did with another six-year-old boy illustrates how artistic activity can help a child progress from relatively complete withdrawal to establishing expressive abilities in different media and becoming a more productive participant in the classroom environment. The relationship with this boy, early in my career, once again illustrated how different art forms will emerge naturally within the therapeutic setting. I was originally asked to work with him because his teachers felt that he had skills with the visual arts, but as our work unfolded, drawing and painting stimulated far more comprehensive expression in dramatic improvisation, movement, and storytelling.

When referred to expressive art therapy, the child was totally nonverbal and thus unable to become involved in the basic activities of the first grade classroom in a public school. The teachers were alarmed when two months into the school year, he became increasingly immersed in private fantasy play. They described how he made strange noises while playing which he later described as "monster sounds."

Figure 16.

Monster dramatizations and fantasies are common with young children and not necessarily signs of emotional problems. However, this child was frightened by adults. His creative expressions conveyed fears of being hurt by forces outside of himself. I sensed that there were connections of some kind between his monster figures and adults.

One of the first pictures that he drew (Fig. 16) depicted a large shark swimming after him.

In response to my questions, he began to talk about the picture in a barely audible whisper. He said, "The boy was at the beach with his mother and father, and he swam out too far, and the shark came after him, and got him, and ate him, and his mother and father were sad."

Soon after making the picture of being pursued by the shark, he painted a circle resting on a blue horizontal line which he described as "a ball on the water that got away from a boy because he threw it too far, and it went out into the ocean."

The boy's artworks and the imaginative and descriptive statements that he made in response to them revealed that he had considerable expressive potential, conceptual aptitude, and insight. I determined that the main purpose of our work together should be the provision of opportunities for creative expression. I was impressed with the way he immersed himself in the process of painting and drawing, and how he responded without hesitation to my invitations to engage his pictures.

In these first sessions, I was simply trying to encourage the boy to talk after making pictures, to use his voice, and speak to another person. Since I was not thinking in terms of stories and creative enactments, I was taken aback by the imaginative statements that he made and how they tersely gave a dramatic coherence and purpose to the whole composition.

I began to feel that perhaps he retreated from contact with other people and hid within himself as a form of protection. He was clearly capable of making meaningful contact with others but nevertheless withdrew into himself. He lived in an ocean community so it was natural for the sea to be a familiar part of his imagery and sharks were ubiquitous in the pictures of all the children in the school as a result of the recent release of the film *Jaws*.

In a later picture, he drew another shark with an open mouth swimming up to a ball. "The shark is going to bite the ball and pop it. Someone threw it out too far."

Sharks, the sea, floating balls, and "too far" were consistent themes in these first pictures and statements. In addition to images of sharks, he also created pictures of monsters.

The teachers felt that this expressive activity with me was having a positive impact on his more general behavior in the classroom. He was now working on projects and he stopped using self-immersed monster fantasies to separate himself from classmates. He was communicating with others through creative expressions and using them as a basis for establishing relationships. The monster pictures and stories ended after he drew a picture of me as a monster, confirming my belief that this theme was connected to a fear of adults.

He began another series of imaginative pictures that always began with the drawing of a mound in the middle of the page. After making the mound shape in each drawing, he added an elaborate network of inner passageways.

In response to Figure 17, he said: "This is a mountain with orange trees and tunnels that people use to get to the top to have a sun-tan. It's a fun mountain. Some kids come up and play. They throw rocks! They bury rocks. They put rocks on a pile. They make a hole. Then they put rocks inside it. Then they fill it up. Then they go down the mountain. (PAUSE) They play with rocks because it's the only thing they can do. I wash them off at home and put them in a bowl with fish."

This was the first of many stories about rocks, tunnels, digging holes, and putting the rocks in the holes. His family had meager financial resources, and he told me that he played with rocks all the time because there was nothing else.

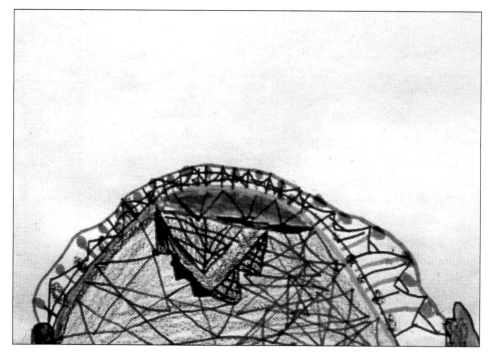

Figure 17.

I was struck by the resourcefulness and complexity of his fantasy life which he had not previously revealed in such detail. He demonstrated how the imagination makes use of the most basic materials to fashion vital and engaging creations.

It also became apparent that it was important for this child to have the opportunity to work creatively in a one-to-one relationship with an adult. He was at first lost in the larger classroom group which seemed to make him retreat even more into himself. He needed to begin expressing himself in a secure context where his strengths with the creative imagination could be affirmed and used as bridges to more comprehensive communications with others.

In subsequent pictures and stories, the boy moved beyond the repetition of rocks, holes, and tunnels. It seemed like these places were a private and protected inner sanctum of the imagination and that he was now ready to explore a larger context of expressions in the outer world. He continued to draw the mound at the bottom center of every picture, but it became less significant and gradually disappeared.

The later pictures started with images of airplanes and developed into violent battle scenes and dramatizations of war. He began to act more aggressively in making these pictures and in responding to them. When drawing, he made forceful vocal sounds of explosions, roaring engines, and bursts of movement. The whole process was a lively dramatic enactment. As he became immersed in the spontaneous drama, he often stepped back from the table or easel and used his body to act out scenes he created.

The making of pictures set the stage for self-initiated dramatic play. He seemed to appreciate the responses and support that he received from me and other children who were fascinated by his creative dramatizations. At this early point in my career, he helped me to realize how all of the children were using the creative imagination and different forms of artistic drama to respond to their pictures as contrasted to adults who tended to use more literal and descriptive narratives.

Six months had passed in our work together, and he was noticeably more articulate and responsive to the total classroom environment. He was transferred into a special classroom where there were only five other children. His teacher supported his verbalizations by making tape recordings of his voice and playing them back to him. He greatly enjoyed making and listening to the tapes which affirmed how much he could benefit from attention, affirmation, and the more general objectification of his experience and expression. The move to the special education resource room was designed to build upon the skills and interests that he showed in artistic expression and the work that we did in responding to the pictures.

Figure 18 provides an example of his expressive battle art. Note the small mound at the bottom of the page. This was the last of the mound pictures. These combat scenes stimulated more elaborate and animated stories.

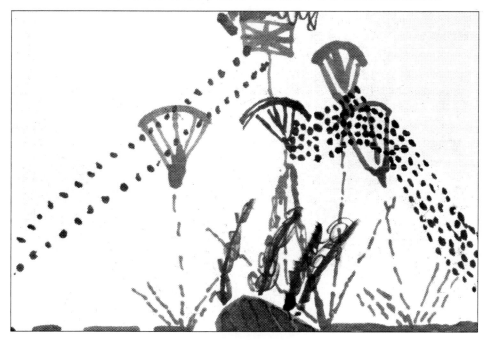

Figure 18.

"This is a pool of burning blood," he said. "These are bombs at the bottom. The good guys are coming down in parachutes, and they are going to fall into the bombs and into the blood that the bad guys put there. The guy in the middle is carrying the guns and they can't get to them to fight back. (PAUSE) I would like to be a dead guy. (PAUSE) These two guys are getting murdered. Look at this–the men are falling and getting bombed up. They both got bombed up at the same time. They all got murdered. But the good guys that got killed got operated on by doctors in the army, and they got better, and they came back and got the bad guys."

His teacher walked into the room and he said spontaneously to her, "Guess what team got killed, the good guys or the bad guys?"

At this point in our work together, his language and verbal expression had developed markedly from the first sessions when he would only make soft, whispering, and very terse statements in response to my questions. Through every phase of our work together his creative expressions were always self-initiated and as he became more relaxed and confident, his art became more complex and forceful.

He extended the venue of his battle art from earth to outer space with Figure 19.

"The rocket bombed up into the sky and saw guys shooting people and some guys smashed into him, and he got on fire, and then the world bombed

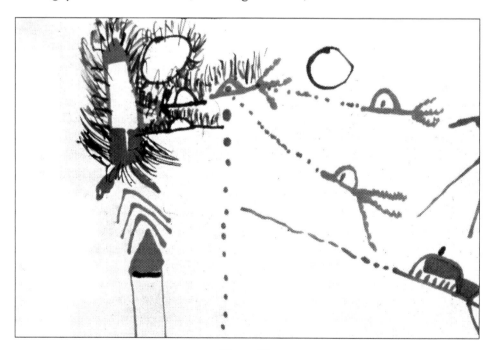

Figure 19.

Figure 20.

up. Then the police and fire engine went on fire. Then the rocket and everything fell."

He acted out an inferno of total devastation where even the keepers of the
social order (police and fire engines) were destroyed.

The story and picture that he shared with me in our last session continued
the battle enactments but were more focused on protected and "safe" places.

He described Figure 20 as "an airport with a place on top of the building
where they watch the men. That plane is the bad guy (right) and that one is
the good guy (left). That's the stuff to put out the fire on the good guy's plane
(lines connecting plane to bottom left). They're shooting from inside the
building because it's safe in there."

This drawing and accompanying story suggest that he is able to bring the
battle under control and "put out the fire." In addition to strengthening his
expressive skills and confidence, our sessions helped this child develop inner
discipline and organization. He enacted previously repressed emotions and
the results were consistently positive. He expressed fears and vulnerabilities
and was able to manage the process with skill and sensitivity. Expressive
vitality and coherence emerged from spontaneous expression rather than
harmful chaos and destruction.

Communication was consistent through every phase of our work over the
course of the school year and there was a steady development in the quality

of both his creative and verbal expressions. The last two pictures that he made (Figs. 19 & 20) are skillful and clearly rendered drawings that depict complex and vivid action.

Children's war dramatizations generally serve an important form of expressive release. Through art, they confront the reality of wars both outside and inside themselves while coming to grips with the harm and devastation that can result. Imaginary battle enactments were particularly productive in the work that I did with this young boy. As he vented his aggressive feelings, he simultaneously practiced managing them in a creative way that always resulted in a more general sense of calm and competence when the process was completed.

Expressing and fully dramatizing fears and aggressive fantasies was the essence of the expressive arts therapy process with this child. The arts helped him emerge from autistic withdrawal and through drawing, storytelling, and dramatic improvisation, he learned how to enact his feelings with other people. The characters in the battle creations are always men with the ability to do both good and evil and the boy's imaginary enactments played out ambivalent feelings towards these characters. He showed the same ambivalence towards his monsters, which were objects of fear and affection. The men in his battle pictures are both the "bad guys" and the keepers of social order.

From an archetypal perspective, the boy's expressions can be viewed as embodiments of mythic themes involving battles between heroes and dark forces. In this sense, they are much more than just war pictures. The tensions were never resolved with any sense of finality and this once against fits the mythic reality where opposing forces form a creative partnership. In his art, the boy separates from his usual behaviors, enacts the mythic journey into imagination, and returns to the daily life of the classroom.

Witnessing this journey through the imagination gave me one of my first exposures to how the expressive arts therapy process can both heal the soul and strengthen a person's capacity to function more effectively in the world. The boy also taught me how even young children with serious disabilities have an innate tendency to brilliantly enact universal and yet highly individual dramas of the imagination. There was a distinct depth and wisdom conveyed by the contents of his expression.

When he took the risk to express himself completely, the boy discovered that he was always grounded in the action and discipline of making art and a supportive relationship with someone who witnessed and affirmed his expressions. He was able to let go of his restraints and allow the spontaneous flow of imagination to occur while demonstrating an ability to direct his expression. Every time he confronted his fears of going "out too far" or being devoured by monsters and other malevolent forces, as well as the potential within him to do harm, he returned intact and better for it. As Dennis McCarthy suggests in writing about monster enactments in children's art, healing occurs when we no longer stifle but begin to engage, express, and transform the energy of the feared image (2007).

On the most concrete level, expressive arts therapy gave this boy the chance to freely exercise and express his imagination in a positive way; develop his inner ability to control emotions and actions; establish self-confidence based upon real competence and mastery with various artistic media; establish a respected identity for himself within the classroom group; and achieve a new comfort when interacting with adults.

As an expressive arts therapist, I learned from this boy how verbal expression, creative stories, and deeply significant dramatic enactments can emerge naturally from the process of making pictures. The different media of artistic expression build upon one another and carry the imagination to places that may not be possible to reach through the use of only one mode of communication.

This boy was my teacher and his highly imaginative process of making art and responding to his pictures has informed everything I have done in the expressive arts therapies since first working with him over thirty years ago. He showed me how people sometimes have a deep need, almost a compulsion, to respond to their paintings and drawings in imaginative ways. The art object acts as both a stimulus and as a companion in furthering discovery within the realm of imagination. The picture is always there. It patiently stays with us through our inevitable motions of approach and avoidance and then generously reveals itself when we let go and open to the wisdom of these creative explorations. Within expressive arts therapy the art object also acts as a tangible anchor that grounds us in the immediate physical world as we descend into inner musings. The artwork is an intermediary object and a helper, an abiding presence that accompanies us through the flux of free expression.

But perhaps most importantly, this boy taught me how the process of therapy is most effective when it is directed by the child himself with the therapist acting as a guide and keeper of the art and healing space. Like D. W. Winnicott, I have realized how the most insightful and transformative moments happen unexpectedly and as part of the flow of creative expression when therapists help children learn and discover life for themselves.

More attention must be given to how children can heal themselves within environments that promote discovery. My belief is that young children retreat from the world or become immersed in destructive actions because they are not given the opportunity to learn in creative ways with the support and love of adults. Therefore, the fundamental task of expressive arts therapy is one of creating environments where the missing core of healthy experience can take place for children and all the other people who are longing for this kind of creative inquiry and transformation.

If we therapists can empower and recognize young children as our teachers within a process of reciprocal influences, then we can contribute to a deeper mode of healing that happens when people in need are able to influence and transform others and not just themselves. I may have helped this boy by coming to his school each week for a year and giving him the chance to express himself through the arts, but he may have done more for me. Our work together has had a lifelong and formative influence on how I approach expressive arts therapy.

Efforts to heal and be healed are part of a constant ebb and flow of losing and gaining awareness. The goal is never achieved with finality. The most abiding sense of well-being tends to come when we realize this impermanence and simply sustain our efforts to live as creatively as possible with the resources that we have. This young boy helped me to appreciate this basic condition of the creative process and perhaps our work together made some small contribution to a positive unfolding of his life and expressive potential.

ADULTS WHO SHOW HOW THE ARTS HEAL

In this section, I will offer descriptions of the work I did at the Danvers State Hospital and the Addison Gallery of American Art together with more recent accounts in an effort to describe how essential methods and concepts of expressive arts therapy have been shaped through practice with others. The primary focus is on my initial involvement with expressive arts therapy since this period has had such a significant influence on how I work with people, my sense of the role of art in therapy, and my development as an artist.

My seminal experiences at Danvers with Anthony, Bernice, Christopher, and Priscilla have been described in a number of previous publications (McNiff, 1981, 1992, & 2004). However, because there is considerable depth and range to their creative expressions, the majority of the works shown here are being published for the first time. I will also offer new reflections on other Danvers artists who informed my first efforts to integrate different art forms within the expressive therapy studio.

A Lifeline during an Intense Disturbance

One of the first encounters that I had at Danvers State Hospital has proven to be among the most unusual expressive arts therapy incidents that I have observed over the course of my career. Bernice, a woman in her late thirties, made intensely expressive art during an extended catatonic period. She was mute and severely withdrawn from any kind of social contact for a number of months. When she returned to her usual modes of speaking to other people, her art stopped.

The work that Bernice did in expressive arts therapy was largely self-initiated and I served as a witness, supporter, and occasional guide. When she was immersed in art, I tried to stay off to the side while affirming what she was doing. People constantly describe to me how this quiet witnessing of artistic experience by another person is a fundamental and necessary feature of the expressive arts therapy experience.

Bernice was referred to the Danvers studio in an effort to draw her out of a catatonic stupor. She would not speak, and her eye contact with other people was minimal. Her movements were extremely stiff, and unless she was asked to move, she would remain motionless in the same chair all day.

From my experience with Bernice, I learned how artistic expression sometimes serves as a temporary bridge to others when other forms of communication are not available. As she began to speak in her normal way, Bernice's artistic expression stopped completely. Although as an artist, I felt a loss in relation to the powerful expressions that Bernice made in the art studio, I accepted this change as part of her overall recovery.

In our first meeting, Bernice was reluctant to draw and she made a picture with random doodles. However, she returned to the art studio on subsequent occasions and became immersed in the process of silently making drawings.

As she became comfortable in the studio, Bernice's pictures were more expressive of inner feelings. She typically began by drawing a face or human figures and then made a series of repeating lines emanating from the central form. Figure 21 demonstrates the expressive power of the drawings she made when unable to speak. On the picture she wrote "Nobody, August ?, 1970."

In a later session, when she was speaking again, Bernice described how this picture expresses how she felt bound and locked within her silence. All of her tension was pushing inward. While drawing, she heavily shaded the elbows to emphasize how they were pressing into the person. The tension-filled facial expression resembled her own face when she sat silently in the hospital, showing only a pained grimace.

Her decorative use of line, form, and color was markedly similar to many of the drawings included in Prinzhorn's 1922 book. I believe that this similarity is a manifestation of universal artistic patterns of expression whereby a composition is constructed by drawing a figure or shape and then repeating the lines to build an overall pictorial configuration. Where the cliché psychiatric interpretations were likely to see anything bizarre or fragmented as indications of schizophrenic thought, I was impressed by the positive way Bernice constructed complex and visually dynamic pictures while working intently at the process of drawing.

Figure 21. Nobody.

When I saw the artworks included in Prinzhorn's *Artistry of the Mentally Ill*, I was intrigued with the similarities to Bernice's pictures, which could have been included in the volume. A half-century after the book was published Bernice affirmed Prinzhorn's core theory that the patient artists were motivated by an innate "urge for expression" that was in this case intensified by her withdrawal from verbal communication. During an intense emotional crisis when speech was not accessible to Bernice, she turned to art and the floodgates of expression were opened. Her pictures and the process of making them provided an emotional outlet, a discipline of creative work, and connections with other people. She was communicating with vitality and intelligence when the more usual ways of relating to others did not exist.

As I worked with Bernice in the art therapy studio, there were many challenges and threats to the progress she was making. The unfolding of artistic expression is rarely a step-by-step incremental process. Setbacks, together with instances of doubt, anger, and frustration, are likely to be features of the overall experience for every person.

After we worked together for six weeks, Bernice appeared to be highly motivated to begin speaking and acting in her normal fashion. But as she spoke to me in what appeared to be a relaxed and comfortable mood, the picture she was making changed into a monster-like figure. She quickly became agitated and furiously ripped the painting apart. She began to destroy all of her previous work, and I intervened, held her, and requested that she save the pictures.

For a week after this incident, Bernice was extremely withdrawn. Although I was discouraged by what appeared to be a major setback to the steady emergence from a severe catatonic state, I sensed that this period of upheaval indicated that Bernice was not yet ready to re-enter the world of usual relations with other people. The healing process required more time. She had to take a step backwards before moving forward in a significant way.

These sessions helped me see how anger and fury are powerful motivational elements that spur us to withdraw from the world as well as act upon it in belligerent ways. Art served as a transitional medium that enabled Bernice to bring what was inside into the outside world, to express her anger creatively. In addition to the affirmations that she received from other people, I feel that an important feature of Bernice's involvement in the expressive arts therapy studio was her ability to witness the power of her artistic expressions and the intensity of the emotional contents that they manifested.

One of the most striking features of this expressive arts therapy experience was the way in which a person who became a dynamo of graphic emotional expression lost the desire to make art when she was "well" once again. When completely withdrawn in terms of language and physical gestures, Bernice still felt a need to express feelings and transform experience symbolically through drawing and painting. When her language was restored, her art was no longer needed.

Three years after leaving the hospital, Bernice returned to meet with me. She described how angry she was when first admitted to the locked ward for acutely disturbed patients and how she had withdrawn because she was afraid of hurting herself and other people. Her catatonic condition was an internalization of her anger and fear. It was also a form of self-restraint, keeping her from acting on her destructive feelings. She described how her early pictures expressed the anger she felt and allowed her to release feelings in a way that would not harm anyone.

Expressive arts therapy provides a way of engaging and transforming these conflicts into affirmations of life. The process is alchemical and different from more linear approaches to solving problems. Jung wrote repeatedly about how artistic images act upon people with palpable and "age-old magical effects" that emit from the expressive power of symbols. He described how the pictures that we make will: "cast their magic into our systems and put us right, provided we put ourselves into them" (Chodorow, 1997, p. 152); and induce a neutralizing "spell" on the conditions they express (p. 176).

Art served many different healing functions for Bernice. Her drawing enactments provided a medium through which she confronted and expelled her demons. The pictures also gave tangible form to fear and anger, helping her to gradually lessen their restrictive hold on her life.

As she communicated with people in the expressive arts therapy studio through her art, we began to show the pictures to other people in the hospital who expressed great interest. Bernice's involvement in art helped to rebuild her self-image and sense of personal value. She first spoke to me only in relation to her pictures and the process of creating them. As she mastered drawing techniques, Bernice seemed to enjoy the attention that she received from other people and the warmth they extended to her in acknowledging her art. The drawings gave others an opportunity to support her.

My experience with Bernice helped me to completely reverse the general perception of what was then considered "schizophrenic art." Bernice was a person suffering from what can be called a schizophrenic episode, but her art was a profoundly significant manifestation of health and the striving of the psyche to work its way through a tormented time. Where the conventional approach to psychiatric art focused on the revelation of what was wrong with a person, Bernice's depiction of tortured subject matter can be viewed as giving shape to feelings and providing an outlet for expression during a period of crisis. Artistic expression was a lifeline that Bernice used to draw and paint her way back to health.

Awakening the Whole Person through All of the Arts

During my first years at Danvers I had many experiences where developmental patterns in artistic expression were accompanied by corresponding changes in behavior. My work with Anthony began with drawing and painting and expanded to a more comprehensive involvement with all of the arts and other life experiences with the goal of developing his whole person.

I first met Anthony when he was thirty-five and after he had lived in the back wards of the hospital for 20 years. His mute withdrawal and behavioral regression were so profound that he gave the impression of having severe mental deficits. Anthony's records indicated that as a youth he had been an "A" student and a capable athlete but that he was also a very shy child. He was admitted to the psychiatric hospital at age 15 for serious emotional disturbances of an unknown origin. Electroshock therapy and the general conditions of institutional living increased his withdrawal, and for 20 years he rarely spoke. Past entries into his file indicated that he would mumble, "I don't know," in response to questions that were addressed to him.

Anthony was part of an expressive arts therapy group that I organized for men living in one of the locked wards of the state hospital, a place where the most withdrawn and disturbed patients passed year after year with virtually no therapeutic treatment other than medications and various forms of

Figure 22. Scribbled Figure.

restraint. He spent his days pacing or lying in a fetal position and it could be said that over the years he successfully conformed to the expectations of institutional life.

In previous publications I have described how Anthony progressed in his art from many months of making quick and repetitious line drawings of a human figure (Fig. 22) to creating skillfully rendered paintings with a distinct style. This consistent and dramatic development in artistic expression helped to stimulate a more comprehensive awakening of his total life experience.

He made bold contour drawings of objects in the studio that stunned me with their intelligence, skill, and aesthetic sensitivity (Fig. 23). I tried to build on this ability and engaged him in making pictures interpreting photos of works of art (Figs. 24 & 25) and a photograph of a man holding a child (Fig. 26).

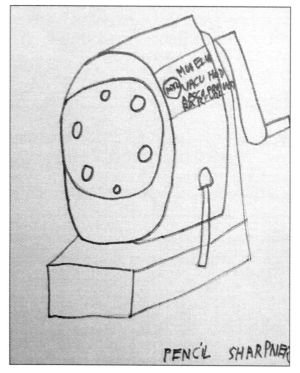

Figure 23. Pencil sharpener.

Figure 24. From Ben Shahn.

Figure 25. From Picasso.

Figure 26. Grandfather and infant.

Figure 27. Portrait of Christopher.

Figure 28. Portrait of Shaun McNiff.

At my urging, he created portraits of other people in the studio (Figs. 27 & 28).

If I was not physically present and encouraging Anthony to make a picture, he would do nothing. Everything he created in the visual arts was part of a close relationship that we developed. I "coached" him, encouraged looking closely at objects, and taking time to render what he saw. As I watched him draw and paint, I began to internalize his style of expression and it felt almost like the pictures were coming from something that existed between the two of us even though he made every mark on his own. As I will describe in the next section, this collaboration with Anthony had a major impact on my own artistic development.

We listened to music while working and he would occasionally stop for a moment and walk through the studio humming. Music and body movement thus emerged naturally as important elements in what became a multisensory expressive arts therapy process.

Since Anthony never spoke, I developed ways of reinforcing his expressions and connecting with him through touch—pats on the back, hand shakes, an arm around his shoulders, and so forth. A sense of camaraderie was established as I became increasingly involved and fascinated with his artistic expressions, his overall demeanor in the studio, and his ways of relating to me. I viewed myself as a kind of transitional figure in that he continued his severe withdrawal in relation to other people and hospital staff. In drawing and painting and the more extended relationship with me as an agent of these activities, Anthony began to show distinct gifts for creative expression and he started for the first time to initiate activity in other areas of his life.

Toward the end of our first year of working together, Anthony began to utter words in stream of consciousness speech. Some of his statements were quite dramatic. He said to me, "I have been dead for a long time," and a moment later he continued, "Dr. Crush got me in Waltham . . . Waltham shocks."

While talking about "getting shocked," he held his fingers to his temples where the electroshock electrodes were placed. He began to speak to me about his father, who had died of a heart attack shortly after he was first admitted to the mental hospital. With clear and intelligent handwriting, he wrote the names of the people in his family, childhood friends, street names, and other neighborhood sites. He would regularly look at me, ask me who I was, and then refer to me as his father (I was ten years younger than Anthony).

Time for Anthony had stopped when he was first hospitalized, and he constantly referred to the year as 1953 and gave his age as 17, thus denying the years that had passed since he was admitted to the hospital. He did not want to accept the death of his father. At other times, he would refer to himself as an infant, and he curled his body up on the floor.

Anthony's artistic development drew significant attention within the hospital, where staff and other patients were taken aback when they saw him producing sophisticated drawings. The entire process was astounding to me as a beginning expressive arts therapist. I met with Anthony's mother who visited with him at least one day a week over his 20 years of hospitalization. She was amazed and spoke of how he always stood in a corner, paced, and never spoke when he was with her.

Anthony's tangible growth within the visual arts gave an indication of the potential that could possibly be extended into his total being. As with others in the studio, it became clear that he might benefit by expanding what we were doing in the visual arts to other expressive modalities. He confirmed the importance of total sensory involvement in expressive arts therapy and helped me shape this new discipline in response to the conditions of his life and natural needs for communication.

As we continued our expressive arts therapy work, I observed Anthony's excellent physical coordination, and began to engage him in movement activities. I noted that if I met him after breakfast every morning and did a series of physical exercises, he became much more alert and motivated. After a year of this morning exercise, his body became trim and fit. He also had a fine baritone voice that we began to develop. I would sing statements to him, and he would sing them back to me playfully. These games not only revitalized his voice but increased his spontaneity when speaking.

He had not spoken for so long that he was intrigued with the vibrations of his vocal chords, and he touched them with his fingers while singing and talking.

After our second year of working together, he took a job in the hospital laundry and our focus changed to social responsibility, his physical appearance, and self-initiated action. We were able to have Anthony taken off a locked ward for the first time in over two decades, and I joined his mother and brother during their weekly visits. Anthony began to speak with her and kissed her frequently. Being a devoutly religious woman, she was convinced that this was a miracle.

As we continued to work with paintings and drawings, I tried to keep expanding the range of our expressive work. In addition to reading literature, we read the newspaper aloud in the morning. It took more than a year for him to stop saying the date on the newspaper as 1953. One day I decided to eat lunch with him and observed his voracious eating habits. Anthony devoured plates of food in seconds, preferring his fingers to utensils. With the financial support of his mother, I began to expose him to the "art of dining" at a number of different restaurants. The going was very difficult at the start, but his interest in eating turned out to be a strong motivation for developing a certain degree of table etiquette.

As Anthony's comfort outside the hospital continued to improve, I began to take him to visit with his mother at home on a regular basis.

All of this progress with Anthony was not without incidents. We involved him in a summer camp and on the first evening, he walked away and was returned to the hospital by the state police, who found him walking along a major highway. The police said that he was very cooperative and clearly stated his name. When asked for his address, he gave the street number of his childhood home. This incident and a number of similar events took place during a period when he was probably not quite sure whether or not he wanted to give up his retreat of withdrawing into himself. I also think that he was trying to show us that he could be independent and initiate bold actions on his own in response to feelings he was experiencing as manifested one evening when he ran away from the hospital after we had a disagreement in the art studio.

I worked closely with Anthony most every day during my last two years at the hospital. After leaving, I saw him once a week for four years in an expressive arts therapy group that we held at the Addison Gallery of American Art. These sessions allowed us to maintain our relationship, and I was able to engage him with a number of Lesley University graduate students who were participating in the group. The weekly meetings also allowed us to sustain his artistic expression, but as time went on, it appeared that the development of his ability to relate to others became more important than making pictures. He was also personally interested in relating closely with the other staff so we involved him more in drama, movement, and activities focused on interpersonal communication. It seemed that the visual arts were associated with his relationship with me, and he was not as motivated to paint with other people. Each of his new relationships thus developed its own rhythm and communication style.

However, we observed that without the daily attention I gave Anthony at the hospital, he began to regress. I was able to interest other therapists in working with him, and they continued many of the rituals and activities that we did together.

These experiences with Anthony over a ten-year period confirmed my belief that expressive arts therapy might connect to activities that include shaving in the morning, relearning how to ride a bicycle, eating in a restaurant, and driving through a forest with an appreciation of how these experiences further sensory awareness and a person's more general interaction with the world.

Drawing and painting served as bridges from withdrawal to life with others. The visual arts provided a transitional mode of interacting with another human being in a context that demanded more than the perfunctory patterns of institutional life. Anthony and I had a shared interest in art and I believe that his expressions helped him to change his self-image, his confidence, and his willingness to become involved in an expanded circle of human relationships.

I learned how withdrawn institutionalized people desperately need attention within compassionate relationships. Anthony benefited from another person taking an interest in the totality of his life. In the early 1970s, this kind of relationship was significantly absent in mental health institutions for severely disturbed people. It was not possible to delineate where his illness began and ended in relation to what I perceived as the pathology of the large mental hospital environment.

No matter how dedicated and skillful individual staff members were during this period of institutionalized care, they were still required to work within a context that rarely supported and reinforced their efforts. The institutional environment fostered the autistic dependence that Anthony embodied. Within the expressive arts therapy studio we created another kind of milieu that offered distinctly different opportunities for expression. I think that our expressive arts therapy studio had a positive impact on the whole institution as well as the individual participants in our sessions. The work that we did in the studio certainly gave many people in the outside community a more hopeful sense of what was possible in terms of creative expression within a psychiatric hospital.

As Anthony and I began to make progress within our relationship, my goal was to help him extend his trust and capacity to communicate with his family and other people within the hospital. I discovered that changes in his behavior were largely due to my perseverance and commitment to him rather than skill. I believe that he also experienced genuine enjoyment within our expressive arts therapy sessions, and he basically found that there were many things in life that he could experience and enjoy.

While working as an expressive arts therapist within a state hospital setting, I had a number of similar experiences where artistic growth precipitated development within the whole person. I also discovered that the process of giving attention and support to another person within a creative and mutually fulfilling relationship tended to be the single most important aspect of the work that I was doing.

Development in Art Making and in the Person

I first met Christopher when he was 56 and after he had been living in a state hospital for 35 years. He told the story about how he was having a cigarette with a group of patients outside another Massachusetts state hospital and was taken back in with them and had been inside ever since. In the

1950s a lobotomy was performed on Christopher and hospital records stated that the surgical procedure did not produce changes in behavior.

The history of Christopher's original admission shows no indication of severe emotional disturbance. It describes how he was arrested for vagrancy in New York City and after being kept in jail for an extended period of time, he began to act aggressively and was then sent to the mental hospital and never left the system.

When we began to work together, Christopher was completely dependent on the hospital and this institutionalization was his major emotional difficulty. He could not conceive of living anywhere else. The thought of leaving the hospital was frightening, and he would begin to act inappropriately whenever that possibility was suggested to him. He avoided all therapeutic programs and spent his days wandering about the hospital grounds.

It was this wandering that first brought Christopher to the hospital studio. He joined our open sessions where he sat off to the side and observed people working. He would not participate in our group activities and began on his own initiative to draw with pencils and watercolors in an isolated corner of the studio.

His first picture was a stereotypic Christmas scene that he drew over and over again. He progressed to repeating numerous mandala designs, varying the patterns slightly with each picture, and over time the compositions conveyed considerable aesthetic sensibility (Fig. 29). In a latter session, he made a drawing of his pack of Bugler tobacco and I could see that he had the potential to become involved with drawing from nature in a more focused way.

He went on to draw personal representations of artworks painted by well-known artists (Figs. 30 & 31).

This process of responding to the art of others was a transitional stage for Christopher. His work was consistently original and uniquely expressive even when making renditions of other pictures. As he became more confident and spontaneous in his drawings, I encouraged him to focus his attention on objects and people in the studio.

Life drawing and making portraits of others was an important social event for him (Fig. 32). He was in control of the flow of interaction. People were attentive and interested in what he as doing, and the eye contact, together with the general energy between him and the person that he was drawing, was quite intense. The drawings themselves were remarkably inventive and stimulating. I was a frequent subject of his portraits (Figs. 33 & 34).

Christopher also produced pictures of groups working in the studio (Fig. 35) and a series of self-portraits where he established a keen sensibility to his own distinctive features and expression (Fig. 36).

Figure 29. Mandala.

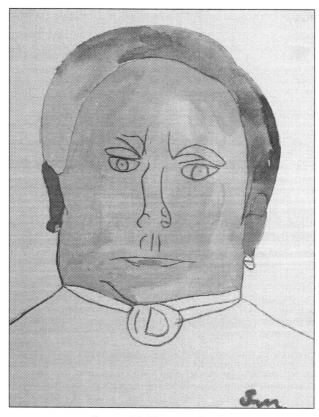

Figure 30. From art book.

Figure 31. Figures from Picasso.

Through the process of drawing and painting Christopher showed how someone appearing to be one of the most institutionalized residents of the hospital had a considerable genius that could be shared with others. His art had a profound impact on me as I will show in the following sections and in many ways the "therapy" that I did with him evolved into a significant and lasting artistic partnership. Christopher was a savvy and easy-going man who seemed to enjoy watching me delight in his expressions. He affirmed how personal fulfillment is tied to being able to give something of value to others. My role involved setting the stage for him to influence and relate to people.

Within the studio, Christopher developed a reputation as a fine artist, and after a year and one-half of expressive arts therapy, I began to exhibit his art in leading galleries. His drawings and paintings stimulated significant public interest as I will describe in the following description of his exhibit with Priscilla.

All of the various aspects of the expressive arts therapy process helped to transform Christopher's self-image. He became more interested in life outside the hospital and I would try whenever possible to take him with me on trips into the community. On a number of occasions, he walked away from

Figure 32. Portrait of Tony.

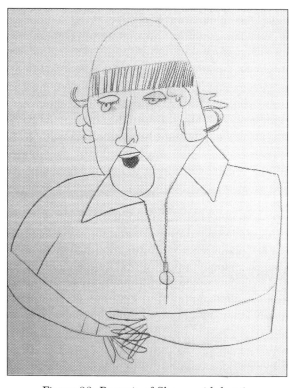

Figure 33. Portrait of Shaun with hat 1.

Figure 34. Portrait of Shaun with hat 2.

Figure 35. Studio group.

Figure 36. Self-portrait.

me and spent three to four days exploring the outside world before returning to the hospital. The staff continued to support my efforts to take him into
the community and we interpreted his actions as an indication of an interest
in leaving the institution. After two months of preparation, he did leave the
hospital.

As with Anthony, Christopher's expressive arts therapy experience stimulated a more complete development of the self. They both taught me how
what we do in art cannot be separated from the total therapeutic process.

Transcendent Beauty

With many children and adults, I have observed how the arts provide opportunities for healing through the creation of sensually pleasing expressions. The aesthetic dimensions of expressive arts therapy enable people to transcend the sometimes harsh and painful conditions of their lives and experience well-being in the real realms of creative imagination. I would like to describe the work that I did over a ten-year period with a woman whose approach to art is oriented toward experiencing beauty. The artist is Priscilla Hathaway and she has agreed to be mentioned by name so that she may receive the recognition that she deserves for her creative achievement.

When I worked with Priscilla, her creative expression was a stable element in a difficult life that had been spent largely in residential mental health institutions from childhood. She was in her thirties and active in all forms of artistic expression. In addition to working with the visual arts, Priscilla wrote poetry, composed music, and danced with enthusiasm. I will focus here on her painting, which has been her primary artistic focus since adolescence, and her poetry.

Priscilla first became committed to art while attending a therapeutic school that emphasized creative expression in its curriculum. Although her art was supported during her schooling, she received little formal training. She became aware of the world of art by reading art history books, and she is particularly drawn to the work of Van Gogh, Gauguin, and Georgia O'Keefe. Within her paintings, Priscilla creates a bright and vivid world of color and sensual action that contrasts sharply to the austere state hospital environments where she made the images. Her pictures are often religious and they express archetypal themes of physical and divine love, good and evil, deliverance from suffering, the celebration of human life, and the family. She would regularly describe to me how she could not have love and happiness in her life and therefore created it for herself in art.

Priscilla has referred to her pictures as children and says that the artistic process for her is characterized by both struggle and fulfillment. "When I start a picture I'm afraid that I'm going to fail or goof up. But when the picture is halfway through, I begin to enjoy it. I start to see that this goes here and that goes there, and so on. It's like a mother carrying a child in her womb. She never knows whether it will be born deformed or a beautiful, healthy baby."

In response to my question as to why she made art, Priscilla shared this statement with me: "When I make art, I forget my pain, and I feel closer to artistic men and women and to the Lord, who is the first creator . . . artists are special people because they are always creating beautiful things for others to see. Art is for me an escape from one world into a more perfect one

. . . art helps me to feel relieved from my feelings of guilt and self-abuse. When I create new shapes and forms, I feel a sense of accomplishment. It makes me feel important and just as good as the next person . . . art gives me a sense of freedom. My mind is not captivated by the worries of the world when I am working. I think art is God's world . . . when I am sad, I can look at one of my pictures and see beauty . . . when sharing my art with others, I feel important, secure, and among friends. I do not want to spend my whole life locked up in a mental institution. I am the master of my own decisions when making art."

Priscilla's art has repeatedly served as a means of transcendence and she consciously used creative activity to find freedom and beauty during periods when these feelings were conspicuously absent in her relationships with other people. The process of creation and the pictures that she produced helped her to deal with feelings of loneliness and isolation from other people. Her art has helped to fulfill desires for a love relationship and she described how in the absence of being loved by another person "in this world" she is able to create love "in artwork" (Fig. 37).

Her pictures also create imaginary places, such as those shown in Figure 38. Priscilla expressed her deepest longing in many paintings of families enjoying themselves in landscapes far from the often cruel and painful world of inner emotions and conflict. She would also create pictures expressing her passion for music (Fig. 39) and dance.

Priscilla's reputation as a fine painter strengthened her self-esteem. We were able to exhibit her art in galleries, universities, and at professional association meetings across the United States. The support and attention that she received helped her to begin to place more value on herself, her life, and her sense of what she has to offer other people. Because of the time she spent within various psychiatric institutions and the resulting negative effects on her self-image, Priscilla needed the affirmation that she received from others through her art.

People sent Priscilla letters, poems, and other communications in response to the exhibits we organized. These responses were a vital part of the overall expressive arts therapy experience because Priscilla was for the first time consistently receiving the message that she had something valuable to give to people. Over the years that we worked together, she was always insecure, and from time to time she was very confused about how other people perceived her. Her art served as an aesthetic antidote to these sometimes overwhelming insecurities and the difficulties of the past. Priscilla ultimately left the hospital to live in a community residence in large part buoyed by the daily discipline of creative expression in different media.

In addition to expressing idealized and fantasized emotions and scenes in her art, Priscilla was a master of finding beauty in the most routine and often debased features of life within a locked and crowded state hospital ward. She

Figure 37. Horse and lovers.

Figure 38. Picnic under trees.

Figure 39. Piano player.

transformed the bleak conditions into a world of vibrant color and forms that express the essence of real people, places, and things (Figs. 40 & 41).

Figure 42, one of the finest paintings that I have witnessed being made in my career in the arts, is a portrait of a Christopher whose work is described earlier in this chapter.

Priscilla's art has been completely self-initiated and self-sustained. She perceived me as a fellow artist with a deep appreciation for her art. Prior to my meeting Priscilla, her art was of interest to staff members at the hospital, but they would refer to her pictures as a representation of psychotic imagery. They felt that since she had many personal difficulties, her art was but another manifestation of psychopathology. Because the staff were so negatively conditioned by pathological approaches to art, it was difficult for them to perceive the intelligence, strength, and imaginative depth of Priscilla's expression.

Figure 40. Ward group.

Figure 41. Woman on the ward.

Figure 42. Portrait of Christopher.

In my work with Priscilla, I tried to fulfill her vision of working together as artistic colleagues. As a beginning artist and expressive art therapist, I faced a number of personal challenges in taking on this role as I will describe in the following chapter. However, there was never any doubt about how the seriousness and originality of Priscilla's expression inspired me and informed my approach to expressive arts therapy practice as well as my development as an artist. She helped me see how much she needed me to treat her as a fellow artist, and help provide the dignity and respect for her gifts and creative achievements that gave a purpose to her life.

In our work together, Priscilla was able to carry on a relationship that emphasized her artistic strengths. No matter how disturbed she might have been on a given day, she could always develop a sense of control, order, and personal meaning through her art. It was an absolutely dependable form of communication. Priscilla took pleasure in my continuous excitement about her art, and she felt that our relationship evolved around, and recognized, her most personal imagery.

As we continued our work together in the studio, and as her trust in me developed, I found myself taking on a new role as her artistic advocate inside and outside the hospital. It was very appropriate for Priscilla to center her life and her future plans on art. With her talent and commitment to the creative process, she could be secure in the realization that she had the ability to make creative and valuable contributions to the lives of other people while finding her personal fulfillment in art.

Priscilla always asked me to include her poetry when I showed her art. She creates poems, music, and dance with fervor equal to her visual art. The subject matter of her poems and pictures is consistent, and they tend to reinforce one another as shown by the following poem.

City Child

The lonely city is stained with dust.
The cold wind blows in from the sea.
The wind cries out: Come! Oh come, warm daughter
sweet, with an angelic face.
Blare your golden fiery trumpet!
Sing the blues in every lonely city street.
Give the soiled workmen soul food.
They sing low with strong, stout hearts.
Tired babes are crying by the market sides . . .
I sigh: Yes God, I notice them.
A fat flock of speckled pigeons,
feathers as soft as the wings of butterflies
are stirring the torn papers with flapping wings . . .
I sigh, deep inside: God grant me wings!
I long for the end of the road, where paradise begins.
A new land, stirred by the fire of love's allegiance;
the fire of poetic artists, friends of whom once
chanting, hailed like soft-caped royal deities,
like kings and queens of another world, the
land of creativity, the blood roots of sweet sensitivity.
That love star of infinity. The Union of grand liberty.
I listen to the trumpeteers play their silver trumpets.
Their music makes me want to cry. Their music makes me
long to soar. Their sweet wild tunes make me long to
rest my tired head on my departed mother's lap again.

The clapping of the people's hands makes me want to draw
forth a lover. So mad are my desires, so starved is my
passion. But I stand alone. Is this really my freedom?
Is the city dwelling my prison? Low I join the gathering
crowds anyway . . . like a sad, sweet-eyed wanderer. I let the
music of ceremony flood my longing heart. The young, dark-haired,
black-eyed mothers hold the children, starry-eyed, in their arms
like doves with deep throated breasts, full with the beauty
of fertility. The image of their love, like a satin veil,
soothes my broken lovesick spirit. For a short time, the wind
swirling the papers tugs at me and I hear my own thoughts cry out:
Little woman, who are you? The city stands erect like God.
The city lies chained to the hearts of men.
The wayward tide is the fateful way of life.
Vain men mock, vain men walk on.
City child, my city child,
where are your friends?

The poem conveys many of the themes expressed in Priscilla's paintings and other artistic expressions—longing for love and relationship, transcendence of loneliness, the presence of artist companions, a personal dialogue with God, the music of all of the arts combined in celebration of beauty, artistic expression as a channeling of passion, and life lived in a sensuous physical world.

Priscilla was practicing total expressive arts therapy before I arrived at Danvers State Hospital. She was far ahead of me and the expressive arts therapy discipline in so many ways in relation to her natural approach to using various forms of artistic expression for the purpose of healing and furthering well-being in herself and others.

Within the expressive arts therapy studio, I was able to enlarge Priscilla's community of artists. Building on the positive response to the 1973 exhibition, *Art Therapy at Danvers*, which traveled to museums, galleries, and universities throughout the Northeast, I organized an exhibit featuring her art and Christopher's at The School of the Museum of Fine Arts in Boston.

Robert Taylor, the senior art critic at the *Boston Globe*, selected it as the best small exhibit for 1974. From Taylor's response and the reactions of others viewing the show, it was clear that this recognition resulted from the aesthetic quality and authenticity of the work presented and not because Christopher and Priscilla lived in a mental hospital. Their living circumstances no doubt furthered the originality and distinctness of their expression, but being locked in dismal psychiatric wards were conditions to be overcome and not to be romanticized as a source of creative originality. Rather than seeing themselves as victims, Christopher and Priscilla transformed their harsh environments into transcendent works of beauty.

The Wellspring of Improvisation

Leah, a woman in her late fifties, with whom I worked for many years at Danvers and the Addison Gallery, was my most influential "teacher" in discovering the powers of spontaneous movement, voice, and dramatic improvisation.

In one of our group sessions, when Leah was about to take her turn alone in the center of a circle dance, I observed that she was tapping her foot before entering the movement space. I encouraged her to start her dance by repeating the tapping movement and building upon it with other gestures.

"Try and stay with the tapping motion Leah and don't think about anything else," I said. "Do it over and over again and see where it leads you. Make it louder or softer and add other movements to it with other parts of your body if you feel the urge."

The simple tapping gesture gave Leah a concrete focus and starting point. As she began to move, she established a rhythmic sound pattern with her foot. I and other group members joined her in making this rhythm with our feet and hands. As the rhythmic sounds grew clearer and stronger, Leah's movement expression unfolded into a sustained and highly imaginative dance in sync with the rhythmic sounds that she initiated and which the group maintained. Her every gesture displayed a precise sense of timing and the different aspects of her dance emerged as part of an interrelated whole. The group interaction created an energy that carried every one of us beyond our initial inhibitions. We became part of a rhythmic pulse that grew from movement and returned energy to it.

When I worked with Leah, we were immersed in the use of video within expressive arts therapy as I described earlier. We discovered how the presence of the camera served to motivate her movement expression. Viewing her dance during playback reinforced the significance and power of her bodily expression. Video playback also served to make everyone more aware of the sound qualities of the dance. The video helped us hear sounds that were missed when we viewed the original movement, perhaps because the visual qualities of dance tend to be more dominant during the original movement experience.

As our work continued in subsequent sessions, Leah became a leader and a source of inspiration for others in the dance and movement area. She was masterful at picking up a long stick or other object and not only moving with it as a prop but using it as a musical instrument during her dance. As her dances progressed, she drew in other group members and helped them move to the rhythms she established.

Leah taught me and my expressive arts therapy students many lessons about how dance and rhythmic sound can emanate from virtually every movement that becomes an object of concentration. She would build a dance from a single finger moving and making contact with a surface or by gently rocking her head in a rhythmic pattern. She thrived on the responses that she received from group members and became a reliable catalyst for our collective expression.

When I first experienced this kind of group movement and sound improvisation, it felt like magic. I discovered how the key to success was the identification of a simple movement pattern or rhythmic sound that we then sustained. The expression emerged like a stream that ultimately maintained its own life and momentum.

A Pencil and Scrap of Paper

While working with adult psychiatric patients, I observed how they used poetry more than any other art mode to express themselves spontaneously. Poems were written during solitary moments or in times of crisis and most people simply put them away with other personal belongings. If I was meeting with someone in the art studio or walking through a ward, a poem might be presented to me for comment.

I discovered how all that a person needs to create serious poetry is a pencil and a scrap of paper, or even more basically, we can work with just memory if writing materials are not available. This accessibility is one reason why poetry is such a universal way of artistic healing.

Writing poetry involves introspection, the heightening of perceptual awareness, and the expression of emotion through language, all of which lend themselves naturally to the therapeutic process. It is interesting how poetry therapy is one of the smallest of the expressive arts therapy disciplines when the healing dimensions of the poetic process have such a deep, universal, and long history. Yet poetic speech can be viewed as permeating all of the expressive arts therapies.

Spontaneous poetry is often written in anger as a form of protest, as an expression of longing or loss, and as personal affirmation in the face of stressful situations. Poetry enables us to do something creative and life-affirming with bad situations. The poetic process uses difficulties as sources of energy and creative transformation. Mary, a woman in her late thirties, living in a state mental hospital, shared this poem with me and described how it was a response to the "craziness" of the ward environment.

J2

locked in seclusion
when you don't feel well
help call
men come over
throw you in room
take your clothes off
and give you medication:
Stelazine
Cogentin
Mellaril
Thorazine
Navane
Fearsol
with a needle
go to sleep
unconscious
like dead
wake up in cell
no bed
just a mattress
no sheets, no pillows
no nothing
it's a shame
this never happened to me
it happened to Beatrice
she was tapping on the window
scratching her face . . .
calling my name: "Mary, Mary, I'm sorry!"
and asked me for a cigarette and
got wise again.

I was taken aback when I read this poem written by a person who rarely spoke. She expresses empathy for another woman together with an insider's insight into the dynamics of a mental hospital ward. The poem demonstrates how an apparently mute woman can compassionately witness another person's experience and use it as a source of creative expression.

Mary took the time to respond, to do something with her feelings and observations of another woman's plight. The poem affirms how the human spirit continues to manifest itself and brilliantly transform abhorrent situations outside the awareness of most people. In creating this poem, Mary taught me what the arts are capable of doing in giving voice and dignity to what would otherwise remain unspoken and unacknowledged.

Giving Voice to Pain and Loss

Very often the poem will burst forth out of its own inner necessity. Poems written spontaneously during periods of emotional distress tend to convey intense emotional energy and the most genuine communication of things that must be expressed.

I worked closely with Peter, a man in his late forties, who was a writer and graduate of an Ivy League college. He had been hospitalized as a result of a severe depression that ensued after his son, a Vietnam veteran and a paraplegic, apparently took his own life by driving his car off a highway bridge. The son was conceived during a brief relationship and never knew his father until he returned from Vietnam and contacted him. They shared an apartment and became very close.

The abrupt death was shattering to Peter. After many weeks of acute withdrawal in the hospital, he first expressed his feelings about the loss in a poem.

> So you're gone; your laughing eyes,
> your friendly mouth, your strong and gentle face
> soft haloed in copper that sunned to brass,
> your voice a bard muted, your wild sweet smell
> that came from no bottle, no can, no jar,
> all atomized in a micro-instant. I ask not Why:
> we could not hold you here, your heart too big,
> your lovely mind in a manic world, a body broken
> senselessly.
> But on your *birthday*? A child of twenty-four?
> You probably never thought of it, just wanted Out,
> decided it was Time. Be FREE my son!
> And laugh and sing and RUN again
> without obscene appliances. And now I know
> you're with me now as never then
> while on I still must go.

Not only did the writing of the poem serve as a way of releasing and transforming pain and loss, but Peter repeatedly read the poem to me and others and became intensely emotional as he felt the impact of his words and the sound of his voice reading. I learned through this early relationship with poetry how the process of witnessing and supporting the expression of another person plays an important role in the healing process. There are many different dimensions of poetic healing that include the making of the poem, reading, and receiving the responses of others. Whenever possible I try to create environments where these different dimensions can complement one another.

What strikes me most about the place of poetry in expressive arts therapy is how people experiencing life crises will autonomously turn to this medium as a way of dealing with their emotions and finding a way to live with unthinkable situations. The person's spirit rises from the destructive situation and affirms life through the poem. Artistic expressions are manifestations of what might be viewed as an inner necessity, as the only way that a person can respond to otherwise overwhelming conditions. At the deepest levels of the psyche, the universal creative urge responds instinctively to threats to our existence.

Connection to the Archetypal Dimensions of Life

I have observed how creative expression has served this transformative necessity throughout my years of expressive arts therapy practice, but perhaps nowhere more dramatically than in the work I did with the poet M. L. O'Connor. While undergoing treatment at the Dana-Farber Cancer Institute, M. L. took solace in her poetry and used it to help her deal with excruciating pain and torment resulting from experimental treatments that she was receiving. She described how her poems took both herself and the staff at Dana-Farber into "archetypal" dimensions of experience. Like Jung, she discovered how healing occurs when the pain she was experiencing is related to more universal human phenomena and difficulties shared by all people. The poem in this respect takes on a very personal and particular function, while at the same time transcending the immediate clinical context and connecting to the larger, mythic dimensions of experience.

M. L., who typically focused on love and beauty in her poems, felt that she had to express the truth of the pain she was experiencing. During a period when she felt "desperately ill," M. L. concentrated on the mythic figure Inanna, a figure in the Sumerian pantheon of ancient Mesopotamia whose descent into the underworld involves great suffering. When she was "aching beyond all aches" during a clinical trial, M. L. could not speak, but she "kept thinking of Inanna" and she wrote the following poem about the ordeal.

Inanna

> I cannot soar
> when the sea sick sky invades
> all senses, and
> my stomach retches out the ill taste of everything, and
> my mouth and throat are full of salivating sores, and
> I cannot swallow
> though I thirst

when all is gray, and
there is no horizon in the dark death cave
I cannot rise

Darting figures prod and pull, whispering
to feign dying
to endure this underworld
where I am loathe to find
nauseous and empty next to Death
no escape from pain
dreams heavy and hopeless
no light nor love
nor any memories save the wracking moment
when Death turns its face
thinking I am his

But I hold on
to nothing
  nothing calls
  nothing sings
I hold on
  a trace heart beat
    for no reason
I hold on
  barely hearing the whispers of Enki's envoys, as they
drag me through the gates

And since I am so much dead
Death does not know
I have escaped

M. L. described how this poem conveyed what she felt in her body. She told me how she found support in how the little things that Inanna made came to save her and maybe the poems and pictures that she made during her treatment could help carry her through "the gates."

After starting an arts program for other patients at Dana-Farber, the cancer spread throughout her body and when close to death, M. L. described how "There may have been a time in this sickness when my attitude, my mind intentions, and my art kept me alive."

She went on to say how she had now come to a different place where acceptance of death gives her satisfaction: "I can honor what life I have but I am no decision maker. The decision is someplace else . . . There is a time to be with the moment and honor every sacred thing that is happening."

During this entire period of cancer treatment and the subsequent process of dying, M. L. spoke of how poetry connected her to the larger, archetypal realms of life. Her suffering, and the poetic expression of it, became a source of transcendence.

Being Seen and Heard

A woman in one of my studios who was struggling with extreme fear of expression and insecurity described how profoundly healing it was for her to read her poetic expressions to other people who listened compassionately and without judgment of any kind. She said that it was as though the poem did not exist until it was read to someone else and reflected back to her in a response. She felt that the same applied to emotions aroused by the poem.

As I observed her read insightful and moving poems, I realized how we often do not become aware of what we know until we express these things and have them witnessed and affirmed. In many ways, writing and other forms of artistic expression precede the recognition of knowing. The making of art is a thoroughly intelligent process with its own unique epistemology, but I repeatedly see how most of us need to be witnessed by others and receive their observations in order to become more aware of what we have done and what we are capable of doing. In this respect, the poet Vincent Ferrini said to me, "The 'I' cannot see itself." We need others in order to discover ourselves.

In my experience, it is not just the responses that I receive from others, but more often, it is the total process of conveying my ideas and expressions to them, the interplay of communication, that helps me access thoughts and insights. I find that I think through conversation and dialogue with another person as mentioned earlier when describing my relationship with Paolo Knill. The connection with another is like the making of positive and negative links that permits the flow of electrical currents. My thought tends to be more static when it circulates solely within its own sphere. Creators generally need to get outside of themselves and into contact with other people and things in order to access the resources that lie within themselves.

People suffering from severe trauma, depression, and various disorders of thought are often locked into themselves. The severity of the emotional difficulties is typically connected to the degree of isolation and the absence of creative flow with others and the environment. Thoughts and feelings may be plentiful within the person, but they tend to stay confined and unexpressed.

Creative expression in complete isolation can have great value as the world's artistic history suggests. In this respect, solitary art can also heal outside the context of therapy and social interaction. For me, the defining difference between private artistic expression and expressive arts therapy is how the latter establishes a supportive environment where creative expressions can be witnessed and affirmed by others.

I worked for a number of years with a young man in a hospital expressive arts therapy studio and later in a community program. He was a literature and psychology student who took his poems seriously and used to share them with me regularly. He experienced intense visionary experiences that the hospital environment tended to view as psychotic hallucinations and this disregard for phenomena that he considered sacred only augmented his depression and autism. As our relationship grew, it became clear that he needed someone to hear, value, and respond to his writing and to accept the personal validity of his visions. So much of our work together was based on me witnessing his expressions and respecting them. He also helped me realize how the expressive arts therapist's identity as an artist who brings the values of art when responding to a person's expression within a clinical setting can help to further appreciation of its significance. When working within a hospital, I always valued and respected the core mission of the institution, but I worked hard to help staff understand the full significance of artistic expressions and be wary of making stereotypic psychological judgments about them.

The following is an example of this young man's writing and the intense, sensory and dreamlike quality of his visions.

> . . .We are animals, searching passion
> so unconscious are we of the pluck, a
> plumefeather in my cap, a pip and stockings,
> lilies in the pond, a single frog croaking,
> nature resplendent, O' clear Liliwana,
> oh doll of the sea. I have searched you,
> you have searched me. In the dusk of our
> life we are but wanderers, searching for our souls,
> the animal within, the phony without. I look
> for no other, my treasure is here on earth, you
> have brought me solace. Winter grief and fallen
> sticks, dried up dates and yesterday's tears,
> the ache within, the penniless. Tonight I saw
> an angel carrying a basket of bread. Lay down
> upon the earth and love, the sky will rumble.

As we worked together in the art studio, I realized how deeply he felt about life experiences and how his poetry clearly conveyed his "searching passion," his longing for loving relationships. I did everything I could to let him know how I heard, saw, felt, and witnessed what he was saying.

I also went to other staff members and spoke to them about his poetry and encouraged them to take it more seriously and as a manifestation of health rather than as a literal expression of hallucinatory experiences. He was speaking metaphorically and sometimes brilliantly and the mental health institution was taking him literally, no doubt with good intentions, because he did not have the ability at that time to navigate effectively between the different realms of his inner and outer experiences.

My work with this young man confirmed how important expressive arts therapy programs can be for people who are experiencing deep emotions and personal crises and who have few outlets for their expression and virtually no affirmation of the thoroughly healthy efforts of the distressed soul to make meaningful contact with others and the world. In this particular case, the disturbances and "inappropriate" behaviors intensified as the young man's poetic ways of expressing them were not appreciated by the mental health systems.

When we began to work together, I tried to accept his writing and validate his efforts to create and give value to his life. Over time, this approach strengthened and sustained our relationship. I was able to bring him into contact with other artists who affirmed his work, and on a number of occasions, I involved him in poetry readings that supported his efforts to express himself through his own unique language.

When he first read his poems, his voice was barely audible. I would sometimes speak back to him in the same whispering voice and he would smile because be could barely hear what I was saying. These playful interactions assumed a larger role in our overall relationship and he began to exercise his own considerable gifts of humor and spontaneous expression. He raised the volume of his voice in response to my coaching and on certain occasions, he even read loudly and with anger that he had always repressed and which seemed unfamiliar. I often asked him to repeat his poems, to vary the intonations of his voice in order to express different emotions and feelings. The involvement with poetry became a basis for a necessary immersion in therapeutic voicework. The reading of the poem is in this respect a musical, lyrical, and dramatic performance. One art form is constantly working in synergy with others.

He went from reading his poems alone with me to sharing the work with the larger studio group which gave him the opportunity to exercise his voice in different and new ways and to expand its range and power. Being witnessed and supported by the studio community had a tremendous impact of this young man. Since many of his emotional difficulties were related to the struggles he had with social relationships.

Support and trust played an important role in our work together. When he first shared his visions with me, he said that he had not described them to other people because he knew that they would belittle them and not believe that what he was saying was true. I told him that I would accept his definition of what was true for him. From that point, he continuously shared his work with me. For several years after we completed our work together in the hospital studio, he maintained contact with me and sent copies of his poems, affirming the importance of having the work witnessed and supported by another person.

During this period, I had started to work closely with the Addison Gallery of American Art, as described earlier, and this young man became one of the most influential people in helping us develop a complete integrated arts approach to therapeutic practice. He welcomed the video camera as a witness to his reading of poems. Poetry, video, and dramatic enactment were integrated naturally in the work he did in the studio.

The feedback from the camera reinforced the complete poem—its sounds, pauses, and rhythms as well as the interrelationships of words, lines, and the overall composition. Video helped us all to experience the total expression of the poem which included the way it emerged through the posture and expression of his body moving in space as well as his voice and the dramatic enactment of its presentation before the group and the camera.

Over the course of the extended work that I did with this man in expressive arts therapy, I learned that art heals by giving opportunities for the expression of our difficulties and aspirations. The poem rarely takes away or fixes deeply rooted problems and afflictions, but it does express, transform, and put them to use in the service of life.

As Stephen Levine says in *Poiesis: The Language of Psychology and the Speech of the Soul,* "The task of therapy is not to eliminate suffering but to give a voice to it, to find a form in which it can be expressed" (1992, p. 15). The arts make the languages of soul available to us when we need to voice the suffering and longing of the soul.

Total Expression with All of the Arts

Throughout my career, I have discovered how focused and quality attention is a prerequisite for every aspect of expressive arts therapies. As a group leader, my personal practice has increasingly centered on being as attentive as possible to what other people are doing. I say to myself when I enter a studio session, and especially if I am distracted, annoyed, or wanting to be somewhere else, "Right now, this particular time has to be the most important moment in your life. If it is not, if your thoughts are elsewhere, then you will not be as effective in helping others."

I also find that I have to be keenly interested in what people are doing in my groups and then show this interest through the quality of my concentration. My attentiveness in turn helps group members to focus on immediate experiences, to move beyond their distractions and scattered thoughts and to deeply connect with what they are doing.

In my work with creative movement, I strive to demonstrate this focused concentration by paying close attention to the most common movements of daily life—demonstrating the process of walking into a circle, standing, sitting on a chair, moving with an object in my hands, or tearing a piece of paper with as much concentration as possible. As I show this way of being in relation to movements, it helps others to adopt a similar attitude and focus.

In his classic book, *An Actor Prepares*, Constantin Stanislavski described how giving close attention to an object "naturally arouses a desire to do something with it" and the subsequent activity then enhances the observation of its qualities (1976, p. 72).

In my work moving with objects in expressive arts therapy, I always begin by encouraging people to take time to closely contemplate the thing that they will engage before beginning to move with it. I ask participants to look deeply at the forms and characteristics of an object, to sense its expressive qualities, and to then begin to move in response to what they see and feel.

I find that intense concentration of an external object can be the most helpful way to liberate expression and generate feelings of well-being. The object of attention becomes a partner that helps us transcend preoccupations and blocks to expression. Sometimes these partners function as muses, subtle liberators, motivators, or sources of enchantment that operate upon us in unplanned and unexpected ways.

One of the most transformative experiences I had with helping a person move within expressive arts therapy involved work that I did with Richard, a young man in his late twenties who had been admitted to the hospital during a period of acute emotional disturbance. I started to work with Richard right after he arrived and continued our expressive arts therapy relationship throughout the one year that he was in the hospital and for three more years in a community-based expressive arts therapy program at the Addison Gallery.

Although interested in becoming engaged with various forms of creative movement, Richard was unable to move his body in anything other than rigid ways, shuffling his feet across the floor with a robotic gait. His posture was painfully stiff and he rarely bent the trunk of his body as he moved. Everything about his movement in space was sharply vertical. He even found it difficult to move his head and his eyes were always peering straight ahead. If he wanted to change his view, he did this by moving his entire body.

Richard joined us in creative movement and painting sessions, but his gestures were severely hampered by the more general condition of his body. When he first spoke to me after our early sessions, he said that he experienced a constant and intense burning sensation in his stomach and chest area; that the pain was terrible and it made it very difficult for him to move. He wanted to be with us in the expressive arts therapy studio and came faithfully to our sessions in spite of his limited range of movement.

As the group was viewing a video playback of a creative movement experience that happened a few minutes earlier, I noticed how Richard carefully watched the tape. His first expressions of emotion were in the form of smiles and eye movements in response to viewing himself moving stiffly with others. In subsequent sessions, I observed that he began to move his body with some degree of spontaneity while viewing the tapes. I also noticed how he showed an interest in the operation of the camera. I offered to demonstrate how to use the equipment and he was intrigued.

During our group sessions the video camera was always operated by professionals or by me and graduate interns. In keeping with the therapeutic principle of correspondence discussed throughout this book, we felt that it was necessary to assure a certain degree of aesthetic quality and perceptual clarity in the video presentation in order to encourage a parallel effect on viewers. We were also dealing with chronic mental patients and others in states of acute disturbance who were often agitated and in need of attention, so involving the patient artists in the videotaping process was not a focus of our work at the time.

After the third month of Richard's participation in the hospital expressive arts therapy program his movement was still rigid and severely limited. At this point, he expressed an interest in running the video camera and we decided to involve him in the recording of sessions.

Operation of the video portapak, which was a heavy and more cumbersome technology than the small devices used today, required fairly demanding physical coordination, as well as the integration of visual, motor, aural, and tactile senses.

The portapak was strapped over Richard's shoulder and his fingers had to press the appropriate recording buttons, as well as manipulate the camera with its different light and focus adjustments. When operating the equipment, he had to follow the flow of movement within the group with his eyes and body, framing the action with the camera, and all the while coordinating the various technical operations I have described.

As he became more familiar with the video technology, he experimented with the process of "in-camera editing" and recorded various thematic aspects of the group's movements—hand, foot, and facial expressions or he would follow a particular person through a group movement experience.

Richard described how he forgot himself when he was behind the camera and how it became completely fused with his body. He said, "The pain goes away when I am shooting videotape. I am so busy concentrating and being challenged that I forget my pains and how afraid I am to move."

Toward the end of our first year of work together, Richard became skillful and continuously interested in using video equipment. The portapak became his creative partner and it involved him in a form of combined art and movement therapy.

The rigid quality of his bodily gestures began to change gradually to a more fluid and easygoing style of moving. We felt that his intense concentration on the recording of dance movements helped him to internalize their rhythms. His own body movements in dance sessions showed this new fluidly.

Richard's verbal expressions began to develop in a parallel relationship to the visual quality of his videotapes. We discovered that this previously mute and physically immobile man was a very intelligent, articulate, and artistically gifted person. Over time, his sense of rhythm became apparent, and he began to move in a noticeably smooth, lively, and creative manner.

During the third and fourth years of our work together, Richard spent less time videotaping and became increasingly interested in dance and drama. After his second year with us, the pains were gone altogether, and he began to attend the expressive arts therapy sessions as a volunteer. He helped in videotaping as well as assisting less functional participants.

It can be argued that it is impossible to separate one art form from another within the context of truly integrated expressive arts therapy. In Richard's case, the need to expand limited movement expression was addressed through his fascination with another artistic medium. Video, in this respect, served as an object of concentration as described earlier, as a transitional medium and therapeutic bridge that enabled him to gradually restore his movement expression in the world. The making of video was a channel for the more elemental and all-pervasive regeneration of Richard's physical movement.

As we often see within expressive arts therapy practice, concentration on expression within a particular medium will help to dissolve obstacles to expression in other areas. This factor offers one of the most pressing justifications for encouraging the use of multiple media when using artistic expression in therapy. For example, I repeatedly see how people who are reluctant to speak will turn to the visual arts to communicate feelings as demonstrated by the work of Bernice, shown earlier in this section. When the primary mode of expression is restored, the transitional medium tends to fade as an object of concentration. As his natural proclivity for movement was restored, Richard immersed himself in it and gave less attention to using the video camera.

In my own life, I find that I move amongst different art media in ways not dissimilar to the experiences of Richard and Bernice. I tend to intensely concentrate on different modes of expression for sustained periods of time and then shift to another in a cyclic or seasonal way. I will always return to my primary modes of expression after a hiatus. Perhaps Richard's experience can help us understand how the different media of artistic expression support and complement one another. In his case he used video to cultivate and renew his ability to move freely and creatively in the world.

Paradoxically, we sometimes find that concentration on a visual art medium will enhance movement or vice versa. The indirect route may sometimes offer unexpected access to the core of an expressive medium. The same things apply to problem solving and invention where approaching an intractable situation from a new perspective may offer the insight needed to bring resolution. Expressive arts therapy thus offers a kind of cross-training that activates all of the channels to creative expression. The creative imagination rarely proceeds in straight lines. What might at first appear foreign may have the most to offer in advancing a particular goal. Practice with multiple modalities strengthens a person's total expressive capacity and, in my opinion, furthers discovery and change.

But I must emphasize that even as we shift from one artistic medium to another, movement continues as the primary source of expression. As Wilhelm Reich emphasized in describing the limits of language in psychotherapy, "the living organism expresses itself in movements" (1973, p. 140). Language is a form of communication that in Reich's view can sometimes obstruct the body's ways of knowing and healing.

Susanne K. Langer spent her lifetime studying how the different artistic modalities offer ways of communicating that are distinctly different than language. In her culminating three volume work, *Mind: An Essay on Human Feeling*, Langer describes how both human experience and the physical world, from microbiology to art, involve a continuous sequence of actions, "acts," that build upon one another in dynamic and creative ways.

Striving to integrate the historic split between mind and body, Langer suggests that the microscopic aspects of life show "rhythms within rhythms," a "matrix of acts within acts" that creatively shape our worlds (1967, p. 274). Therefore, we might find that subtle shifts in action, small changes in the things that we do, relying less on one particular way of approaching a situation, might alter the course of action within a particular domain of life. Also, we might find that varying the structure of actions in one area of expression, may yield significant effects in another. Human experience is a complex of influences like the natural world where the whole "texture of activities" (Langer, p. 311) and linkages amongst experiences will often bring change in unlikely and expected ways.

As I reflect upon my work with Richard, I see how his healing and return to a full life outside the hospital environment can be viewed from both the perspective of Reich's emphasis upon "moving outward" into the world (p.

140) and Langer's vision of "acts" making new life by reinforcing and advancing one another. It is intriguing to imagine, as Langer did at the end of her life, that all of the things that we do within the expressive arts therapies contribute to chemical, biological, and psychic activities that heal, renew, and remake our worlds.

Richard's experience shows how the process of change in expressive arts therapies will generally unfold according to the unique conditions of individual sessions. We will never know as we begin our work what combination of expressive actions will ultimately help an individual person to progress and heal.

What I can say with some degree of confidence is that everything that we do in expressive arts therapy is based in creative movement and action. The experience of Richard and the others described in this chapter also suggest that the people we serve will benefit if we make available a spectrum of artistic media so they can integrate them in ways that further their well-being.

PERSONAL ARTISTIC EXPRESSION: "IT'S ALL RESEARCH"

Students and beginning expressive arts therapists are especially interested in how it is possible to integrate their personal artistic expression with a life of service. They often ask me: how I am able to make art while working full time in so many other areas; how my art has been affected by work with others; how creative expression can inform and improve professional practice; whether it is possible to truly integrate art and service; is it important to keep artistic practice as a separate and private domain; do I have a personal relationship to art as a healing experience; and how the quality of my expression has been affected by expressive art therapy practice?

Although I can answer these questions with references to my expression in dance, voice, percussion, performance, creative writing, and various forms of improvisational drama that I use in my practice, I will focus my responses in this section on painting, which has always been my primary artistic discipline outside the expressive arts therapy studio. This examination of a single medium will hopefully generate principles that inform experience with other forms of artistic expression. But I must emphasize that even though painting has been my sustained artistic discipline, dance, movement, and rhythm have always been part of my core orientation to expression. Poetry has also been an important form of creative expression as demonstrated by the writings included in a later section.

In keeping with this book's emphasis on the formative power of early experiences, I attempt to show how I was genuinely influenced by the

Danvers artists described in the previous section of this book and by my efforts to understand how expressive arts therapy related to my experience as artist.

At the Start

I began a relationship with expressive arts therapy as an aspiring young painter. In college, I studied abstract expressionist painting in New York City with Theodoros Stamos and then "progressed" to the kind of minimalist imagery that was current in the late 1960s.

After graduating from college, I sublet a spacious artist's loft in SoHo for the summer and progressively minimalized large canvases to a subtle stripe across the surface, cadmium yellow on white or vice versa. The most logical culmination of this aesthetic concept was to stop painting altogether. I called my father in August and asked if he could help me get into law school. He said, "Great, let's do this for next year." I replied that I wanted to go in September.

A detached retina discovered when I tried to enroll in the Marine Corps Platoon Leader program at the start of my sophomore year at Fordham in 1965, before I grasped the dimensions of the Vietnam War, exempted me from the draft at a time when I was marching in Washington against the war. The Army draft official saluted me when he read the medical file and Marine Corps documents my father prepared. It was a crazy era when everything was inverted. Bobby Kennedy was going to be my college commencement speaker and he was shot days before the event, which became a memorial service.

I attended law school for a year and a half; worked in my father's law firm, which I enjoyed; but ultimately felt that I had to get back to art. I got a job in an ironworks plant, learned how to weld and cut iron, made minimalist steel sculpture, but after a few months spent largely in a toxic spray-paint room, I determined that I needed to make more than $2.25 per hour.

I applied for a job as a social worker at the nearby Danvers State Hospital since I had worked for the New York City Welfare Department in Brooklyn during my summer living in SoHo. I went for an interview, discovered that psychiatric social workers had just been required to have a master's degree and after the personnel director looked at my resume, he asked whether I was interested in the recently vacated art therapy position.

Although I had never heard the term art therapy before, I was intrigued and sensed that I could use this opportunity to further my commitment to art and social service. I interviewed with other staff; gave common sense explanations of how making art could be therapeutic; and left the hospital as the new art therapist.

As I have written previously (1992), my grandmother, Margaret Tyndall, had been a volunteer at the hospital for 20 years and the director of personnel was then director of volunteers. He admired my grandmother and fortuitously enabled my life work to grow from her service to others. She was a skilled maker of things, far more technically competent than me, and engaged the patients in various forms of creative activity. The poet Vincent Ferrini would often say to me, "No accidents," when talking about this kind of convergence in a person's life.

While working in the ironworks, I prepared applications to MFA programs at UCLA and other schools and was not admitted. I was a history major in college and the absence of formal study and the time in law school no doubt raised questions about the reliability of my commitment to art. In retrospect, the rejections were key factors in the unfolding of my career.

Within the hospital studio, I found that the conceptual principles informing my personal artistic expression had little relevance to what people were doing. There was a gulf between my immersion in contemporary art world trends and the more organic and archetypal creations of people in the studio.

As I helped Anthony, Christopher, Bernice, and Priscilla, whose work I described earlier, and other artists perfect their ways of expression, I found myself being influenced by them. I was their teacher and they became mine, introducing me to authentic and natural ways of making art. This was the beginning of my movement away from what I progressively perceived to be superficial fashions in art. It has been a difficult process because I admired the gallery world and especially Stamos and the New York art community. I discovered my personal vision of artistic expression when I left New York and immersed myself in what most considered an unattractive and foreboding mental hospital north of Boston.

During my first year at the state hospital, I was making large paintings in my home studio in response to circular configurations in my steel sculptures (Fig. 43).

I was relating to New York conceptual trends in my art, aspiring to make large scale sculptures. Figure 44, Found Sculpture, is a photograph of concrete sewer pipes awaiting installation near my family home in Salem, Massachusetts. These "found" forms epitomize the type of sculptures that I hoped to construct when I serendipitously began to practice expressive arts therapy.

I sensed how the direction of my art was thoroughly alien to the expressive interests and needs of people in the hospital studio who were struggling with the most elemental conflicts and pains of existence. I had not found a way to fuse my personal art with what I was doing in expressive arts therapy.

Figure 43. Interpretation of sculpture.

One of the first integrations of my work as a therapist and artist happened when I started to make pictures of the circular forms in my paintings and sculpture with wax crayons and the elemental school paints that I was using at the hospital. If I was going to encourage others to make art with these resources, I had to see what I could do with them myself.

Painting on paper for the first time since childhood, I applied forceful pressure with the crayons and became involved with an entirely new and more physical way of making pictures in keeping with what I was doing with people in the hospital studio (Fig. 45).

Shifts toward more innate expression happened through the use of rudimentary materials rather than by making changes in the subject matter of my art. I was painting the same designs and shapes but in a more visceral way. Broadening the media of expression, in keeping with the principles of expressive arts therapy, had a transformative impact.

Figure 44. Found sculpture.

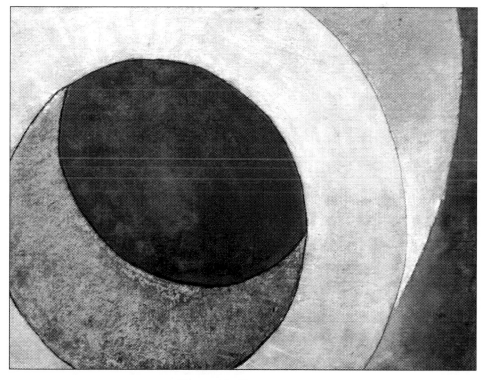

Figure 45. Crayon resist.

An Early Challenge

In writing a chapter for a book on the self-disclosure of psychotherapists (McNiff, 2008), I was prompted by Andrea Bloomgarden, one of the editors, to describe a difficult experience that I had in relation to my personal artistic expression in therapeutic work with others. Dealing with this question, I realized how my relationship with Priscilla, whose art I presented earlier, challenged my self-confidence and self-image as a beginning artist and expressive arts therapist.

As described above, there was a gap between what we were doing in the hospital studio and my personal expression. Priscilla was ten years older than me and I realized that her style of expression was in many ways more developed than mine with her paintings evoking Van Gogh and others. She constantly asked me to show her my art and I was reluctant to do this.

I was trying to establish a professional distance as "her therapist," making it clear that I was there to help her. I had never considered bringing my personal art to the studio and felt that this might bias and confuse the work of others. But on an emotional level, I was also protecting myself from the possible negative judgments or the perception that my creative expression was out of sync with the art being made in the hospital studio.

I told Priscilla how I studied painting in New York City with Stamos who was close to Mark Rothko and other abstract expressionists, but this only increased her persistence in wanting to see my art. I did not realize at this point how Priscilla desired to be part of a community of artists, how she was genuinely interested in relating to me as a fellow artist, and that perhaps in this particular case, my role as her expressive arts therapist may have called for this. I continued to work with Priscilla for over ten years and ultimately my practice of expressive arts therapy realized her vision of artists working together in a supportive studio space, perhaps in keeping with what Pat Allen later described as the "artist-in-residence" model of therapy (1992).

As I helped Christopher and Anthony develop their ways of painting figures and scenes during this period, I internalized what we were doing together. As a devout abstractionist, I began to paint figures in the studio from life and memory just like Anthony, Priscilla, and Christopher (Figs. 46, 47, & 48).

Anthony and Christopher made paintings and drawings of me as shown in the previous section and I reciprocated (Fig. 49).

After leaving the hospital to start the Lesley graduate program, I returned often to paint together with a group of people, something I was not able to do when leading groups and directing the studio. My art world moved from New York to the mental hospital where I found inspiration in authentic and universal ways of expression.

Christopher's bold lines, colors, and compositions had a strong impact on me and I was mesmerized and inspired by Anthony's ability to catch the

Figure 46. Danvers man 1.

Figure 47. Danvers man 2.

Figure 48. Leah on couch.

Figure 49. Anthony.

expression of a subject with quick, minimal, and decisive line drawings. The intimate manner in which we worked over the years in the Danvers studio, afterwards at the Addison Gallery of American Art, and when I returned to the hospital to paint together with them, created bonds of expression that sometimes felt like we were creating as partners. I moved away from painting on canvas for a number of years and worked almost completely on paper with the same kinds of water-based paints, oil pastels, and ebony pencils that we used in the expressive arts therapy studio.

The Art Alchemy Series

"I tell you: one must still have chaos in one, to give birth to a dancing star."
Friedrich Nietzsche, *Thus Spake Zarathustra*

One of the most important periods in my development as an artist and expressive arts therapist occurred in the late 1970s when I felt that the demands of my professional work were at odds with my desire to create and live as an artist. I recall consciously asking myself; why not apply what I do with the arts in therapy to myself?

I was seriously considering leaving the expressive arts therapy field, just as I had left law school, and once again committing myself completely to art. It occurred to me that the conflicts I was having could become the subject matter of my art and my research. If I changed my idea about the nature of art, I could in fact live it with my whole being.

This period turned out to be a crucible in which my emotional struggles forged a permanent partnership between art and healing. I liken these experiences to the vision quests of shamans who find their vocations and methods of healing through their own crises and disintegration.

My experiences with artistic expression during this transformative period address many questions that students ask about the relationship between personal art and profession practice, self-healing through art, research, and the artistic identity of the expressive arts therapist.

The first personal art healing experiment happened after our family had moved into a large and uninsulated old house just before the energy crisis of the mid 1970s. I was working in an attic crawl space and experiencing considerable stress that peaked when I put my foot through a pristine plaster ceiling. It occurred to me after a period of dismay that I could make my attic project into an artwork, in sync with the projects of my conceptual art colleagues. At this time, I had become closely involved with conceptual artists Don Burgy and Don Huebler through my work with Christopher Cook at the Addison Gallery.

My attitude toward the insulation project immediately changed as I began to photograph the rolls of fiberglass insulation, the attic space, the tools I was using, and the hole in the ceiling. I even took apart some of the work that I had completed in order to make "before and after" photographs. I discovered how aesthetic perception could completely change my attitude toward what had been a horrible experience. I put my afflictions to use and explored how a sense of purpose and value can transform negative feelings. I called this process art alchemy.

I also began to apply these transformation principles to my painting as a way of dealing with the conflicts in my professional work. It seemed that I was spending all of my time in meetings at the university and with professional groups. It occurred to me that I could do something creative with my inability to have time in my studio by approaching the meetings as a source of expression. I made small drawings in the sessions with the support of my colleagues and I found that this helped me be more focused and attentive within the discussions (Figs. 50, 51, & 52).

The pictures—often showing a scattering of papers, exit signs over doors, tables drawn with bold converging lines, and weary people—channeled my exasperation and the turmoil I was feeling into a new dimension of aesthetic exaltation. My attitude toward the meetings changed completely and I actually started to look forward to them. I was living on Cape Ann, north of Boston, where so many of the great artists during the past century traveled to paint (Hopper, Hartley, and others) and I was sharpening my pencils for meetings in cities.

The meeting images became a primary focus in my art over the next few years. I not only continued drawing in the sessions, but brought the meetings into my studio where I amplified the sketches into large paintings (Figs. 53 & 54).

The project integrated expressive arts therapy practice with my personal artistic and emotional life. I made all of the studio paintings quickly on unstretched canvas which allowed me to work efficiently during this hectic period of integrating art with work. The project was in many ways a single, conceptual art piece and I exhibited the paintings as one day art events at the Addison Gallery and the Hartford Art School. There was a nomadic quality to traveling with the paintings rolled into one compact package that filled large galleries at both sites.

The "art alchemies" series helped me to formulate what has become my core theory of how art heals by transforming emotional conflicts and maladies into affirmations of life, using disturbances as fuel for creation. It also helped me realize how it is possible to integrate art making into every aspect of my life and work, even during the busiest times.

Figure 50. Morning meeting at the college.

Figure 51. AATA Board meeting.

Figure 52. AATA business meeting.

An Expanded Notion of the Self-Portrait

In a correspondence with Bruce Moon, I wrote, "My female figures, animals, and landscapes are as much of a self-portrait as the literal ones painted before the mirror" (personal communication, December 6, 2007). The same applies to my ways of moving with materials, the colors selected, and other purely aesthetic aspects of art.

The "self," in a psychological sense, is generally considered to be a configuration of a person's essential qualities and a consciousness of one's being. My sense of the self is inseparable from relationships with others, things, and the place where I live. Inside and outside are always working together. My self-portrait is thus an ongoing interpretation of relationships with these varied phenomena, mediated by imagination and my particular manner of expressing myself.

When I paint the rocks surrounding my house, the sea, human figures, and other things, either directly or from memory, I am mediating them through my perceptions and gestures. I am opening to their influences and perhaps becoming more aware of how they shape my sensibilities, what we might call my inner being. Self-portraiture becomes an expanded awareness of oneself in relationship to life and the antithesis of ego-centrism since the self becomes less isolated. It exists as a distinctly autonomous character, but always established by its relations with otherness.

Figure 53. Meeting mania.

Figure 54. Late night AATA Board meeting.

I first became aware of how artistic expressions convey this reciprocal relationship between me and others when making portraits at Danvers State Hospital. My drawings and paintings of artists in the studio combined perceptions of them with my own unintentional self-portraiture. As I became more relaxed making art together with my hospital colleagues, I was no doubt susceptible to subliminal influences taking place outside consciousness as my imagery merged with theirs. I saw the same qualities in my pictures of meetings.

These experiences taught me how the deepest forms of integration occur unintentionally and how every form of expression carries certain traces of our artistic DNA and self-presentation. Yet the self-portraits that I make are themselves autonomous. Although closely related to me, they can be likened, as I have said before, to offspring, fusions of my being and other elements. They cannot be reduced to me alone.

When I expanded my practice during the 1980s to leading studio retreats outside the context of mental health institutions, with a larger cross-section of society, I was again influenced by the people with whom I worked. As artists in my studios made pictures expressing imaginative and deeply personal experiences, my own expression unfolded in relation to the environmental influences.

Painting more from imagination, I made pictures that integrated memories, dreams, relationships, and whatever figures and compositions emerged from spontaneous gestures (Figs. 55, 56, & 57). I have felt closely connected to these imaginal "others" who often embody the more subtle features of the self and its relationship to the world.

The more direct self-portrait continues to intrigue me and I still strive to catch distinctive qualities of the physical self as first experienced with Anthony, Christopher, and Priscilla (Fig. 58). All these images can be viewed as a composite self-portrait expressing the many different aspects of the self.

Within the psychotherapeutic community, we are prone to limit the domain of inner expressions to conflicted and emotionally challenging contents. After so many years of being part of this viewpoint, I found myself repressing expressions of beauty, pleasure, and whimsy and dismissing them as forms of superficial and aesthetic avoidance which denied the true nitty-gritty of the psyche.

I have made a conscious decision in my painting to explore the more pleasurable and dreamlike features of expression as essential components of my more complete interpretation of the self and its relationships with the world (Figs. 59 & 60). The pursuit of beauty has been a consistent and primary feature of how art heals in my personal experience and I think that we need to give more attention to this feature of expressive arts therapy.

I believe that our most intimate expressions of self are conveyed by these aesthetic sensibilities. In my art, I continue to hold the abstract expressionist

Figure 55. Figures in doorway.

Figure 56. Bass player.

Figure 57. Annisquam pasture.

values instilled in me by Stamos and I strive to integrate them with more figurative and psychological themes. He taught me how the essential qualities of paint and expression carry beauty and meaning. Stamos helped me see how depth can be on the surface of artworks. He said to me once, "When I look out at the world, I see alizarin crimson." His core being was a reflection of color that he gave back to the world. The artist's vision thus offers a paradoxically mystical and organic sense of the self merging with the elements of nature.

In the early 1980s, I discovered the art of Charlotte Salomon who has significantly informed my understanding of how art and healing can be integrated through an expanded notion of the self-portrait. In addition to offering one of history's most compelling accounts of how art heals, Salomon's paintings and drawings continuously inspire my own expression.

Working alone from 1941–1942, before being killed at Auschwitz at age 26, she painted her entire life story in a series of 769 spontaneous and imaginative paintings. Her art demonstrates how every authentic expression of inner and outer experience continuously creates and recreates the self. As I study Salomon's art, it is the style of her expression, its visual spontaneity, breadth, and vitality, as much as the content, which expresses and affirms the creative self (Salomon, 1981; Felstiner, 1994).

Figure 58. Self-portrait.

Figure 59. Flute player.

Figure 60. Village Hall.

My own history as a painter suggests how the purely physical elements of expression may convey more of the self than the subject matter of an artwork. The overall process of artistic expression, a person's lifework, is also a more complete self-portrait than a single object. For me, the paintings yet to be created hold as much of the self as those that already exit. They express a sense of desire that is never finished and forever emerging in relation to the changing context of life.

Artistic Expression as a Way of Knowing and Research

My research into the nature of the expressive arts therapy process is inseparable from my personal artistic expression as demonstrated by the Art Alchemy series and this discussion of self-portraiture. My early writings questioning the validity of diagnostic art methods and the labeling of expressions according to pre-existing psychological concepts were also informed by my experience with art. Realizing that the art diagnosticians would say that I was simply shielding myself from seeing "what was really going on," I trusted my instincts, common sense, and experiences with others and began to systematically challenge the validity of theories and methods which essentially held that everything we express will reveal hidden pathologies. My lifelong studies of the psychology of interpretation and efforts to establish more creative and accurate ways of responding to artworks have always been shaped by a personal sense of artistic reality.

At the start of my career, I was relatively alone within the American Art Therapy Association in giving significant weight to the artistic identity of art therapists. There were a small number of us who shared this view and one of my early presentations to an AATA national conference in 1978 was entitled "The Art Therapist as Artist."

During this period, I began to establish the idea that expressive arts therapy practice and theory could be grounded in artistic practice. *The Arts and Psychotherapy* (1981) viewed "artistic exploration as psychological research of the highest order" and in *Educating the Creative Arts Therapist* (1986), I presented An Artistic Theory of Mental Health and Therapy upon which our profession can be based.

In the late 1970s, when I began to view expressive arts therapy as a survival of ancient healing practices (McNiff, 1979), this notion which is now widely recognized and generally taken for granted had not been broached. The art therapy community and the other creative arts therapy disciplines were at that time far more focused on being credible clinicians. There was no attention given to identification with universal and primordial creative processes and little interest in the use of personal artistic expression as a mode of research, as a primary element of practice with others, and as a necessary form of renewal for therapists.

Edward Adamson had earlier suggested that art therapists needed to maintain an active artistic practice in order to effectively cultivate the curative forces within the studio environment, but he was largely overlooked as art therapy began to develop professional and educational standards. However, art therapy has made tremendous progress in recent years in supporting the artistic identity of art therapists in response to the leadership of Arthur Robbins, Bruce and Cathy Moon, Pat Allen, Lynn Kapitan, Cathy Malchiodi, Howard McConeghey, Michael Franklin, Sr. Kathleen Burke, Gail Rule-Hoffman, and others establishing a new generation of educators and leaders.

In the mid 1980s, I grew increasing uncomfortable with the use of other people's art and experiences as a way of presenting and researching methods and the essential phenomena of arts healing. As my interests moved toward depth psychology, I found that I could take greater liberties in showing my own expressions and reflections than I could by writing about other people.

I also discovered that I could penetrate more deeply into the dynamics of the creative process and the archetypal aspects of my discipline with "firsthand" inquiry.

In *Depth Psychology of Art* (1989) and *Art as Medicine* (1992), I used my own paintings and drawings as a form of art-based research in demonstrating different ways of reflecting upon images. Like Jung, I was committed to researching the dynamics of the psyche and the creative process through direct personal inquiry which engaged challenging situations and emotions. I took risks in showing my art in these books and making myself accessible to the kinds of projective interpretation that I had always challenged. But I was actually more concerned that it would be viewed as self-serving. I tried to emphasize how the presentation of the art I made is not about me but about expressive arts therapy methods and the phenomena that I am engaging.

To my surprise, the response was overwhelmingly positive and I later published *Art-Based Research* (1998), which explores the approach to inquiry that unfolded from this creative experimentation. In the book, I also emphasize how my graduate students had over the years helped me to see how personal art-making could be used to research the work that we do in expressive arts therapy. In keeping with my own teaching, they wanted to use their art as a mode of inquiry at a time when I had not completely crystallized my thinking about art as research. Ironically, it was my "art-based" theory and practice that modeled a new process for the students, but the way I viewed student research projects had not caught up with what I was actually doing. This gap demonstrates how the expressive arts therapy process operates and how our creative expressions are characteristically a few steps ahead of the reflecting mind.

Pablo Picasso said, "I never made a painting as a work of art, it's all research" (Webb, p. 243), so these ideas about art as research are not new. However, the arts and therapy communities have historically been so thoroughly tied to traditional social science methods of research and the more general notions of scientism that we have not appreciated our own unique potential to further human understanding.

Students and therapists not only want to learn more about how the creative process heals by researching their own artistic expression, but they want to receive the therapeutic benefits in their own lives. Arts-based research is an emergent discipline of inquiry that furthers the unique attributes of the expressive arts therapies while also giving therapists a vitally needed medium of self-care that recycles its personal benefits back into the work that serves others.

A Circulation of Creative Energy

My own artistic expression has affirmed how there is usually no single moment of healing or fixing when dealing with the human psyche. In keeping with the dynamics of the creative process, there are epiphanies, instances of insight and synthesis, and unforgettable discoveries that become part of the ongoing process of living. The expressive arts therapy experience is a succession of creative acts, expressions, and responses, all working together to foster well-being.

I have also learned from my practice of expressive arts therapy and from my personal expression that art heals through the flow and exchange of creative energies that act upon us in ways that cannot be planned in advance. As I say in *Art as Medicine,* "the medicinal agent is art itself . . . an infusion of imagination and awareness rather than a specific answer" (1992, p. 3). Whatever credibility I have in making this assertion can be attributed to my personal experience in making art and then having my insights validated by others.

Repeatedly I observe how the creative process finds it way through the thickets of our emotional lives in ways that are inaccessible to the linear movements of verbal explanation. I view the artistic expressions of therapists as vital elements of this process, part of the larger dynamic of discovery and creative transformation that I have learned to admire and trust (McNiff, 1998). Deep artistic healing happens when both clients and therapists let go and trust the wisdom of the creative process and the psyche's power to treat itself.

Whatever we bring to helping others through the arts originates in our personal history of creative expression. My experience suggests that this reciprocal process can be sustained throughout a career in ways that advance both the practice of expressive arts therapy and personal artistic expression. By keeping our relationships to art alive and vital we can transmit its strongest essence to others.

IV. UNIFYING ELEMENTS FOR ALL MEDIA

> Self examination may divide each art from the rest, while their mutual investigation reunites them in their inward effort. Each art has its peculiar force, which cannot be replaced by that of any other. Finally, the peculiar power of the different arts may be coordinated, and this coordination will eventually lead to an art which we may glimpse even now–the truly monumental art.
>
> Wassily Kandinsky, *Concerning the Spiritual in Art* (1970, p. 40)

STRUCTURE AND FREEDOM

There are endless ways of practicing expressive arts therapy. Each of us develops a personal style, preferences, and interests which can change over the course of a career. My methods strive to help people express themselves in the most complete and effective ways. I generally work with groups and sometimes large communities of people so my approaches to expressive arts therapy have been shaped in response these contextual factors.

Beginning expressive arts therapists, and especially students, are interested in learning more about what they can do with people, what particular activities and materials they might use, and how to engage participants in responding to artistic expressions. When I started my work, I had this same priority. I closely watched what therapists, teachers, and leaders did, observing the subtle aspects of how they handled themselves. I probably learned the most by viewing things that I did not like such as overly directive activities and interpretive responses that interfered with the natural unfolding of a person's creative expression. I admired leaders who created environments where people worked seriously and passionately and I strive to do this myself.

My work with students has deepened my appreciation of the issues related to structure and freedom in expressive arts therapy. The concerns that students express about what to do with other people when they are placed in leadership roles have revived my own appreciation for investigating the most basic aspects of structure. Beginning therapists tend to feel a keen sense of responsibility and fear of causing confusion or harm.

146

I discourage dualistic and strict divisions between directive and nondirective ways of working with people in the expressive arts therapies. We can be very directive and simple when introducing methods that support freedom of expression and complexity. As a teacher, I try to further understanding of the often paradoxical relationship between structure and freedom, direction and unplanned arrivals, while discouraging over-identification with either extreme.

In helping others to express themselves, I think of myself ideally as a minimalist. As a leader, I value restraint and the significance of what I do not do. I try to direct sessions and introduce structure in the most basic way to encourage the maximum range of expression. But if necessary, I will initiate whatever level of structure is needed to help people begin to express themselves and hopefully, as I have experienced in the unfolding of my personal methods of expressive arts therapy, they will move beyond these more directive beginnings to increasing levels of creative autonomy.

Experimentation with Structures

During the first years of my practice, I carefully recorded what we did during sessions. I experimented with different artistic processes while giving careful attention to how people responded to the activities. In my work with chronic mental patients who were generally unable to motivate themselves, I discovered the importance of structure introduced by the therapist. I kept recording in my journal how "structure liberates."

Paradoxically, I found that clear direction and tight limits helped people express themselves with greater spontaneously. If the situation was totally open-ended and if participants were invited to do whatever they pleased, in most cases, little would happen or people would revert to the most automatic and habitual expressions. The introduction of something new and concrete offered a fresh starting point, something participants could engage in different and imaginative ways. I also observed how people who were largely incapable of autonomous gestures or who for various reasons resisted opportunities for expression, benefited from the alter-ego of an another person who assisted them in taking initiative.

When I explored the use of different structures within the visual arts and more particularly with drawing and painting, there were two main types that I used: formally oriented activities and content themes.

Formal structures included drawings and painting where participants were asked to work exclusively with straight lines, dashes of paint, curved lines, or other types of marks. I suggested repeating the same gestures and making gradual variations from the basic strokes. Thematic structures might involve the introduction of a concept or emotion (i.e., together; separated; close; distant; random; ordered; calm; turbulent).

My suggestions were always intended as open-ended stimulants and starting points for expression and I discouraged explicitly personal directions such as–draw your fear, your pain, and so forth. At this early point in practice, I realized that it is far more effective when people express these emotions on their own accord rather than in reaction to contrived conditions.

I did similar things with movement and dance. I proposed a formal structure such as the arms and upper body moving in horizontal or vertical patterns and asked the group to work with the basic expression in different ways. I usually came upon the particular gesture by observing how a person in the group was moving, called attention to it, and asked the whole group to work with the movement. We also moved in response to conceptual and emotional themes–fast, slow, high, low, flowing, tight, light, heavy, joyful, serious, and so forth.

With musical instruments and vocal improvisation, we repeated and built upon sounds and rhythms that we heard in our environment and worked with themes–hushed, carefree, cautious, delight. We might also listen to a piece of classical music or read a poem and identify a theme or quality that we then expressed in another medium.

It was fascinating to see how people explored the same gesture or emotion in drawings, movements, sounds, dramatic improvisations, and poems. The process of interpreting a formal or emotional quality generated a very natural and coherent way of using varied art forms.

The Emergence of Integrated Arts Experiences

The overriding goal of my early work was the most complete activation of a person's and a group's creative expression. This fundamental purpose has been sustained over the years in that my role as a leader and expressive arts therapist has always been one of cultivating the creative powers of others. Once the flow of creative expression is activated, therapeutic and life-enhancing outcomes emanate from it.

The objects and various expressions that people make are vital aspects of the overall experience. The "products" of art are necessary contributors in the larger "process"–the different dimensions work together. A commitment to process need not diminish the things that emerge from the experience. If we perceive these expressions with curiosity, respect, and even sacred attitudes, the complete art experience will unfold naturally.

The integrated arts dimensions of my expressive arts therapy practice emerged with very little conscious planning. I was open, curious, receptive, and prone to experiment while striving to create an imaginative and expressive environment. This way of working contrasted to those who were oriented to fixed and predetermined procedures. From the start, I approached everything I did as a practitioner researcher, trying different things in an effort to support expression and then documenting how people responded.

I was also keenly interested in relating to both individual and group needs. If a person showed an interest in a particular form of expression or a special ability, I tried to reinforce these possibilities rather than limit the creative work to one medium. My overall orientation was one of responsiveness to the total range of expressive opportunities existing within the environment, the group, and the individual.

I discovered that participants in our sessions were less apt to become stuck in their resistance to a particular mode of expression when focused on shifting from one medium to another. I have observed over the years how people think less about being judged when moving amongst different art forms, especially if the overall environment generates a sense of relaxation, adventure, and creative discovery. Perhaps the foreignness and newness of the multimedia process takes them to a new place where they are not as prone to apply old attitudes about whether or not they can express themselves effectively in drawing, movement, voice, and other art forms. It becomes clear as we work with varied media that the primary purpose is the promotion of expression and imagination rather than the assessment of a person's ability in a particular art form. When the sessions are literally focused on the "exercise" of creative gestures, like a physical workout in a gym, there can be a shift away from intimidation and negative memories that stifle creative expression for many people.

We experience a sense of wonder and insight on both cognitive and emotional levels by doing unexpected and imaginative things with expressions in varied media. The process of moving from one medium to another becomes the primary focus and this helps to establish an expressive flow that can be more difficult for the average person to sustain within a single medium. There also tends to be a quality of playfulness and a sense of experimentation permeating the atmosphere when engaging different art forms.

When the process of expression is expanded to include a number of different media and the many creations that emerge from this work, we are less likely to become fixated on a single thing. The varied expressions establish a creative ecology, a holistic process which is apt to have more of an impact on people than any particular psychological or therapeutic insight. When I first experienced these effects within sessions, I started to view the art studio as offering a creative milieu therapy, a healing and restorative energy, a therapeutic community of images and expressions, all of which constituted the real essence of expressive arts therapy. The artistic medicines were in the environment and they acted upon us. I felt these effects myself and in keeping with the principles of art-based research, my personal reaction significantly informed what I did to help others.

As described earlier, my work with children strongly affirmed the value of integrating the arts and creating environments that inspire and support an ongoing process of creative expressions. Children will typically use different media in natural and spontaneous ways—making sounds while they paint; telling stories about their pictures; enacting dramas as they work with clay and other three-dimensional materials.

Child psychotherapy has always been an integrated arts process in which varied media of expression are made available to children so that they can play and express themselves imaginatively in the presence of a therapist who creates a safe and supportive space. The overall environment of the therapeutic milieu, whether it is a consulting room, studio, or community, enables the child to practice ways of interacting creatively and effectively with the world.

As I began to work with groups of adults outside mental health settings, I learned how the process of mixing media and shifting from one art form to another had the same positive effects that we observed within the hospital studio. These shifts between media often occurred in response to expressions that appeared spontaneously in a person's art or when relating to feelings or problems experienced by individuals or groups. There was a prevailing sense of wanting to engage the condition, take it to another place, change one's relationship to it, and use it as a source of expression. Rather than trying to talk our way out of a fixation or stuck feeling, we just did something different with it and the physical actions established the basis for a corresponding shift in consciousness and emotion. Changing media and ways of expression becomes a means of changing attitudes, attachments, and actual behaviors.

This approach to integrated arts expressions is in sync with classical healing practices based on principles of correspondence, similarity, and like producing like which will be discussed in the next part of the book. For example, if we want to introduce changes in our lives, we enact situations that involve changing from one thing to another. We can alter how we feel about a problem or a situation by exploring different ways of relating to it and expressing it.

The Simpler, the Deeper

Everything should be made as simple as possible, but not simpler.

Albert Einstein

When it became clear that these deeper currents of expression and healing were happening on their own accord within my studios, I gradually moved away from introducing specific formal tasks and emotional themes. I found that the average group of adults from a cross-section of society did not require the same structures that I used with chronic mental patients. Leader-initiated themes and exercises began to feel superficial and manipulative. I felt that I was biasing the forms and contents of people's expression and I also gradually discovered how the imposition of a theme might actually block and hinder the expressive process as well as the emanation of forceful and intimate expressions that significantly deepened the overall experience.

I gradually began to trust that whatever needed to emerge would manifest itself in a free and open environment. I perceived my role as cultivating the overall atmosphere of creation; instilling a deep sense of safety, respect, and attentiveness to one another. In keeping with the principles of Eastern medicine, I realized how the expressive process would go where it needed to go if we could minimize blocks, obstructions, and fears.

I continued to appreciate the importance of structure, but I embraced a much simpler and basic approach to it. People in my studios describe how there is a complete freedom to express whatever they please but that the overall environment has a clear and very strong organization in terms of what we do together as a group. They smile and say, "You are extremely structured, but we can do whatever we want."

Within groups I will plan the media and materials we use; decide when to shift from one art form to another; and coordinate the more general organization of the session. My focus has thus moved from structuring the contents of a person's expression to the larger context of leadership and shaping the overall sequence of actions, watching the clock, communicating basic principles of operation, and supporting people through the various phases of their expression.

When people paint, I ask them to concentrate on their movement and perhaps focus on the repetition of gestures. I suggest the same things with creative movement, vocal improvisation, writing, and performance. "Make a gesture of some kind," I say, "and try to be immersed in it as completely as possible. Keep it simple and concentrate on what you are doing in the present moment. If you start to plan, you will lose your power. Try and express whatever emerges with as much conviction as possible."

Together with a focus on simplicity, I stress the importance of repetition as a way of letting go and accessing our most natural ways of expression. If we can relax and exercise free and authentic expression, we are more apt to engage our most intimate and poignant concerns. Repetition is rhythmic and especially important with movement and vocal expression, but I have found that repeating gestures and images has the same liberating power in the visual arts, poetry, and performance art. As we do something over and over, it begins to shape itself and take on its own form independent of our thoughts about what it should be.

I must emphasize how the focus on simplicity throughout this book does not involve a denial of the complex nature of human experience and the intricacies of artistic expression. As Rudolf Arnheim states consistently in his studies of the psychology of art, creative expression involves a dynamic tension between simplicity and complexity, order and disorder (1954, 1971). I have discovered how a focus on simplicity helps to hold and channel unsettling and confusing aspects of the creative process whereas complicated activities are more likely to generate superficial expressions. As demonstrated by the discussion in the preceding sections describing expressive arts therapy with children and adults, therapeutic goals will emerge from the structures and processes of artistic expressions.

In my work with people from a cross-section of society, we attempt to further kinetic sensibilities that have been taken for granted and overlooked for years. We start with the same elemental gestures and approaches that were so helpful in the hospital studio. I have found that experienced artists can also benefit from a return to fundamental movements as a way of renewing and enriching their relationships to their disciplines.

In a recent session, an experienced painter accepted my invitation to stay with a single gesture through two whole days of studio work. She made one gesture over and over again with different colors and textures of paint on large surfaces. The process was difficult for her, but she stayed with it and ultimately produced a lively series of pictures that not only furthered her sensitivity to the kinetic underpinnings of paintings, but also helped carry her to a new phase of creation.

This experience also shows how restrictions on movement can advance expression. The limitations on the artist's movement enabled her to invent new ways of moving and gain a deeper understanding of the painting process. The annoyance and struggle with the process also carried her into a more complete partnership with it. She embraced anger and frustration and used their energies to intensify and sustain the repetition of the painting gestures. The limitations of the process fortified the artist's inner engagement with it. No longer able to use her usual skills and techniques, she had to surrender to the restraints and discover how a new partnership with rhythmic gestures could influence her expression.

It was also clear to this artist after her two days of "painting" that the primary reality of her work during this period had been "movement." She gained a firsthand realization of how important it is to value all of the modes of expression when focused on a particular artistic medium. If we limit movement in expressive arts therapy to the confines of dance, we miss the larger and more important creative movement opportunities in other areas of our lives.

The increasing breadth of my experience in expressive arts therapy has reinforced rather than reduced my original sense of how structure helps to liberate expression. Changes in my relationship to "the structure and freedom ratio" have more to do with the relative amounts of structure that is required in particular situations.

With most of the adults with whom I work today, I find that there is a productive tension attached to giving considerable leeway and choice in relation to artistic directions and decisions. In the mid 1970s, I wrote in my journal about the "motivating tension" needed to restore healthy rhythms to our lives and how this tension can fuel creation. I also observed at the start of my work how there are people who are in such personal chaos or withdrawal that they cannot tolerate additional tension or they have insulated themselves from it completely. In the practice of expressive arts therapy, we need to make ongoing assessments regarding the degree of structure to be introduced in response to the demands of the varied situations encountered in our work with others.

The range of conditions that I experience generates different ways of introducing art materials. These environmental factors are constantly shaping how I structure sessions. The needs and abilities of participants will determine the extent to which I stand back and hold a space through my attentiveness to the environment or the degree to which I am "hands on" in assisting people with the most basic aspects of expression. The making of these decisions is the essence of diagnosis and assessment in expressive arts therapy. Within the studio, evaluation and planning are an ongoing and creative process, a dynamic interplay between making observations and responding to immediate and changing circumstances.

WITNESSING OTHERS AND RESPONDING TO EXPRESSIONS

My group sessions have always been organized to support individual persons, partners, or small groups working before other group members who act as witnesses. We will often move together as one group or make rhythms and vocal expressions as a unit, but the sessions are primarily constructed around everyone having the opportunity to both express themselves before the group and practice serving as witnesses.

I have discovered that one of the most effective ways of enhancing creative expression is to focus on how we watch, witness, and respond to what a person does within the studio environment. I emphasize how the silent witnessing of another person's performance within a group can be just as important and active as expressing oneself. The witness is needed to establish the exchange of creative energy and expression. This function can be fulfilled by one person or by a community of people.

Giving Attention to Others and Creative Responses

The palpable sense of creativity in expressive therapy studios is, in my opinion, established by the community of people working together, paying attention to one another, and responding to each other's work. This is the defining therapeutic quality of the environment and I have discovered that it also has great appeal to artists who desire something other than other than the classic "critique" from other studio participants. Artists participate in my studios in order to experience a group environment where others accompany them on their journeys without distracting judgments and support them during periods of uncertainty, loss, and even destruction, when they let go of familiar expressions in order to take their art to new and perhaps more challenging places.

Artists throughout history have, of course, demonstrated how the creative spirit persists without support and in the face of adversity and there are many who make art alone as a way of healing and who do not necessarily receive attention form others. Artistic expressions and objects can in these situations become companions and witnesses to our life situations, giving solace, support, and affirmations of our desires.

In contrast to these solitary instances of art and healing, the expressive arts therapy experience can be defined as a context where there will be at least one other person who will attentively witness an individual's expression. The role of the witness is among the most essential components of the professional therapeutic relationship, perhaps even more primary than that of a guide since the latter role is often subsumed within the act of giving support and attention. When working with groups of people, the therapist expands the community of witnesses by demonstrating how to concentrate and give complete attention to the expressions of others.

In my role as a leader, one of the most directive things that I do is to request complete and silent attention from witnesses as they observe another person working. Participants describe how this attentiveness generates a sense of sanctity and shared commitment.

I also establish straightforward guidelines and "rules" for giving feedback, discouraging judgment, and asking that witnesses describe what they experience while watching a person perform or present their artistic expressions. As Rainer Maria Rilke advises a young poet in his classic letters, artistic expression is an act of "infinite solitude" that is best touched and held through "love" and not "criticism" (1984, p. 23).

It is fascinating how experienced artists and other people who are less familiar with the creative process actually find this type of feedback helpful in terms of ongoing efforts to refine and further the quality of their expression. Each of us has a natural critical faculty and the studio environment offers a place where this critic can relax a bit, let down its guard, listen to how our expressions are influencing others, and thus receive information that will enable us to be more effective in advancing expression.

If a person's artistic expression upsets or confuses a witness, the communication of this kind of experience is welcomed as part of the legitimate give and take between artists and their audiences. We avoid comparative judgments, overly conceptual analyses, and projective assessments of "meanings" by witnesses. I encourage people to be descriptive in saying something about another person's art, to pay careful attention to the expressive characteristics of the phenomena, to observe with respect and appreciation, and to give responses that offer something useful to the artist.

To free the witness from trying to determine what another person might need from a response, I describe how as an artist I appreciate the most sincere account of how my expression affects another person. The same applies to a person's needs for reactions in therapy.

When I watch other people expressing themselves in my studio, I do everything I can to put aside distractions and as stated earlier, make what happens the most important thing in my life at that particular moment. I try to channel all my energy and concentration, and immerse myself fully in the other person's creation. As Jung emphasized, we practice looking psychologically and deeply at the expressions of others and find that this application of energy helps to further the creative process for everyone involved. The witness who gives complete attention is transported, moved, and changed in ways that correspond to the experiences of the artists. Everyone in the group travels with the creative process and, at times, our most significant therapeutic experiences occur in quietly witnessing and supporting the expressions of others. These opportunities for varied dimensions of creative expression and participation are among the qualities which have kept me closely attached to group and community practice.

The place of the witness has grown increasing prominent in my work over the years. Early on, I realized that there are limitations to responding to our own artistic expressions and to those of others solely through verbal descriptions and explanations. Descriptive narratives have an important place in expressive arts therapy, a necessary role, but they access a fraction of our creative and responsive sensibilities. When I describe something in words, I speak from a relatively habitual frame of reference.

As I explored ways of integrating the arts in my studios, I learned how we can go deeper in our responses, access new creative insights and expressions, and even communicate what we experience from an artwork in more comprehensive ways, when we respond through various artistic media. Jung spoke of his methods of active imagination as giving people the opportunity to imagine further; to take the dream or the artistic experience into new dimensions of imagination and discovery. My experience has affirmed Jung's insight and I have come to believe that the cultivation of the ongoing process of creative expression is the essential purpose of expressive arts therapy.

I describe this discipline as responding to art with art and as I have emphasized previously, the potential ways of doing this are wide-ranging. I will often vary the sequence of creative activities, perhaps beginning with movement and vocal improvisations and then responding to these expressions with poetry, painting, storytelling, or dramatic improvisations. Every sequence of expression has its particular features which contribute to the overall experience of integrated arts therapy. The combinations and creative permutations are truly endless and this richness of possibilities has been a primary reason why expressive arts therapy has strongly sustained my creative and research interests. I witness people being touched and transformed by these experiences which continuously affirm the significance of the work.

Creative Responses to Visual Art Objects as an Example of Arts Integration

In my studios visual artworks generally serve as points of origin and sources for creative expressions in other media—movement, drama, poetry, sound improvisation, imaginal dialogue, performance art. Although this pattern may be simply an expression of my particular leadership style and interests in the visual arts, I feel that there is also something significant in having a physical and constant partner and artistic companion through the various phases of integrated arts activity. The artwork serves as an abiding presence, a place to which we can return again and again for inspiration and suggestions for further expression. Like a dream, a painting also conveys a certain degree of mystery and open-ended interpretive possibility which motivates successive and ongoing waves of creative response.

From the start of my work in expressive arts therapy, I have observed how visual art works naturally elicit interpretive responses. Spoken language, stories, and written text are perhaps the most common and spontaneous media used to respond to visual images. Young children innately write on their pictures with a desire to name and define what they have created and this process of combining pictures and text can be viewed as an archetypal phenomenon that appears throughout history.

As described earlier, I systematically used all of the arts as stimuli for encouraging speech and conversation with severely withdrawn psychiatric patients during my first years of practicing expressive arts therapy. As with current efforts to engage dementia patients in multisensory activities to arouse different aspects of consciousness and an overall interplay of perceptual faculties, I focused on how artistic expressions could help people make meaningful contact with the physical world. I felt in the early 1970s that the varied perceptual activities would enhance once another, that using different media activates a holistic process where the coordination of multiple senses could do much more than one alone.

Artworks acted as catalysts for human interaction and communication. The creative process served as a springboard for a more comprehensive activation of a person's interaction with the world. We used various kinds of speech in responding to art objects, ranging from straightforward description to more imaginative responses—stories, fantasies, and encouraging the figures and forms to speak about themselves and their expressions. These methods of responding to art through creative uses of language have continued as a core element of my practice. I have constantly tried to invent new and more imaginative ways of interacting with art through language since this will always be such a fundamental aspect of expressive arts therapy practice. In recent years, I have given more attention to responding through less common modes of interpretation—movement, sound, voice, ritual, and performance.

In my studios where the goals are concerned with deepening and sustaining creative expression, my most basic interpretive activity is to involve people in responding to their paintings and those done by others with movement improvisation lasting for at least a minute-and-a-half or two minutes. "Paintings and drawings," I say, "convey movement, energy, dynamic relationships." I feel that my paintings have more to do with kinetic qualities and vital, emotional relationships amongst forms and colors than with verbal communication. Yet we unthinkingly tend to reduce pictures in therapy to narrative and verbal language-based concepts, a way of reacting to art objects that limits our perception of their expression.

I repeatedly observe how I can learn more about artists' relationships with their pictures and three-dimensional objects when they move in response to them rather than when they talk about what they did. Again, I affirm the place of stories and narrative in response to artworks, what I call creation stories, but I find that these accounts are more apt to repeat what the artist already knows. Responding to art with spontaneous artistic creations, in this case through movement, elicits the unexpected. When introducing this way of responding and providing the structure for the experience, I say, "The only thing that you can do wrong is start to plan what you are going to do before you do it."

Before responding directly to an artwork with movement, I often invite individuals and groups to repeat the essential gestures that were used to make a painting or drawing. I ask people to take a moment before they begin, to remember the process of creating, and to get in touch with their bodily memories of the movements and gestures. This exercise always tends to be well-received and it helps people enter the domain of expressive movement with a direct connection to memories of gestures and bodily sensations that are immediate and unique to their experience. They can begin with a movement sequence that they know and can clearly perform.

I encourage members to take liberties with their original gestures and not feel bound to moving exactly as they did while painting or drawing. A shift has been made from painting to dance and movement so the new art form should have all the freedom it needs. I suggest that people might want to amplify or diminish their beginning gestures, change speed or intensity, or let the movement progress to a new form that may not have existed in the visual art work.

In group studios, all of the participants might repeat their individual painting gestures at the same time as a group dance or smaller groups of three to five people take turns stepping in the center of the space and make these movements together while others witness their expression. The movements tend to serve as a warm-up and preparation for a more direct, individual engagement of particular artistic images.

When moving in response to individual art objects, I ask people to try and immerse themselves in their images, to contemplate them for 10 or 20 seconds before beginning. I suggest looking at the images in purely sensory ways and to then let movements interact with the pictorial configurations. I encourage keeping expressions simple, repeating gestures, and allowing movements to emerge naturally from the repetition.

"Try not to do too many things," I say. "You will engage me and the other witnesses more completely if you stay focused on a gesture and let it build progressively upon itself. If you try and script what you are doing, you get caught in the plan and lose contact with what you are doing in the moment. If you move with this simple focus, the expression will be perfect."

In my studios, we generally sit in a circle and place artworks on the floor in the center and the artist moves in response to the image. Participants are encouraged to stay closely attuned to the image, engage it as a partner in movement as opposed to taking an inspiration from it and then making a separate dance. The expressive quality and depth of the movement is typically determined by the artist's ability to stay closely engaged with the image.

The composition and visual qualities of the art object present movement patterns to artists who respond to them with their own movements. The process might begin with the artist moving in sync with a particular gesture in the picture. Emphasis is always placed on improvisation and having the freedom to move in whatever way best serves the purpose of relating to the image. We do not encourage a literal and strict choreography in response to pictorial and structural configurations presented by the artwork. The movement response might relate to the whole of a picture, a particular part, or a sequence of movements which respond to different aspects of the artistic image.

I cite the archetypal psychology dictum "stick to the image," and say, "If you can stay connected to the image as completely as possible, it will carry you and take you where you need to go. Think about your movement as responding to a partner, as being led and informed by the artistic image, as a way of paying attention to it and interpreting it through the body rather than words. The image was made through your movements so now respond to it with them."

We similarly respond to images with vocal improvisation and sound, often encouraging the person to combine movement and sound. When introducing the process of interpreting artistic expressions with voice and sound, I underscore how sound cannot be separated from movement and how the simple sounds of the body breathing can be an important starting point for expression. Sound emerges naturally as we move in space and make art objects. I will use the repetition of words and brief phrases as a way of giving form and structure to vocal improvisation. This engagement of language is closer to movement and sound improvisation than descriptive narrative as described earlier.

In my studios, we work with all art forms and also respond to images with performance art, ritual, poetry, stories, and imaginal dialogue. These various media will be discussed in other sections of this book dealing with particular art forms. However, I must emphasize that in my practice the individual media are always informing one another and establishing different kinds of connections in relation to the circumstances of the particular context.

The divisions amongst media that appear in the organization of this book do not necessarily reflect the conditions of practice. As Wassily Kandinsky emphasizes in the passage cited at the start of this chapter, "Each art has its peculiar force, which cannot be replaced by that of any other," and the separation of art forms enables us to study the unique features of each (1970, p. 40). However, in life and in the expressive arts therapy studio, the powers of these different art forms can be joined to further expression and a more comprehensive creative experience.

Within the expressive arts therapy experience, we are always differentiating one artistic experience from another and appreciating the unique qualities of each. But a distinctive feature of the therapeutic environment is our primary emphasis on the whole effect, the total expression of the artistic space and the impact that it has on participants.

Cycles of Response

I have learned when a person takes the risk of acting before other group members, that it is important to receive a response from another person. If time permits, I make sure that we always give artists who might be moving, making sounds, uttering words, or enacting spontaneous rituals, the opportunity to select another person in the group to give an artistic response within the same medium.

For example, if a group member is making a dance or ritual in response to a painting, I ask the person to select another group member, prior to working, who will give "a response to the response." In this way, the person selected to respond becomes an integral part of the whole enactment and is given the opportunity to prepare in terms of intention and focus.

The discipline of the artistic response involves an immersion in the present relationship with an image and then allowing creative expression to emerge spontaneously and naturally. Sometimes, and especially if the group is small, more than one person can respond, and in these situations, the cycles of creative expression become more pronounced and varied.

I emphasize how the respondents must be free to relate to the painting in whatever ways engage their imaginations and sensitivities. And again I describe how artists like to see their pictures activate the imagination and expression of another person and how this kind of creative response is the most affirming and personal thing that we can give to another.

We try to free people from the tendency that many feel to give a "correct" response and the assumption that they must figure out what the artist or the painting really needs from them. In all forms of the arts and especially in therapeutic settings people are apt to reduce creative expressions to psychological explanations. Of course, artistic expressions have psychological qualities and meanings, but works of art are primarily gestures, forces, conveyances of emotion, efforts by one human being to connect with another, activations of imagination, and many other transmissions of life that cannot be reduced to concepts and language.

I call attention to responding from the heart and the creative imagination and how this type of genuine communication can often be the most psychologically compelling and deep way of influencing another person. I welcome whimsy and playfulness and try to eliminate all expectations. Therapeutic environments have a tendency to make people feel that they have to be profound, deep, and psychologically penetrating in their responses.

I establish a few ground rules such as not altering or damaging an artwork in giving a response. I also stress that although we are free to express ourselves as imaginatively as possible, the purpose in giving a response is to acknowledge and affirm the other person's art object. Our response is part of a larger intention which serves the well-being of others and supportive relationships.

I say, "What I need as an artist is 'your' most natural response and perhaps my artwork feels the same."

These exchanges of expression teach us that what matters most in therapeutic and artistic environments is the sincere communication of sensibility and support from one person to another. The responsive artistic expression typically becomes a moving ritual of affirmation. I try to help participants realize how much they give when they respond to one another's art with sincere emotion and creative interest. It is the effort and generosity of spirit that contribute to the overall therapeutic and creative impact of the experience.

Artistic Responses and Expressions by Therapists within Sessions

Within the expressive arts therapies, there are significant differences in the degree to which practitioners introduce their own creative expressions into sessions. The nature of the particular medium being used can significantly influence the therapist's involvement. For example, when working with dance, music, vocal improvisation, dramatic improvisation, and other art forms involved with bodily action in the moment, I am always using my own creative expressions to demonstrate and prompt others to create with these media or I will become engaged with collaborative improvisation to support the expression of others. I will do the same with poetry, uttering a verse, passage, or phrase that I make up in that moment to demonstrate or to respond to a person's expression.

As suggested throughout this book, many therapeutic methods utilizing dance, music, vocal expression, and drama are completely based on an exchange of creative expressions between therapists and clients. Object-oriented artistic modalities such as the visual arts and creative writing tend to be more solitary and therapists will often take on the role of facilitator and witness rather than participating directly in the creative process. However, therapists might make visual artworks or write poems within sessions to further the overall creative energy of the space, demonstrate how to use media, prompt free expression, respond to others, or simply be more completely involved in the overall process of communication.

As described in the earlier section dealing with children and expressive arts therapy, D. W. Winnicott perceived psychotherapy as an overlapping relationship between the play of a therapist and a client. If clients have difficulty playing, then accommodations need to be made in order to help them become immersed in the creative process. But if therapists are unable to play, Winnicott says explicitly that they are "not suitable for the work" (p. 54).

I agree completely with Winnicott. As someone who views the expressive arts therapy as offering modalities which should be accessible to every therapist and client, I believe that being able to play, explore, and be immersed in artistic expressions while in the presence of others is a prerequisite for practice. Winnicott feels that "only in being creative" can a person discover "the self" (p. 54). This same criterion of creativity applies to establishing therapeutic relationships. However, circumstances and the demands of a particular context often do not allow us to engage in this kind of cocreation. For example, when I am working with a group of people making art objects, and especially if the group needs assistance, I cannot create my own art since I have so many other things to do with materials and watching over the space. This was especially true when I was working with groups of seriously impaired people or with troubled children. I was kept busy organizing the studio and attending to the needs of participants.

In many of my residential studios, I will make art during breaks and this participation is always well-received and viewed as having a positive impact on the overall environment. People appreciate seeing that I am affected and inspired by the work. They tend to be intrigued by my expressions and welcome them as part of the larger therapeutic and artistic milieu. My creations are viewed just like all of the others generated in the studio and they become part of the larger community of images. I might also make a painting or write a poem after a session and bring it to the next meeting as a communication of how I am being influenced by the group or a particular situation.

When alone with one other person or with a couple, or in a small group, there are many reasons why it can be useful for the expressive arts therapist to make art objects during the session. If we view our paintings, drawings, photos, and other visual art constructions as forms of expression and communication, just like spoken language, dance, and other art media, they can become important parts of the more general exchange between people. These artistic expressions can be created to offer direct responses to the artworks of others or they can be made as part of the expressive arts therapist's more general contribution to the creative milieu.

When I was working with the psychiatrist and author Robert Coles in the 1970s, well before art therapists became seriously involved in discussing the practice of responsive art making, he described how he always made art together with children (McNiff, 1976, pp. 123–124). Referring to himself as "no great artist" but as someone who likes to draw, Coles felt that his participation helped the children feel comfortable with him as he scribbled and painted earnestly but without taking himself too seriously. Art therapists tend to have more difficulty becoming involved with art-making in playful and less self-conscious ways. If we can think less about ourselves and what we might be revealing, we can start examining how the therapist's immersion in the process of expression might help others.

Coles spoke of how the children often felt a sense of "relief" when encouraged to make art alongside an adult and not experience pressure to talk. Interactive drawing was also helpful when children resisted expression or kept repeating the most stereotypic forms.

Describing his artistic ways of engaging children who were feeling stuck, Coles said: "The only way I can deal with them is in a nonverbal way; by noticing what the child is drawing and responding with my own drawings. If I see a child who is being stereotypical, I go out of my way to fill my paper up with a blazing sun, which any child can do, or just put color on the paper without any interest in form or structure, which is very easy for because I'm not very good at form and structure anyway!"(p. 124).

He goes on to emphasize how he is "constantly responding" to the child's art with his own and "adjusting" to his sense of what is needed in the moment. Sometimes the child's proficiency with art challenges him to "work harder" in his responses and in other situations he will intentionally lower the threshold of his drawing skills to be more empathetic.

When I am making art within therapeutic sessions, I try to stay both attached and detached from my expressions, all the while perceiving them as secondary to my primary focus on the other person. My artistic movements and efforts become part of the larger process of creation that is taking place within the therapeutic studio. This orientation is very different from the attitude that I have when working alone in my studio.

In training expressive arts therapists, I encourage them to practice this way of being in their art and not in it at the same time. The approach goes contrary to many ingrained instincts regarding the making of art and it can be more challenging for people who are very serious about their expressions. When my art-making is less self-consciousness and subordinated to another purpose, it can be personally helpful. New expressive elements, themes, and pictorial qualities are apt to arise from outside the scope of my usual creative patterns.

If one of the goals of expressive arts therapy is mutual creation and more comprehensive communication through the arts, we might ask if therapists are withholding important therapeutic elements by completely refraining from artistic expression. Within the art therapy discipline, there is an increasing interest in therapist's making art in response to images made by their clients (Moon, 2000; Fish, 2005). Students are asking many interesting and probing questions about the process which will no doubt be an ongoing area of research within the expressive arts therapies. Since I work primarily with groups, I am more focused in my practice on ways that group members respond to and affirm one another's' expressions. I am apt to become involved in responsive art-making only to demonstrate and introduce the process to others. But I am intrigued with the growing interest in responsive art-making by therapists within art therapy, and I believe that it can significantly enrich the discipline.

There is a tendency within the visual arts to see the art object as closely identified with the self, whereas with movement, sound, drama, and even poetry, the medium is perhaps viewed more essentially as a form of expressive communication, as a language and mode of interaction between therapist and clients. Therefore, the questions that art therapists ask about their self-disclosure when making art with clients might not be as much of a concern for a dance therapist who is always moving with other people and responding to their expressions during a session, or to a music therapist whose basic mode of practice involves mutual improvisation with individuals and groups.

When students express concerns about self-revelation when making art together with clients, I call attention to how every expressive gesture that we make when moving or speaking presents something about who we are and how we act within the world.

I believe that many of our most revealing expressions are "on the surface" of self-presentation in full view of others and not necessarily kept in hidden recesses of the psyche. I encourage students to distinguish open and generous expression in the arts from the discussion of private experiences, memories, and concerns. Artistic expressions do not have to be tied to the latter. When expressive arts therapists communicate through color, line, forms, figure, and imagination, they are showing their artistic styles in much the same way as they show themselves when sitting with another person, walking across the room, playing, or participating in spontaneous exercises with movement and other more physically demonstrative art forms.

One of the most significant barriers to transparent and ongoing co-creation in the expressive arts therapy experience is the feelings of insecurity that therapists sometimes have about their own artistic abilities which tend to vary greatly. I venture to say that many therapists do not always feel confident in using their self-expression to serve the expression of others. There might be a sense of inferiority in relation to one's skills or experience and fear of disclosing this potential inadequacy.

When therapists ask whether or not their skills as artists make a difference within the expressive arts therapy experience, I refer to people like Robert Coles and I adapt Winnicott's "good enough mother" idea to being a "good enough artist." The spectrum of expressive arts therapy experiences is endless and there is room within our discipline for people with varying degrees of skill with artistic media. For me, quality expression by therapists has more to do with authenticity and being "good enough" with the materials of art. Drawing narrow boundaries around who can and cannot use the arts in therapy limits what I see as the universal language of creative expression that needs to made as accessible as possible to people in need.

Graduate students and beginning expressive arts therapists need to become familiar and comfortable with their artistic expression, know their capabilities as well as their limitations, and realize how their art will add to the interplay of transferences, perceptions, influences, and ongoing communications that form the basis of therapeutic environments. I encourage the same kind of awareness toward a therapist's personal art-making in sessions that is applied to the use of spoken language, striving for the best possible aesthetic interaction between self-expression and restraint.

On the basis of my personal experience, both as an expressive arts therapist and as a trainer, I feel that the major challenge facing beginning therapists is the vulnerability, discomfort, and uncertainty commonly felt when sharing their own artistic expressions. Consequently, training programs will often make ongoing self-expression by students and receiving responses from others a major and ongoing part of the educational experience. We all need to know more about how our expressions affect others, how we feel and react when others respond emotionally to our work, and generally develop the ability to ground ourselves when interacting with others in this way, especially when showing our most personal artistic expressions. Continuing education and professional supervision in expressive arts therapy similarly focus on these core issues.

If a picture, poem, or another art object is made by a therapist in response to one made by a client, this can be viewed as an integral part of the therapeutic process, a thoroughly human interplay of perceptions and expressions. It is possible that for some people, the artistic response will carry more significance than verbal communications. It might also be meaningful for a client to respond artistically to an expression that a therapist makes in a session. All of these interactions convey in concrete and accessible forms the intersubjectivity that occurs between human beings. If therapists are able to stand back and view their artistic expressions as different languages and forms of communication, they can use these resources to supplement spoken language in exploring problems and challenges in living.

As the expressive arts therapy field continues to evolve, the linear notions of individuals responding directly to one another might be increasingly replaced with a more complex interplay of interactions. For example, my colleagues Lori Vance, Paula Conrad, and Stan Strickland have created therapeutic community programs for adolescents in the Express Yourself centers in Massachusetts and Milwaukee. In these programs, artists, therapists, and children work together over an extended period of time to produce an annual multi-arts "culminating performance" (P. Conrad, personal communication, December 10, 2001). Staff and participants create together as part of a whole that emphasizes collaboration and cocreation in every aspect of the program, a way of working that challenges artists as well as participants to let go and become something larger than individual expressions. As I emphasize throughout this book, I believe that this more comprehensive circulation of creative energy, in cooperation with others or within our personal expression, is the most fundamental force of art and healing.

THE CREATIVE SPACE

When I was being trained in group psychotherapy in the early 1970s, my psychiatrist supervisor always said that we should never assume that a gathering of people in a room is "a group." He felt there needs to be a degree of purpose and commitment to one another and to the work being done in order to become a group. I believe we can say the same thing about a therapeutic and creative space.

In a 1995 essay, Keeping the Studio, I describe the expressive arts therapist as a "caretaker" and "keeper" of the studio, whose primary responsibility is to "to kindle the soul of the place, to maintain its vitality, and its ability to engage people" and infuse creative spirits and influences (p. 180). The creative space is more than a carefully designed physical area where people work together in the arts. It is a place that generates the creative spirit in the present moment. A particular setting might have a long history of creation, but in order to become a true creative space, it has to be perceived by the people within it as capable of generating and supporting the creative imagination. The creative space is never given to us as a basic assumption of practice. It is something that we make every time we create with others.

In addition to C. G. Jung, D. W. Winnicott (1896–1971) is an important ally of expressive arts therapy within the psychoanalytic tradition. Winnicott viewed psychological health as "living creatively" and sickness as a mechanical acquiescence to some other person's or institution's wishes which conflict with our own creative urges (1971, p. 65). I would expand this definition to include forces within a person that undermine creativity.

The goal of therapy for Winnicott is the creation of a "holding environment" where people are given the chance to be creative, let go of unauthentic self-images, and shape "the true self." In keeping with classical definitions of the imagination discussed earlier, he called this space an "intermediate area" that is both psychic and physical (p. 11).

In my opinion, Winnicott's greatest teaching for the expressive arts therapy community is his realization that the therapist "holds," cultivates, and supports the creative space in which people experience their own transformations and deep discoveries, often by surprise–"It is not the moment of my clever interpretation that is significant" (p. 51). Winnicott describes with dismay how often he obstructed "deep change" with his "need to interpret" and that he experiences "immense joy" when a person "arrives at understanding creatively" (p. 86).

I try to impress upon therapists in training how we need to practice patience, "trusting the process" of expressive arts therapy (McNiff, 1998), and learning how to give room to others so they can naturally realize their creative potential. We work together with others to establish a space that conveys and arouses imagination and then let the process unfold.

The Celtic tradition recognizes "thin places" as areas where the distinctions between domains of experience are relaxed and liminal, where people can cross with greater ease from one realm to another. I like to imagine the expressive arts therapy studio as a thin place where the usual separations between inner and outer experiences, between personal and communal expressions, are minimized and where thresholds to creative expressions remain as open as possible. I take great satisfaction when we establish this kind of atmosphere within the challenging environments that generally characterize our practice.

Expressive arts therapy can be imagined as a discipline which encourages these subtle distinctions between artistic media. Within an integrated arts context, expressions overlap and merge and the usual separations that characterize the arts in society, and which we have generally ingrained within ourselves, become more permeable. Since so much of the creative process involves the making of new relationships between previously separate entities, the integrated arts experience tends to generate a palpable aura of novelty and imagination within the studio space.

Evoking Creativity through Percussive Rhythm

Experiences with music have had a large effect on how I approach the influence of environments on expression and how different art forms can support one another. In the beginning of my expressive arts therapy practice, when I was working at Danvers State Hospital, I introduced recorded classical music or jazz as a way of creating an aesthetic atmosphere, relaxing people in the studio, arousing emotion and sensibility, and motivating expression. I used music only within the self-contained environment of the open studio at the hospital and not when working in other spaces, inside and outside the hospital, where silence and the sounds of people making art and speaking with one another had their own positive influences on expression. I have not used any kind of recorded music for over 30 years.

Through my experimentation with shamanic and percussive music in the late 1970s, I began to explore the use of drumming in my studio groups while people worked individually with various arts experiences. I introduced only the most basic and simple rhythms with the goal of creating a supportive pulse as people made art. I was surprised to see that people responded favorably to me drumming while they worked with the visual arts or creative writing.

As the process of me playing percussive music became a defining feature of my studios, I tried to develop ways of keeping the rhythms simple and always in the service of the expression of others. In one of my studios, a young man took over the drums and began to display his musical virtuosity and it was clear that the rhythms were all about him and his skills and they were not supporting the artistic expressions of the other people in the room. Participants became distracted and I learned a major lesson about the role of rhythm in the studio; how sounds need to be sensitive to the rhythms of people expressing themselves in other artistic media; how the rhythm accompanies and supports the movements of others rather than dominating the space and calling attention to itself.

As with my experiences with sound and dance, I discovered how simple and repetitious rhythms helped people release the basic gestures of artistic expressions. As I make rhythms, people in the studio move their brushes in sync with them and I will also respond to the sounds of their movements. Painting and drawing are themselves rhythmic processes which can be assisted by the larger cadences of an environment. We feel that we are part of a larger pulsation, an environmental force, which empowers our individual expressions.

Aside from giving me something useful to do while people are making art in my studios, I have seen how drumming and creating rhythms with a mbira and other percussive instruments has had a significant influence on the more general therapeutic and creative milieu. Participants have described how the rhythms help to create a sense of safety within the studio space. In keeping with its archetypal function of summoning expression, the drum helps people relax their minds and focus more on rhythmic movement and expressing themselves from the body.

I have always been intrigued by the way indigenous communities describe the drum as the shaman's horse which serves as a mode of travel between worlds. In our studios, rhythmic expressions support the artist in letting go and gaining access to new dimensions of expression. The rhythms help the images to emerge and they create a common pulse which fosters a unified purpose in the studio. Everyone, including myself, is assisted in discarding distractions by focusing on the rhythm and allowing ourselves to be carried by it.

The immersion in rhythm creates a distinct sense of sacred space within a thoroughly mundane setting. Participants tell me when I am making supportive rhythms that they know that I am completely present and caring for the space and that this contributes both a sense of sanctity and protection which helps them to take risks with their expressions. I believe that the presence of rhythm during the art-making experience establishes a core process of arts integration and cooperation that sets the stage for making shifts between media when we respond to artworks with movement, voice, and ritual. Rhythm helps to lower resistance to expression and it supports people in moving more naturally amongst realms of experience.

Recognizing that the way I use drumming and percussion in my studios is a highly individuated practice which emerges from my particular artistic history and interests, I can, however, draw more universal lessons from these experiences regarding the primary role of the creative atmosphere in expressive arts therapy.

As I stated earlier, I have become convinced that the medicines of the arts are largely generated by the milieu in which we work, even when creating alone. We construct a creative space in our writing, imagining, moving, singing, playing, painting, and drawing which acts upon us. My use of drumming and rhythm is just one way of establishing a creative space. The making of this arts-space might be as elemental as a writer sitting in particular chair or going to an area designated as a place for creation. There is distinct ritualistic dimension to work with every artistic medium, a reliable sequence of actions, things that artists do to focus themselves, engage the present moment, elicit inspiration, and get the process moving.

Individual artists have their unique rituals that are used to elicit the muse and enter the zone of free expression. Groups and teams of people similarly use rituals and other devices to designate and activate the creative space, to prepare and open themselves to optimum performance. In my group studios, percussion is a primary way of activating expression and generating a creative milieu, but there are many other things that I do—sitting together in a circle at the start of each day and at various intervals during the day, assuring moments of silent contemplation and pauses between artistic enactments, making sure individual people are acknowledged and welcomed in every phase of the work, giving ongoing and focused attention to the various forms of artistic expression that emerge, and so forth.

Paolo Knill starts his groups by lighting a candle and placing it on a piece of fabric together with stones and other natural objects in the center of the room. When I have worked many times as a leader in an ongoing group after Paolo, I always feel somewhat sacrilegious when I move these altars off to side. I do this because for me, the empty space of the circle is a defining quality of my work; it welcomes and will hold the expressions that we will make together. I do the same thing with studio spaces where I prefer empty walls and no art hanging from previous groups.

Yet I am intrigued with how groups, even those who have been deeply involved in the work with Paolo, support me in moving their communal altar. They realize that my actions are symbolic of a change in leaders, the beginning of a new phase in their work together, and the need to make yet another creative space that will be defined by what we do together in the present rather than through memories of what they had done previously.

In my experience as a group leader, I am also keenly aware of how the sense of creative space that we may have established together in a prior session needs to be constantly remade and regenerated. In keeping with my earlier lessons about creation in groups, I never take the creative space for granted and realize how it must be cultivated in a sustained way until we end our work together.

When I am tired or perhaps reluctant to get back to the job in the studio, I have moments when I wish that the work did not require this persistent effort, but I always realize that the space, like the creative process, is dynamic and constantly moving, and never static. My primarily discipline as an expressive arts therapist is one of showing up with a commitment to making the creative space in every new meeting so that it can do the work that needs to be done. And unfailingly, I discover, even when I resist being totally present to the work, that once the environment of creation is established, I too am healed, refocused, and energized for the work ahead.

Welcoming All Images and Difficulties with the Process

The creative space is open and receptive to all of the new images that will emerge to define and empower it. When the first images arrive as people are painting, I always feel that we have begun to establish our distinctive studio environment that will carry us further in our expression and work together as a community. The varied creative actions of the group and the emergence of images and other forms of expression are primary contributors to the milieu and the unique characteristics that distinguish an arts-based creative space from communities oriented towards discussion.

The building of a safe and vital atmosphere is significantly affected by how we respond to the emergent creations. In my experience, the tone and confidence of a studio space is established through early and consistent affirmations of expressions. I tell groups how people have a keen instinctive sense, an ability to psychically smell whether or not a place is supportive and accepts honest expression.

When I begin studio sessions, I typically say something about how disturbing and difficult expressions are welcomed. I describe how images in our dreams and artistic expression are not there to hurt us. Other people hurt us and we hurt ourselves, but this is not the purpose of the intimate images that emerge from our psyches. They might frighten and annoy, but I have found that these reactions are part of their deeper purpose, their way of getting our attention, moving us into action, calling out for responses and changes in our lives, offering invitations to transform their power.

It is important to convey the same acceptance of chaos, confusion, and fragmentation if they appear in a person's artistic expression. These forces and states which challenge self-control can be even more threatening than what seem to be malevolent images. The creative process continuously affirms how remaking experience may require a comprehensive deconstruction of the current situation and prevailing attitudes. The psyche may need to be turned inside out in order to regain a sense of its vitality. Within expressive arts therapy, we establish safe and predictable environments that will anchor and support people when it may be necessary to let things fall apart in order to be made anew.

We all deal with self-censorship in our expressions and decisions about what we communicate or when we let ourselves open to the unknown. Readiness and timing are greatly respected in the studio and, as stated earlier, I will never push or directly elicit private personal expressions or try to instill threatening emotions. Although I appreciate the place of tension, destruction, and chaos in the creative process, I do not introduce these conditions as a leader. I try to establish an environment where people can create with the chaos and conflict that already exist within them. Participants are free to follow their inclinations with the understanding that the studio is a tolerant and accepting place that does everything it can to hold and affirm their particular engagements with the creative process.

Safe Places and Affirming the Unusual

Repeatedly, I see people who are afraid to express their unusual ways of viewing the world. Society has done a very good job in making the average person feel that strange and deeply expressive ideas are a form of madness. As I tell my students, if you are going to do this work of cultivating the most authentic expression of others, you cannot be afraid of appearing weird.

My colleague, Margot Fuchs-Knill, who has become an important contributor to the discipline of poetry therapy, focuses on how creative writing values "thinking the unthinkable" and establishing "a counterforce to daily life language" by breaking rules, deviating from all norms, embracing contradictions, and thus giving us new eyes for living (2002, p. 93). She writes: "This house of thought has round windows with an outlook from the unthinkable that spirals in and out."

Without becoming embroiled in the philosophical debate about whether or not language completely controls the way we perceive and understand the world, we can certainly agree that it exerts considerable influence through ingrained habits, attitudes, and ideas. Fuchs-Knill describes how we are "thrown into a given-language" at birth and in her work she strives to help us craft a more personal voice. The poem offers the opportunity "to rage with the echo from the untied life, where the day, stretched into the world" (p. 29).

By giving value to the "unthinkable," we open up and expand the field of play. I cannot underestimate the importance of simply receiving permission to go against the norm, the conventional borders and limits of speech, and then being supported in following instincts and desires. Rules have their place in art as well as life, but within the realm of imaginative expression, they need to be considerably relaxed and take a back seat to our more peculiar and whimsical inclinations.

The poet, like any other artist, tends to access authentic and intimate expressions by taking risks, engaging fears, and revealing the most private imaginings. There can be powerful healing in the process of fully expressing rather than curing away a fear. In her poem, The Writer, Fuchs-Knill (1999, p. 199) offers a challenge:

> Dare to go the path of stones
> slippery and wet
> Dare to long for the other shore,
> for
> you know the place of sounds hitting the bottom.

For some of us, the risky elements of self-disclosure in art offer an intrigue, sometimes more delightful and energizing than threatening. But in my experience, this embrace of risk is far from the norm. Most people find it very difficult and frightening to show their strange sides.

We fear that our dark and idiosyncratic expressions can be used against us or we simply do not want to burden others with murky and strange musings. Even if we feel it necessary to carefully watch our speech in more general reactions with others, poetic expression offers a private context where we can take out the stops and flow with our spontaneous inclinations.

It is essential to create a safe and nonjudgmental environment for sharing this kind of honest expression. We need to create spaces where people can take risks and have them affirmed and respected. The poem asks, maybe more often it implores: "Don't take me literally. I am an expression of imagination, a movement of the soul. Try and accept and enjoy me for what I am."

As Thomas Moore emphasizes in *Dark Eros*, pathology and the nasty figures of imagination are part of the natural world. While I do not deny the soulful qualities of exultation, soul resides as much in our wounds, vulnerabilities, and unusual imaginings. Moore describes how "the darkest and most perverted haunts of Eros have a place in the art of soul-making" (1990, p. 184).

One of the great achievements of expressive arts therapy has been the creation of safe places, where people can open to realms that are so thoroughly repressed in every sector of society. Expressive arts therapy is a discipline that understands and celebrates the complete spectrum of imagination, engaging the dark and the light as necessary partners in the process of creative transformation and healing. Art heals emotional wounds and afflictions by compassionately entering the heart of painful symptoms and accepting them.

Unrecognized Partnerships with the Physical Space

I have always been sensitive to how the physical and emotional characteristics of environments either support or deter creation. When I started the expressive arts therapy graduate program at Lesley University in the early 1970s, we offered courses focused on designing spaces that supported the arts and the creative imagination. Cora Beth Able taught the first courses and she went on to found Adaptive Environments with Elaine Ostroff who practiced movement and multidisciplinary expressive arts therapy. They have since made award winning contributions to the universal design movement, helping the architecture profession and government create spaces that are more accessible for people with disabilities.

However, the more general sensitivity to the effects of the physical space on expression is still largely overlooked in all sectors of the arts in therapy. More recently, I have become involved in the work of Dalia Gottlieb-Tanaka, an architect who founded The Society for the Arts in Dementia Care, in Vancouver, British Columbia. In her doctoral dissertation at the University of British Columbia, Gottlieb-Tanaka combines the fields of architecture, interior design, expressive arts therapy, psychology, and neurology in examining how creative environments can influence people experiencing dementia (2006). Grasping how the physical space is one of our most influential partners in expression, Gottlieb-Tanaka has combined her professional skills as an architect and interior designer with her current focus on expressive arts therapy. She underscores how creative expression is profoundly influenced by the way spaces are constructed and how we arrange things within them.

We are always moving in relationship to spaces, inside and outside ourselves, inside and outside the buildings and rooms that we inhabit. Environmental psychology is helping us be more aware of these partnerships and the larger ecology of expression, but I hope that expressive arts therapists will begin to give more attention to the elemental interactions that we have with the places in which we move and express ourselves.

I have worked with people in the most impoverished environments of state hospital back wards and within optimum studio settings and I am always intrigued and sensitive to how every place has its unique effects on how I and others move within it. The physical space is too often the unseen and acknowledged partner in our expression. As we give it more respect and consideration as a primary participant, we will not only feel the positive impact on expression, but we will contribute to the work of creating and healing in cooperation with the physical world.

Challenging Places

Being able to establish a vibrant creative space within the most unattractive places is one of the most pervasive challenges of expressive arts therapy. If we see ourselves as serving creative expression where it is most needed, we invariably find ourselves in debased, resistant, and unlikely places for creation.

I appreciate working within ideal studio environments and I do my best to encourage them in schools, medical institutions, nursing homes, community centers, and the studio retreat settings where I work. However, the reality for many of us in expressive arts therapy, especially when we travel and work in a nomadic fashion, is that we will often find ourselves in less than ideal surroundings—the annex to a busy hotel and conference center kitchen where I once worked with close to 100 people accompanied by the sounds and "noise" of people talking and working nearby; the session in a public lobby with people walking past and looking; the crowded rooms with posts dividing us from another; the medication room in a cancer center where the artist with an I-V attached to one arm worked with the other on a small surface; the corridor outside the classroom where I met alone with a child; the posh room with new rugs where we try to involve people in painting and making objects with materials from nature without causing damage; the quiet and contemplative painting studio next to a wood-working shop with loud machines or a raucous music group; and other settings that make the private corners of a locked institution with large firm tables feel like a sanctuary.

These are the challenging environments that expressive arts therapists learn to accept and engage. I do not always like these places or look forward to returning to them, but they are often the basis of my work. I have learned how to create from the hard places and do my best to establish a safe, supportive, and creative atmosphere in whatever context I find myself (McNiff, 2003). I have my own personal distractions and annoyances, especially with sound and movement happening outside the confines of a group, and I try to relax in these situations and accept conditions that I cannot change. I have learned that if I am to help others focus and become completely present to the work, I need to do this myself. I cannot model distraction when I am trying to help people concentrate.

When I find myself in these difficult and less than ideal surroundings, I do everything I can to create an atmosphere that supports creative expression. The design of the space in both a physical and expressive sense is one of the most universal and fundamental things that we do as expressive arts therapists. We strive to create spaces where we can work without external distractions and where our own sounds are the only ones we hear; where there is an open area for performance and movement; tables and walls for making visual artwork; together with ample natural light, sinks, closets, storage space for materials and artworks, and opportunities to access the most current art-making technologies.

On the basis of my own expressive arts therapy experience in many hundreds of settings in different part of the world, I can say that ideal studio conditions have been infrequent. Yet these imperfect conditions underscore the importance of the work that we are doing. We are bringing creative expression to places where it is not currently a top priority or where an organization supporting this work lacks the resources to offer favorable conditions. I actually wonder whether perfect studio environments would take away our edge, the relevance of expressive arts therapies in treating whole environments as well as the individual people within them. The medicines that we offer have perhaps risen from the aching needs for creative spaces in our world.

The distinguishing feature of the expressive arts therapy experience is its ability to make a creative space in any context. We create with our immediate conditions and avoid the preoccupation of trying to be somewhere other than the place where we are.

I like to imagine myself like an indigenous person who works with whatever spaces and materials are at hand with a sense that everything in the world is potentially sacred. The most debased places and things may actually hold the greatest potential for transformation (McNiff, 1995). The power that we bring as expressive arts therapists is the ability to engage these places in fresh and imaginative ways, to make them into sanctuaries for creative expression, and to demonstrate to others how to do this in a world where constant impediments to creative expression will reliably present themselves.

Expressive arts therapy brings dignity and creative vitality to impoverished and struggling environments. Even a basement room with pipes, ducts, and artificial light can be embraced and become a source of inspiration and ally in the creative process.

Resistance Is Natural

Creative spaces are characterized by fluid movement between different spheres of experience and receptivity to new presentations, connections, and attitudes. Within my experience, most people, even the supposed "creative types," resist significant change. I describe to students and others beginning expressive arts therapy practice how the most significant dynamic of my career has been the core paradox whereby even people who come to my studios with a desire to express themselves in new ways, typically encounter considerable resistance and even discomfort when given the opportunity to create in completely new and challenging ways. Many individuals who have traveled a great distance to attend one of my studios have confessed how they felt the urge to get right back into their cars or head back to the airport during the early phases of the studio work.

I say to students, resistance to expression is our core subject matter, the phenomena we train ourselves to accept and transform. Resistance is thoroughly natural and something to engage rather than a problem to be eliminated or cured. I have repeatedly discovered how resistance is a sign of getting close to something important, a gateway to the new, or as a student said to me, "an indication of where I need to go." I have thus concluded that resistance is good, a healthy sign of vital instincts and energies. We need to learn how to use its power in service of creative expression rather than as a repressive force.

Nevertheless, I repeatedly observe how the fear that people feel when invited to spontaneously express themselves in front of others even within the most supportive situations can approach the intensity of terror (McNiff, 2006, 2007). These acute fears and feelings of panic often occur when I invite people to explore the most elemental kinds of creative expression such as simply moving their bodies or using their voices in unfamiliar ways. The extreme discomfort is based upon more than just entering the unknown, changing habitual ways of expressing themselves, facing potential incompetence—areas that Hugh O'Doherty at the Center for Leadership at Harvard says we are already "hard-wired to resist" (personal communication, March 16, 2007).

My sense is that the core resistance to expression that we experience in the arts, and especially with bodily and vocal expressions, is linked to bad memories of shame and vulnerability, fears of exposing "too much," losing control, and being engulfed by chaos. We fear that opening to the expression of emotions will result in being overwhelmed by forces beyond our control and unattractive personal traits, what Jung called the shadow that we usually keep under tight wraps. Sometimes the most intense terror is the dread that we might be empty inside and will have nothing of significance to express to others.

The creative transformation of resistances is in many ways the ultimate end of our practice. When we are able to honestly see and do something creative with our afflictions and fears, we experience ways of being in the world that are distinctly different from the cycles of harmful destruction that occur when these vulnerabilities and insecurities are denied and suppressed. The same applies to embracing the significance of ways of expression that we previously did not value.

The effective creative space acknowledges and embraces all of these resistances and blocks, perceiving them as unavoidable aspects of creative expression. The safest and most deeply imaginative studio environments recognize that the creative process may sometimes need demons as well as angels, darkness together with light. Art's transformative remedies and creative energies are not without toxins and tensions. All of these elements are part of the alchemical mix of expressive arts therapy.

I do not think that the expressive arts therapy community, typically driven by efforts to establish, justify, and sustain itself as a viable professional domain, has fully appreciated the archetypal dimensions of the spaces it creates. The expressive arts therapy studio is a realm of integration and creation, a place of health and healing, a realization of the classical ideal of imagination as an intermediate realm, a milieu where we are inspired and supported in taking the risks to do the new things that are the basis of transformation in both our inner and outer lives.

V. DISTINCT QUALITIES OF ART FORMS

This section offers descriptions of what I do with the different art forms in expressive arts therapy. Since students find it helpful, as I do myself, when given a spectrum of possible ideas for application, I do my best to address this need. I encourage readers to be wary of stock methods and to approach these descriptions as suggestions for practice and creative adaption.

Many of the things described in this chapter relate to what has been discussed in other sections of the book. A certain amount of repetition may be useful in service of the goal of gathering together the "seeds" of multimedia practice.

I have organized this section according to individual art media, but as I emphasize in every section of this book, the various senses and art forms are always blending and influencing one another in my studios. Most of the experiences that I describe involve an integration of the arts. The separation according to media does, however, reflect the reality of each art form occupying its distinct place within the context of integrated arts practice.

As described throughout this book, my overall approach to encouraging spontaneous expression in each art form gives special attention to free and exploratory movement as a way of generating imagery, themes, ideas, and artistic compositions. In my practice, the kinesthetic and bodily realm works together with all of the other artistic media and serves as a foundation for them all.

Some might argue that art forms like poetry and creative writing do not involve this connection to body movement. However, there is a clear strain in modern poetry that celebrates linkages to breathe, dance, and various other forms of physical and embodied expression. The visual arts, music, and drama have more indisputable connections to bodily movement, but to the extent to which any art form values the emanation of contents and an improvisational flow of expression, I believe that movement serves as the carrier of these processes.

Whether it is poetry, performance art, dance, storytelling, painting, sculpture, photography, video, vocal improvisation, or drumming, I always begin with a simple focus on the immediate moment and the surrounding space. We establish a point of concentration and let that focus of attention carry us further.

MOVEMENT AND THE BODY

It is his body that is his answer, his body intact and fought for, the absolute of his organism in its simplest terms . . . the house he is, this house that moves, breathes, acts, this house where his life is . . .

Charles Olson, *Tyrian Businesses*

Most people tend to approach dance and movement expression with overly complicated thoughts about what they might be expected to do or even desire to do. I reverse this mental process by starting from the body's most elemental gestures and spontaneous physical sensations. Although these movements are unplanned, they can be characterized by a high degree of concentration upon the emanation of simple gestures in the present moment. I encourage reading the following pages on movement and embodied expression with a sensitivity to how the principles apply to dance and all of the arts.

The Movement Basis of All Expression

When working with the most withdrawn adults within a psychiatric hospital environment, I approached bodily movement as a basis of communication. Even if a person was confined to a chair, we could use elemental movements to communicate with one another and express ourselves—a finger moving, a hand tapping a table, or a foot sliding across the floor. The simplest gestures were starting points for the progressive building of movement relationships.

I found that by embracing whatever a person is able to do in the domain of movement, we can then augment this foundation with other expressions. The most regressed people showed me how to construct an approach to expressive arts therapy that takes nothing for granted. I appreciated every bodily motion that they made and discovered how drawing attention to these expressions, responding to them with movements of my own, and describing observations helped people become more aware of what they were doing and the surrounding environment. Perhaps even more importantly, these elemental movement experiences enabled the participants to express themselves creatively and interact productively with others.

If a person was able to tap a foot on the floor, I repeated this expression and added to it in a rhythmic way, amplifying the gesture and the sound. When working in groups I encouraged others to creatively build upon the expressions of a severely withdrawn person and use them as starting points. Fundamental movements offered a reliable way for people to interact with one another even if they were unable to communicate through conversation.

In the group studio sessions that I led within the mental hospital, we encouraged people to simply get up from their chairs and walk slowly into the center of the circle that we made, to perhaps walk in a circle, take pauses, and stand still for brief moments while the group watched and supported them. I discovered how straightforward body movements like raising and lowering an arm in a mindful and slow manner can have a profound effect on the person making the gesture and those witnessing it.

We recognized how movement and action call for corresponding pauses and reflection that further both relaxation and awareness. The moments of contemplation are as fundamental to the work of art and healing as the expressive gestures that we make. The partnership between action and quiet pauses generates feelings of well-being and heightened consciousness.

When introducing people to various forms of artistic expression, I similarly emphasize the basis of movement in everything we do. I encourage people to think about beginning a dance, musical rhythm, sound improvisation, performance, or painting with simple gestures rather than conceptual expectations. It also helps to approach writing as a movement discipline, to encourage the emanation of words and images from physical actions.

I find that even the most capable people find it challenging to relax and accept their natural and most genuine movements as serious expressions. The invitation to move in front of others is more likely to arouse severe inhibition rather than a sense of excitement. These reactions can be attributed to how we are generally not accustomed to moving our bodies creatively in the presence of others. The average person, as well as many experienced artists, tends to find it difficult to embrace simplicity, breath, the bodily origins of expression, and staying with elemental movements for extended periods of time.

By focusing attention on movement for its own sake and with the realization that artistic manifestations will always emerge from this reliable source, every person is given a foundation for expression. My role as a leader becomes one of persuasion and helping people realize that all they have to do is start moving and then stay with their gestures in order to allow them to unfold. I find that the quality of movement expression is impeded when people begin to think too much about preconceived images, put all of their emphasis on planning, and miss the opportunity to simply immerse themselves in the process of moving in the present moment, and concentrate on whatever they are doing without concern for what will happen next.

For example, my experimentation with the repetition of a movement in a painting or drawing, even if done many times over and over again, suggests that it will ultimately generate subtle variations. I try to affirm these movement patterns and help the most resistive people to vary them in gradual ways. We do the same things with movements of the whole body in dance, always embracing what the person is doing as the source of expression which can unfold into successive moments of creation. We do not have to go beyond the most basic and unappreciated gestures of daily life to initiate dance and creative movement. If possible, we talk about what we feel while moving or what we see as witnesses to the movements of others and these reflections further awareness.

I am reluctant to reduce the total spectrum of a professional discipline to a single essential idea or principle such as movement, but as Paul Valéry declares: "Nothing stands still in the mind" (1965, p. 18). We are constantly operating in fields of kinetic energy where one thing takes shape from another and where the certainty of one moment is easily lost in the next as we shift attention. Having established this caveat, I can report that over my years of expressive arts therapy practice, the movement source of all creative expression has become increasingly primary to my practice. I establish the basis for everything I do with different forms of creative expression in movement and find that this practical and philosophical focus always helps people liberate their expression.

Lifting an Arm

Place an arm in front of your body, hold it, and concentrate as completely as possible on the energy moving through your fingers and your whole body. Let the arm gradually move upwards with the assistance of the strength that you feel in your legs and the support being given by your physical contact with the ground. As you reach a resting point, simply hold the arm, breathe, and enjoy the feeling of tension that results from this extension of your limb.

Do not think at all about what you are going to do next. Let an ensuing movement happen spontaneously, gravitationally, in response to the force that you have exerted in a particular direction. Maybe your hand and arm will fall suddenly or more gradually. Try and let this happen as spontaneously as possible and do not rush the movements. When the arm reaches a resting point, pause, and let another movement emerge from this position.

Continue this pattern of moving in a particular direction, pausing, and letting another movement happen spontaneously in response to the force expended. As you move one way, this gesture sets the stage for the next in yet another direction. Movements emerge from one another, just like breathing.

Creativity becomes a process of letting the gestures happen with the most complete concentration possible. If you can breathe with vitality, you can do the same with movement. Put aside all ideas about whether or not your movements are skillful. I have found that when gestures are made with complete concentration and with the support of the studio group, they will be perceived as beautiful and fulfilling.

Many people like to begin to move with their eyes closed, something which tends to relax inner critics and concerns about being watched by others. I ask that participants place themselves in a stable and comfortable position before beginning. We find that closing the eyes can further the bodily sensation of movement while promoting relaxation. When people are feeling more relaxed, I encourage them to open their eyes and use visual perception to further connection to the gestures.

My approach to movement embraces whatever a person is capable of doing, no matter how apparently insignificant it may be. Every gesture thus carries a feeling of some kind. I constantly discover how what at first may appear to be impoverished or insignificant, can take on meaning when we look at it with compassion and interest.

Expanding to the Whole Body

Use both of your arms to move spontaneously, reaching and extending their range while you stay in place. Feel free to move your hands and arms in similar or differing directions. It is fascinating how it is possible to concentrate on both the separate and unified expression of the arms if we move slowly and mindfully.

Make these gestures with a sense of upper body movements extending from your whole body. Concentrate on feeling supportive connections between your contact with the ground and the way your hands and arms move in space. Hopefully your reflections will further a more complete and fulfilling sense of movement as well as the aesthetic appeal of the gestures.

Even when moving from a fixed position, the legs and their connections to the floor or earth are a primary source of expression. In addition to the obvious need to engage the whole body in dance and creative movement, I emphasize the formative powers of the legs and lower body in relation to painting, singing, reading poetry, and other forms of expression where we are apt to overlook the foundations of expression. We tend to get caught in our thoughts and focus too much energy in the head and lose contact with the creative force that flows from our lower bodies, thighs, feet, and our direct connections to the physical space. This focus on the lower body has proven to be tremendously helpful to people seeking more spontaneous and new ways of moving.

As your arms reach into space, imagine them being directed by what you feel in your feet, calves, and thighs.

Pause when you reach the end of your extension. Use the energy and power converging in this pause to inform the next spontaneous gesture in whatever direction gravity and the impulses of your body take you. Don't move too quickly and try and feel how the movement emerges from your natural instinct to explore a different direction.

An extended dance can be constructed from the simple pattern of staying within a space and mindfully moving the body in a particular direction and into a posture or shape that is informed by the movement impulse; pausing; and then responding to the felt sense of the gesture with another sequence of expression.

Breath

With these first descriptions of creative movement, the body has stayed connected to a particular area in the physical space. I have experienced the boundless possibilities for dance even when we stay in one place in a room and focus on a range of movement possibilities that we typically take for granted. Moving from a relatively fixed position also helps to further security, confidence, and a progressive engagement of more expansive movements.

Where the proceeding descriptions of movement possibilities focused on parts of the body extending themselves in space, I would also like to concentrate on breathing as our most essential physical movement. In considering the movement basis of all forms of artistic expression, we can say in an even more fundamental way that breath is the essential source of all of the body's gestures. Through breath, we stabilize ourselves emotionally and physically, inform our movements from inside our bodies as well as from outside, and further the strength and resilience of expression.

For me, the proof of the primacy of breath is the way we "lose it" when we are overextended, frightened, and tense. My most reliable method of helping people experiencing panic is to gently encourage them to take a pause in relation to what they are doing and to concentrate on their breath. The rhythm of breathing, the essential movement felt inside and outside the body, is the most reliable way of gaining a sense of relaxation, focus, and connection to the environment.

Sometimes it feels that it is almost too simple, too much of a contemplative cliché, to approach breath as a source of creative expression, but I have learned that it needs to take this central role and especially with any artistic expression involving the body and the voice.

Begin by paying attention to the movement of taking air in and letting it out. Do this for a few minutes and let yourself become part of the rhythm.

When you are feeling relaxed and in complete sync with the breath, let it gradually inspire movements that accompany its tempo and sounds. Imagine your gestures moving as partners with breath. As with the movements described above, one action will always unfold into another if we can allow expression to build naturally.

Like many others, I have had a tendency in my career to become so involved with my new experiments that I am apt overlook the fundamentals that should never be taken for granted. As the poet Charles Olson said, he had to learn "the simplest things last." Olson established the basic structures of poetic lines in response to pauses in breathing (1966). Breath is always with us as a necessary and valuable partner in every art form, though it is not usually the primary focus of practice as with many contemplative disciplines.

As I described above, the discipline of breathing is particularly important when expressing difficult emotions. Practice breathing with the disturbance; take it in; and of course "let it go" with your breath.

Breath is in so many ways both the primary gesture and metaphor for expressive arts therapy practice. As a physically-oriented discipline we appreciate its role as the anchor of practice. When we lose contact with breath, or appreciation of its primacy, it teaches us how everything we do in the creative process is grounded in the ebb and flow of losing something in order to regain it anew.

Practice breathing and moving in this way. Slowly make a gesture as you exhale and imagine yourself letting it go as completely as possible and arriving in a place of stillness when you pause. As you inhale, make a new movement which you then hold and ultimately let go with the ensuing gesture.

Continue this process in a sequence of movements, either repeating the same gesture or making different ones. You will discover that creative expression is based as much on letting a gesture go as it is on making new ones.

Maybe you will imagine your entire dance, poem, or painting as an ongoing process of letting go of gestures rather than building them up. This reversal might help counter the pressure we place on ourselves to initiate and construct expression. Artists sense this core dynamic in terms of the process of expression never being finished. Completed artworks are in this respect part of an ongoing movement, an exhalation and letting go, that prepares for the next gesture.

Repetition

As emphasized throughout this book, repetition is one of our most important allies in furthering spontaneous expression. In keeping with the experience of athletes, the psyche tends to do its best work when the controlling mind relaxes and follows the lead of the body's natural ways of responding to particular situations. The practice suggestions presented here in relation to dance and creative movement apply to repetitious gestures and expressions in all of the other arts.

When people create bodily gestures in a dance space, make marks on a piece of paper, or utter sounds, I encourage their repetition, again and again. Try to lose yourself in the expression, I say, so it can take you to places that can never be planned.

I emphasize how a particular movement can be viewed as having a mind and purpose of its own, and that our practice is focused on learning how to engage these natural powers as effectively as possible. As a person repeats an expression, self-consciousness tends to subside and there is an increased awareness of the particular qualities of the gesture.

If we can persist in the repetition and surrender to it, the conscious mind takes a back seat and the expressive force can manifest itself more completely. As I heard John Cage say at an event that we sponsored at Lesley University, if an expression is boring after 2 minutes, do it for 4 minutes, and if the feeling persists, stay with it for 8, 16, 32 minutes and ultimately the movement will become fascinating to you.

Repetition is the basis of rhythm and trance. The controlling mind needs to submit itself to the purpose of the body's gesture, supporting rather than directing expressions. I encourage people to just repeat a movement and try not to be too clever. I suggest that they ask their critical aspects and inner judges to relax, take a seat, and watch how expressions move from the first phases of impulse to refinement. It might help to imagine expression entering the world like breathe. Relax the mind, and respond to whatever seems to be taking shape and build upon it.

When first engaging people in a group session, I might suggest that they slowly and mindfully make a simple gesture or movement while standing in place, and then repeat it 5 or 6 times. My goal is generally one of easing people into the process of repetition and building their confidence in its formative powers. The average person first thinks that repeating a gesture is monotonous and there often tends to be resistance to this. Like a coach, I try to build commitment and belief in what we are doing.

As people begin to relax, I encourage them to keep repeating the gestures, over and over again without counting the repetitions. We discover, in keeping with the John Cage statement, how the sustained movement begins to take on a life of its own. The movement is perceived both as something we make and as an autonomous entity with which we collaborate.

The purpose of this practice is to focus on a fundamental gesture and let its power grow through recurrence and concentration. If we try and do too many things or get complex or clever, we will lose the focus and rhythmic reiteration which increases the impact of the movement.

Begin with gestures as simple as letting the body slowly sway from side to side or gracefully lowering hands and arms while slightly bending the knees and then raising them. I have found, perhaps in keeping with the ancient traditions of contemplative practice and rhythmic expression, that these gestures can be sustained for extended periods of time when we are able to relax and surrender to the movement and its healing effects.

Once people become fully immersed in the process of moving, variations grow naturally from the gestures. I will often encourage subtle changes after the first phases of repetition and the duration of the expressions usually depends upon the person's ability to sustain the rhythmic movement with the expressions ultimately progressing to a natural resting point.

"Let the gestures change themselves naturally," I say. "Watch how something new emerges. Stay with this fresh gesture and as you contemplate it and continue the process of repetition, successive phases of creation will emanate from the movement source." The process can be reassuring to people who have trouble trusting that something significant can happen outside the sphere of their mental control.

The key to this practice is sustained expression, keeping the rhythmic gesture, and allowing it to spin off new forms from its basic structure. And again people will vary in relation to their ability to stay with the gesture.

Repetitious gestures are the basis of trance, as mentioned above, and these gestures can, of course, result in altered states of consciousness, especially if the practice is sustained with a complete focus on replication. Trancelike effects can further relaxation and more complete immersion in the creative process. However, trance for its own sake is not necessarily a goal in my practice.

In my studios, our overall purpose is the liberation of creative expression and perceptual attentiveness to the ensuing expressions as contrasted to therapies that strive to instill hypnotic states. Our aim is generally one of achieving an accepting and comfortable relationship to our expressions; thus the time given to repeating a gesture is generally determined by this purpose. We are also oriented toward the most authentic and complete range of creative expressions; therefore imaginative variations upon repetitious movements are always encouraged and supported.

Moving through Space

We have spent some considerable time in this discussion of creative movement and dance, focusing exclusively on what can be done by staying connected to a particular position in space. The richness of possibilities underscores the endless range associated with any dimension of expressive arts therapy practice. Hopefully, the focus on movement in a fixed place will further an appreciation of core kinesthetic principles that extend to the larger realm of expressions when we move throughout a physical space.

In keeping with my more pervasive emphasis on simplicity, repetition, rhythm, and building confidence by starting with the most elemental gestures, we often begin to move within a space by concentrating on making the most ordinary movements, like taking steps from one place to another. These actions become artistic expressions when an aesthetic consciousness is applied to both making and perceiving the gestures.

I say that if we are capable of moving, even if restricted to a fixed position, we can start to dance. In keeping with the previous section on repetition, I encourage walking with small and mindful steps and then letting the gestures gradually expand by varying the process of walking and embellishing the actions. The results are always fascinating and imaginative as people apply themselves to these elemental dimensions of practice. When introducing creative movement, my bias is toward the most basic and familiar gestures that become the source for more varied expressions that emerge from them. Ordinary people, untrained in dance, can move in this way so the work immediately becomes universally accessible.

I want to stress how trained dancers often tend to need this focus on elemental and ordinary movement as the springboard for new expressions. The experienced dancer often carries a repertoire of pre-existing gestures and skills that can get in the way of creative discovery. Yet at the same time, the proficient dancer who commits to these elemental processes generally has an ability to mindfully sustain expression in a way that can inspire beginners and provide effective modeling.

In addition to walking, I often ask people to simply move from one place to another. I might suggest taking a minute or two minutes to move a distance of ten or fifteen feet. The extended time furthers focus, immersion in the movement process, while welcoming varied and unusual movements.

In my studios, we work in a circle and after warming up the entire group, we take turns moving in the center with group members acting as witnesses. As described earlier when discussing the role of witnesses, the group concentration always seems to energize and help sustain a person's movement expression.

The connection of expressive movement to deep emotions is also significantly influenced by the process of being witnessed by others in a highly attentive context. When a person takes the stage or enters a circle surrounded by others, they are watched in a more complete way and with an emotional investment being made by audience members. The degree and quality of audience and environmental attention always tends to have a corresponding effect on the emotional experience of the person moving. The merger of inside and outside realms is greatly affected by the quality of concentration established by the audience and the artist.

Pauses

As described earlier, I give considerable attention to pauses and periods of reflection as part of the total movement experience. People are generally taken aback by the emotional power and significance of a conscious pause after making a series of movements. The silence and reflective space enables them to be more fully aware of what they have done and more relaxed with their expressions. When the pause occurs in a group of people, it generates a sense of sanctity and deep respect for the preceding expressions.

I use pauses and moments of reflection in a routine way in order to promote the contemplation and appreciation of all expressions. I encourage the person to breathe and take a comfortable and silent pause after every phase of movement. As a group leader or when working with an individual person, I use my own breathing and pausing after a movement expression to help instill this condition in others. This simple period of reflection seems to lower anxiety and helps the person moving feel the lingering effects on the body.

The dancer is then encouraged to move once again in response to what is felt in the present moment. Invariably, the period of contemplation takes the movement to another place, not necessarily better, but generally the pause will further awareness, relaxation, and acceptance. These moments of stillness are especially useful after a person moves in frenetic, agitated, or uneasy ways. The pause helps shift the energy and emotion of the movement to a more grounded moment of reflection.

When a person appears anxious, afraid, or close to being overwhelmed, I suggest taking a pause. Take a moment, I say, and focus on breathing.

In my first years of practice as an expressive arts therapist within a psychiatric hospital for acutely disturbed patients, I worked with a man in his early twenties shortly after he had been admitted. In his first expressive arts therapy group session, he enacted a series of intensely emotional and forceful dances characterized by aggressive, yet well coordinated leaps, turns, and vocal expressions. The dance was carefully executed and controlled in spite of its tumultuous movement.

After the movement improvisation, the man was so aroused that it was difficult for him to relax and contemplate what he had done. I asked the group to take a pause together with him and to reflect upon his expression and how it affected them.

The collective pause assisted the man in doing something that he could not do alone. The others helped him to calm down, rest, and appreciate what he had done. After the pause I asked group members to give verbal responses to his movement, to describe what they saw and how it influenced them. These communications furthered the group support for the man and the responses helped him understand how his expressions were perceived by others.

Partners

As discussed above, every element of movement from our breath to the physical space can be engaged as a partner. The movements we make can also be viewed as companions.

"Concentrate on a gesture that attracts you," I say. "View it as a partner and as a source of inspiration. Relax in its presence and realize that you are not alone. You have something reliable and totally accessible with which you can relate. Revel in what is available to you, what you have right now, and don't be concerned with anything else. You block expression and become distracted by thinking about what is not here. Trust that if you commit yourself to your gestures, if you can concentrate deeply, your expressive powers will be released. If you can give yourself totally to what you are doing, the movement will unfold naturally and according to its purpose."

Although most of what I have said in this chapter about dance and movement therapy focuses on individual people moving alone, or in response to an art object, I want to emphasize how dancing and moving with another person is an essential and popular aspect of expressive arts therapy practice. Dance therapists typically move with their clients and participants in group experiences move in tandem with one another or with larger groupings of partners. From the most common dance therapy activities of mirroring another person's movement to the more adventurous practices of contact improvisation, dance and movement therapy regularly makes use of improvised dances with a partner.

The founding of our expressive arts therapy program at Lesley University overlapped with the experimental work that Steve Paxton was doing with contact improvisation in New York City in the 1970s. This way of moving with a partner or in relationship to aspects of the studio space (floor, walls, furniture, and other objects) was closely attuned to the improvisational methods of expression that we explored in Cambridge. As mentioned earlier, we pursued dance without recorded music and our work with partners focused on moving in relation to the spontaneous ways that bodies connected to one another in an ongoing sequence of movements–pushing, swaying, turning, lifting, dropping to the floor, rolling, and so forth. The dance expression was concerned with the most elemental movements that built upon one another in a sustained flow of expression.

Touch and fusing with another person's movement opened up a whole new world of cooperative dance. Combining and blending with the movements of others was greatly satisfying and helped us get beyond the ego limitations of expression. Dance was perceived as something more than moving alone in space. Other people, places, and things contributed to a process of expression that was still based in the most elemental physical movements.

In addition to approaching dance as a process of exchanging and integrating movements with improvisational partners, I applied these principles to painting and sculpting. I encouraged people to view their movements with brushes, painting surfaces, and the ground on which they worked as collaborators in the process of making something from mutual action. The contact with the brush, the paint, and the surface was viewed as informing the expressive movements that unfold from it.

The basic premise behind all of these movement partnerships is that we never move alone in the world, even when we might appear to be dancing all by ourselves. We are always moving with the forces in our environment— the ground, air, gravity, and so forth. Spontaneous movement with a partner evokes an intimacy and a surrender of control which may be intimidating to many and therefore it is important to be sensitive to these qualities of the creative activity.

In my work with the most unresponsive adults in psychiatric hospitals, I found that moving in tandem with rudimentary gestures became a reliable mode of expression for many people, especially when language was not accessible. It was a significant therapeutic outcome for an otherwise mute person to follow my movements or to be placed in the role of leading and having me follow. The movement activities and the resulting partnership became a bridge that led to other possibilities for relationship with others and the world.

The expressive work that I did with highly withdrawn people was based upon elemental gestures. If a person is able to watch how I move and then repeat it, or better yet do this movement in sync with me, there is a relatively high degree of perceptual, cognitive, and expressive behavior being manifested. When the other person takes the lead and makes gestures that I follow, this immerses us in yet another realm of interpersonal communication. It is like a dance where we take turns leading and following with each role generating its particular therapeutic benefits. Too often in our psychiatric and mental health systems, we miss the opportunity to make use of these apparently elemental actions to foster the interpersonal sensitivities and communications upon which all other forms of human relationship and expression can be based.

In some expressive arts therapy situations, touch can not only be intimidating but forbidden, as I experienced in my work with orthodox religious women. The idea of dance itself can be off limits within certain religious communities so therefore, it may sometimes be useful to refer to the work we do as movement expression and improvisation.

In my practice, I have found that it is possible to move in complete sync with another person without making physical contact. In some forms of movement expression, the power of the work may even be enhanced by this energetic or magnetic way of moving in relationship to others. The absence of touch makes it necessary to be even more sensitive to the gestures and movements of another person. We establish what might be described as a kinetic telepathy that joins us in common expression.

Since severe psychic disturbances are characterized by the absence of sensitive and empathetic relationships with other people and things, this approach to mutual movement and kinetic sensibility can be of great value for people who are detached from the immediate environment. However, touch is generally sustained in even the most withdrawn states and thus offers possibilities for communication and reciprocal expression.

In the numerous psychiatric hospitals that I have visited, and tragically in many nursing homes, people are always sitting, rocking in chairs, walking back and forth, sitting, and sitting, and generally not making meaningful or purposeful contact with other people and things. Over time, the person's body movements, posture, and general appearance tend to reflect the more general character of the institutional setting.

When I began my work in the expressive arts therapies during the early 1970s, the institutionalization of chronic mental patients was itself the most serious challenge that we faced in helping people to live more creative and productive lives. When confronted with the pervasive and serious effects of these pathologies, I concluded that my therapeutic goals and activities needed an elemental focus on helping people enter into meaningful and creative contacts and relationships with their physical context and other people. Nothing about the way a person moves in space or relates to another person could be taken for granted. We began by examining the most rudimentary actions and studying how they either reinforced isolation and institutionalization or helped the person function in more creative and fulfilling ways.

My early inclinations about the needs of chronic mental patients were reinforced by the research of William Condon, which was attracting considerable attention within our community during the early 1970s. Condon's examination of slow motion films of interpersonal interactions revealed a rhythmic "interactional synchrony" between people when they communicate with each other. Through a close analysis of individual film frames, he also showed how emotionally troubled persons are apt to lose this mutual kinesthetic empathy that is maintained by most people in the most elementary of conversations (Condon & Ogston, 1966). The researchers described how "the listener's body moved rhythmically in a dance with that of the speaker" (p. 338). Emotionally disturbed persons are also likely to exhibit a lack of synchrony amongst the different parts of their own bodies with one arm, for example, moving out of sync with the other.

Whether or not one agrees or disagrees with Condon and Ogston's widely cited study, there is no doubt that a focus on movement empathy within expressive arts therapy can promote better relationships with the world, others, and ourselves. All aspects of the physical world as well as the features of our own bodies become potential partners in this practice. The great value of movement in expressive arts therapy is its ability to help us develop these relationships and sensibilities without relying on language and concepts.

My emphasis on the value of movement-oriented activities with withdrawn and severely handicapped people who do not have the ability to express themselves in words does not in any way suggest that these approaches to expressive arts therapy are less effective with highly verbal people. Interestingly enough, I have found that more verbally sophisticated people often use these abilities to avoid contact with their more primary sensory faculties.

Responsive Movement

I chose to work almost exclusively with groups in my expressive arts therapy practice because of the resources and support people can give to one another. I have found that the most effective way of having people accept and appreciate their movement expressions is to have another person give them a movement response to what they have done. These artistic responses and interpretations offer ways of helping others and furthering understandings that are not accessible in words.

For example, I ask the person who has just moved spontaneously for one to three minutes to choose another person in the group to give a movement response within the same time frame. If a group member performed a frenzied dance like the one described above, I repeatedly observe how the person giving a movement response might engage the movement pattern and bring it to a more calm and restful place. The movement response in this respect completes the cycle of movement and returns the group process to a place of quiet acceptance. I find that these responses from others will offer things to the total cycle of movement expression that the original dancer might not be able to do alone, especially when experiencing personal agitation or emotional distress.

In other situations, where the original mover appears constricted and even trapped in a series of bound expressions, the person giving a response might express a gentle unraveling and release of the restrictions. These reciprocal movement expressions offer unique opportunities within the primary language of the dance medium to take the gestures and emotions to another place.

Artistic responses and interpretations do not in my view infringe upon the integrity of the original movement. The response is seen as the expression of another person, a complementary dance that has its own integrity and is not intended to replace or improve upon the first expression. The person offering the response affirms the original expression and offers a related but yet distinctly different and autonomous expression to carry on the process of movement in the group.

I emphasize how there is no correct or incorrect way to give a movement response to another person and how people offering responses need to have the freedom to move according to their own emotional and creative impulses and their sense of what the other person and the situation might need. The process is viewed as sustaining the creative energy of the movement, of dancing it further into yet another phase of artistic expression. The work is guided by an emotional or aesthetic intelligence that manifests itself through spontaneous and improvisational expression.

As described earlier when discussing the more general process of responding creatively to the art of others, I have discovered that people want to receive authentic and imaginative reactions. When I see my expression touching another person and eliciting a creative response, this brings a sense of fulfillment and satisfaction that cannot be conveyed by someone talking about what I have just done.

Although experience with the arts and healing shows how the process of creative expression has the ability within itself to transform conflicts and difficult situations if we can stay committed to the activity (McNiff, 1998), there are times of personal crisis and emotional distress when we cannot do this alone, when we need others to help us through the crucible of creation and renewal. This support and guidance from others can be viewed as the defining quality of the therapeutic relationship as contrasted to solitary artistic expression. Receiving a movement response from another person after dancing is a profoundly therapeutic and affirming experience. It is the kind of activity that distinguishes expressive arts therapy from the more conventional practice of an artistic discipline.

SOUND, VOICE, AND MUSIC

Vocal improvisation and percussive rhythm have been my primary focus in relation to sound and music in expressive arts therapy because I have found them to be accessible to a broad spectrum of people. There are many points of similarity between these two areas as I will demonstrate in the following descriptions. My approach to voice-work is generally rhythmic, building upon the repetition and transformation of elemental sounds and collaborating with varied forms of percussive expression.

Releasing the Voice with Primary Sounds

When working with individuals and groups, I often begin to engage the voice with basic warm-up exercises. These activitiess can actually become the most essential features of the work so I do not want to present them as just preliminary steps toward a higher goal. The most elemental actions in every dimension of expressive arts therapy practice are gateways to the deepest aspects of the work.

The voice, perhaps more than any other expressive modality needs this kind of preparation since most people tend to resist free vocal expression and invitations to make sounds outside the normal range of controlled expressions.

"It is OK to be strange with your sounds," I say. "This is an expressive arts studio where the unusual is welcomed."

If we truly release the range of vocal possibilities, the resulting sounds will be far outside the norm. It is difficult for most people to be comfortable with these expressions so I do everything I can to affirm them and convey how it is natural to resist what might at first seem strange or even bizarre.

I encourage a playful atmosphere as we begin to work and I have people make sounds in unison as a way of preparing and freeing the voice. If I am engaged with just one person in a session, we make sounds together. Collective expression is the premier vehicle for transcending resistance. The group acts as a slipstream which carries the individual person in ways that are not possible when working alone. The chorus of people making sounds together establishes a palpable flow which embraces and holds the individual.

Most people making vocal improvisations for the first time need to be given a sound to repeat and explore. I typically introduce the most rudimentary and guttural sounds in warming up the voice. We might start with an "Ou" followed by an "Ah." I utter the first sounds and have others join me. The Ou -Ah sequence works best when presented rhythmically with the vocal sound being the start of a four-point beat–Ou (2,3,4), Ah (2,3,4). I will clap my hands or slap them against my body and stamp a foot at the start of each utterance and ask the group to participate.

In this experience, the goal is rhythmic repetition. As people engross themselves in making the sounds, they tend to let go and become part of a larger vocal and sound experience which awakens a sensibility to expressions which transcend what an individual is capable of doing alone.

As the momentum of the Ou- Ah sequence builds and as I sense the group becoming one with the vocal expression, I might suggest that we augment the volume or diminish it in rhythmic ways. We might change speed with double time, triple time, and then return to the original tempo.

The clear and predictable structure of the vocal and rhythmic sounds together with the repetition of the expressions makes the process accessible to people. If someone resists at first and does not participate, the sounds continue and they are felt within the body, and if the person chooses to let go and join with the group, it is relatively easy to enter and become part of the total expression.

We might begin to make these sounds seated in chairs and then push them away as the rhythm takes hold. As the feet make contact with the floor and sustain the rhythmic pulse, someone might begin to extend these core gestures into a dance that encourages the individuals to become even more physically involved with their whole bodies.

Anyone familiar with this kind of spontaneous rhythmic experience knows how the pulse of the people making sounds together can transport us to places where we cannot go alone. I feel that a lifelong practice of vocal and musical healing can extend from the most elemental rhythms like those that I have just described. As we immerse ourselves in the flow of musical expression, it will carry us and become the starting point for continual variations and a more complete unfolding of the art form.

Vocal Toning and Elemental Chanting

The process of "toning" together with other people is another elemental mode of vocal improvisation that is widely used in the expressive arts therapies. When I first experienced this process in the early 1970s, I was taken aback by how small and large groups of people would reliably and quickly find common waves of vocalization.

One person begins with a sustained humming sound or drone (oooooo, maaaaa, neeeee et al.) and others join with their voices. Emphasis is placed on sustaining and extending the core sound. Since there is no right or wrong way to make a sound, every person can contribute and all of the elements work together to create a whole. Highs, lows, and all other variations find their way into the overall vibration and convergence of elements.

From the basis of a core harmonic sound, changes are subtly introduced and the entire group invariably follows in sync with the common thread. As the power and stability of the group tone is established and sustained, it has the ability to hold variations, called overtoning, which complement and enrich the primary sound.

Experimentation with toning can be likened to what Carl Rogers observed in relation to groups having a tendency to move toward equilibrium when the overall environmental conditions are supportive. In my experience with toning, there will usually be voices and sounds that are not in sync with the emerging core flow of the vocal stream, but as people listen and stay with the process of making sounds, the mainstream will gather all of the parts into a harmonic unity which begins to take on an independent and sustained expression.

Toning has been used for healing purposes within groups since ancient times. The merger of dissonant elements into a harmonic unity has a corresponding impact on the sensibilities of individual participants.

Play and the Prosody of a Word

In making and exploring a range of sounds with the voice, it is important to have the freedom to play. Although I have experienced the power of cacophony within groups capable of embracing more chaotic sounds, I generally prefer to work within the structures of rhythm and melody as described earlier. With the support of these organizational elements, people are able to let go; experience deep emotions; explore new, sometimes wild and unusual sounds; and always have a formal underpinning that holds the expressions and offers a sense of direction and intention.

In my studios, we have found it helpful to practice vocal improvisation by starting with just one word as a structure and focal point. The word does not have to have particular psychological significance. Anything that comes to mind will suffice. We might begin by working with our names or give words to one another. The emphasis is on play, variation, and using the word as basis for improvisation. By concentrating exclusively on one word, participants are given a clear, simple, and secure structure that frees them to concentrate completely on making sounds with the help of their bodily expressions.

In the poetic tradition, this multidimensional emphasis on pitch, intonation, duration, and rhythm is called prosody, what Ezra Pound called the expression of a poem's "total sound." I apply these elements of prosody to the articulation of a single word or phrase.

I begin by demonstrating ways of improvising and playing with a word, trying to suggest the range of sounds and vocal rhythms that we can make with a simple structure. Generally people tend to quickly grasp the intent of these expressive activities through brief demonstration and do not require extended instruction, perhaps because there is an instinctive understanding in most people of their unrealized vocal potential. I find that participants simply need help in getting beyond the considerable inhibitions that most of us have in relation to vocal improvisation.

I encourage breaking a word into syllables and annunciating these parts in varied and rhythmic ways. For example, the name Malinda can be broken down into three vocal elements . . . Ma-lin-da. These parts can be articulated in varied ways with different emphases–extended or quick, high or low pitch, forceful or soft.

In demonstrating, I might work with all three syllables of Malinda and then explore a range of possibilities with just one of the individual parts and then proceed to others in a sequential fashion. The improvisations can be extended by arranging the elements in different ways and repeating them– Lin-Ma-Da; Da-Ma-Lin; Ma-Da-Lin; Ma-Da, Ma-Da; and so forth. These explorations demonstrate the spectrum of vocal possibilities within what might appear to be the most ordinary and unlikely sources.

As people become more relaxed with the improvisational process, they often begin to sing the sounds. If this does not happen spontaneously, I might suggest singing the sounds and other vocal possibilities.

This approach to singing based upon the repetition and variation of elemental sounds and syllables in rhythmic and percussive ways is very ancient and accessible to every person. By taking the singing process outside the confines of conventional structures and expectations, people are given a fresh, prelyrical platform for vocal expression. A key to success is the creation of a playful and confident atmosphere that supports uninhibited experimentation.

I always encourage participants to make use of their whole bodies and physical movement when making sounds. We practice viewing the abdomen and the lower body as sources of sounds, both low and high. This shift from mental activity and self-consciousness to the most basic physical functions helps to relax expressive restraints and feelings of inhibition.

As we feel more comfortable with these essential ways of exploring the range and possibilities of vocal expression, we might use them to engage more emotionally laden words or phrases or brief passages from a poem. As our vocal improvisations connect with feelings, tensions, and desires, there is a sense of emotional authenticity and depth that I believe is uniquely connected to the voice.

Vocal expression is in this respect a powerful organ of our innermost being. I have discovered in my work with depth psychology that the pain of the soul, in keeping with the early twentieth century discoveries of Alfred Wolfsohn (1896-1962), is closely tied to the voice. Similarly, we have learned how the healing of wounds is furthered by channeling the vocal expression of hurt and loss into affirmations of the human spirit through song. Paul Newham's practice of therapeutic singing and voice-work has linked the traditions of Wolfsohn's work to expressive arts therapy (1993, 1998).

Singing selected words and lines from a poem or from spontaneous statements leads to a larger and more dramatic artistic process that I called "therapeutic operas" in *The Arts and Psychotherapy* (1981), a concept that intrigued Newham. When singing lines or passages from a poetic text, we tend to hone in on poignant expressions, repeating and varying our expression of them. Participants are encouraged to change a text in relation to the flow of emotion and the more general interplay of the improvisational structure which helps us access feelings and other contents that may not reach consciousness through regular speech.

The "operatic" dimension of improvisational voice-work with other people generates many new threads and directions for expression. The sheer energy and auditory impact of the vocalizations, regardless of their contents, can be a powerful source of inspiration and support.

I will take on the role of coach and conductor when I feel it is necessary to help a person stay grounded in terms of breath and the overall expressive process. This conducting process becomes even more necessary when two or more people participate together in a vocal improvisation.

My general orientation is always one of responding to what emerges naturally from people within an improvisational experience, but I will take a leadership role in helping them repeat expressions as described above; take pauses for the purpose of breathing and reflecting; and so forth. We might begin with one person uttering a word or a line and then invite the entire group to participate as a chorus in repeating and singing the passage.

Sound Dialogues and Listening

The play with basic sounds that I have described above unfolds naturally into interactive improvisations between therapists and participants in studio sessions. When helping people explore the range of vocal expression, I will often imitate, echo, or add to their sounds with my own. The interactive element furthers improvisation by supporting and affirming expressions and augmenting creative energy and flow. Receiving an enthusiastic response from another person can be liberating for those who have difficulty initiating sounds on their own.

My work with chronic adult psychiatric patients and the history of utilizing music therapy as a primary therapeutic modality with autistic children confirms the value of interactive sound making as an elemental mode of communication which is accessible when verbal dialogue is not possible. By imitating or "echoing" vocal expressions, we affirm the presence of others and their impact on us. This process, similar to mirror movements in dance, shows people that they are being heard and acknowledged by another person.

When interacting with another person in a musical improvisation, listening becomes as important as the process of making sounds. I have also found that placing more of an emphasis on listening to others within an improvisation helps people to get outside themselves and lessen inhibitions. In keeping with the emphasis on responsive expression throughout this book, we serve something larger than ourselves when connecting with others within a sound improvisation.

All of the possible variations that I described above in relation to the vocal prosody of a single word can be extended through interactive improvisations with another person or with two or three other people relating to one another in this way. The involvement of other people extends the range of improvisational possibilities. I strive to help people stay closely attuned to one another and to listen carefully and thus do their best to establish empathy and attentiveness rather than make disjointed sounds that potentially break the chain of interactions that can progressively build within the exchange. However, the experience of what Mitchell Kossak calls "misattunment" within a musical improvisation can play an essential role in providing a stimulus for awareness, helping us become more aware of what is missing in our experience and what we need to do in a new and different way (Kossak, 2007, p. 22).

The same process of interactive improvisation can be applied to making sounds with objects and instruments. Our immediate environments are usually full of potential sources for music. As a warm-up activity, we might explore the surrounding space with hands, feet, sticks, or stiff bristle brushes to determine the percussive potential. Wonderful individual and group sounds can be created by shaking and moving with unlikely musical sources such as newspaper, cloth, aluminum foil, and other materials. I have also found that people tend to be especially attentive and invested in sounds that are made by personally constructed instruments and generally these media are less threatening than vocal expression.

One of my favorite percussion instruments is a shaker made by putting different amounts or grains, beads, stones, brads, or other small things inside small plastic film containers. These sound sources are endlessly variable and easy for most people to make.

A sound dialogue can begin with two people holding these basic shakers in one hand or in both hands. One person begins by making a basic rhythm, rather than a more complicated series of sounds, while the other watches and listens. After ten or 20 seconds, the originating partner pauses and the other person repeats the sounds. Upon completion of this first exchange, the partners switch roles again and again for at least a few minutes. In this exercise, visual perception helps the witness internalize and hold onto the other person's movement and sound expressions.

After focusing on the replication of sounds, I encourage partners to gradually vary the percussive rhythms as they continue to listen to one another and respond. Partners will often spontaneously merge their sound making and begin to play together rhythmically. This shift to playing together can also be suggested by me as the group leader or by one of the partners. As the two people become immersed in the rhythm, it can continuously sustain itself with either constancy or variation.

In my work with percussive instruments in groups, I will generally introduce a single and unifying rhythm as described earlier. I will also identify a rhythm in another person's expression and ask the whole group to join with it. Although chaotic, non-rhythmic, and dissonant expressions have their place within the larger context of musical improvisation, I prefer to encourage a common pulse. This orientation to rhythm and convergence has been reinforced through my years of practice where I have witnessed the satisfaction that it brings to people.

I must once again emphasize how my methods carry a certain bias which is based on my experience, values, artistic style, and my limitations with certain artistic media. Others may be more inclined to embrace chaotic sounds. For example, I observed my colleague Bob Weiner, a jazz percussionist, improvising freely with a young boy who was making what might be perceived as random sounds on a separate drum set. Weiner's expertise in listening and playing enable him to do something significant with complex and discordant musical situations. It was clear that the young boy was inspired by Weiner's virtuosity and his ability to respond sensitively to whatever sounds emerged, no doubt helped the child play with abandon.

In describing the musical session with the boy, Weiner says, "He is new to it and his spirit is so fresh. His whole body is completely engaged in this thing. I want what he has and he wants what I have." The boy aspires to Weiner's skills and Weiner wants to return "to the simplicity of a child but with consciousness" (2007).

Weiner emphasized how important it is for leaders to be grounded in their own styles and rhythms in order to help others find theirs. The musical dialogue is thus based on working naturally from where we are in our expression, whether it is elemental or highly trained. Those who are inexperienced with the arts need to keep in mind that many experts value the simplicity and newness of their expression. I encourage every expressive arts therapist to stay closely attuned to what the Zen tradition calls "beginner's mind" (Suzuki, 1989). Although the expressive arts therapy discipline is keenly aware of how important it can be for therapists to have artistic skills that enable them to meet certain moments of practice, the work is largely oriented toward accessing the most instinctive ways of being that are available to all people.

The Interplay between Sound and Movement

I have observed how dance and movement therapists tend to work regularly with recorded music which induces different emotional states. In keeping with the principle of correspondence, the qualities of the music will usually have a parallel effect on the person's consciousness and movement. Like most people, I enjoy moving to music and find it to be a source of emotional arousal and creative motivation. But in my practice of expressive arts therapy, I see how recorded music generally elicits conventional social dance responses. I am more interested in helping people communicate emotions through their most personal and authentic physical gestures.

Rather than rely on recorded music, I prefer to work with the sounds that we make with our bodies, voices, physical materials, and musical instruments. This approach to natural and organic sounds heightens an immersion in the present moment and the surrounding space. There are certainly merits to how recordings can arouse the musical imagination and transport us away from difficult circumstances, but I have discovered that my work with others goes deeper when we limit ourselves to natural sounds made from interactions with the immediate physical environment.

My years of cooperation with the dance therapist Norma Canner had a formative impact on my attitude toward the relationship between sound and movement. As a proponent of pure movement, Canner never used recorded music in her sessions and gave attention to the sounds of the body as a percussive instrument and to the voice. Musical instruments were also used to make live sounds.

I work with responsive sound in two ways—by having dancers intensify or simply focus on the sounds that the body is making in space (i.e., breathe, feet on the floor, the sounds of fabric and other materials with which we move) or by having others make instrumental or vocal sounds in reaction to the movements of dancers. I will sometimes accompany the improvisational movement of both children and adults with drums and other percussion instruments, striving to pick up the beat and rhythms of the dance. This responsive use of sound tends to sustain and reinforce the gestures as contrasted to the more conventional use of sound to direct and structure a person's movement.

As we contemplate natural movements, it becomes clear that they are characterized by auditory qualities that are inseparable from the whole kinesthetic experience. The body moving in space will make sounds that contribute to the overall aesthetic experience. When groups of people are painting together in my studios I similarly draw attention to the auditory qualities of their movements. In addition to appreciating the varied sounds of movement, we will often amplify these sounds as a way of deepening and enhancing the expressive qualities of our gestures.

The ability to allow for the emanation of expression in these natural ways goes contrary to the primary instinct of many leaders who feel the need to direct and introduce a structure in order to achieve an outcome and avoid harmful chaos. I had to learn how to relax and develop confidence that movement and sound patterns will ultimately come forward and that the momentum will gather all of us into a common expression. Simplicity once again tends to be the key element of this process and I have observed how skilled leaders will support improvisational expression by encouraging people to stay connected to a particular gesture or sound, repeating it while listening carefully and letting the rhythm develop. As the expression grows in intensity and solidifies itself within the group, I discover how it can then change and gradually gain complexity and morph into new forms of movement or sound that extend from the core rhythm.

In addition to beginning our dances from stillness and the sounds of breath and the body moving, we will sometimes start by making simple musical rhythms that motivate movement. As a six-year-old boy told me at the start of a session when I was using a hand drum, "The drum makes me tingle and want to move."

We might also begin to move in sync with rhythms made with the voice. The sounds are always live and sensitive to the movements of dancers. The dance might start in response to a drum rhythm and as the expression unfolds, the drum will be influenced by the dancer and so forth. There is a continuous give and take between dances and sound much like the contact between dancers.

The dancer and choreographer Paul Taylor described how music "can be aggravating, a terrible whip" that introduces many restrictions of expression. Yet the music can also be essential to the dance in providing inspiration, partnership, and structure.

One of the greatest problems presented by recorded music in therapy is that it does not respond to the immediacy of individual and group emotion. For example, a movement group using recorded music might undergo a striking and emotionally significant change of direction while the music goes its own way and perhaps causes an impediment and distraction to group process.

My personal reluctance to use recorded music stems from how it can exercise too much control over the group's or an individual person's movement. Yet I do recognize how a familiar melody might have a deep emotional effect on a person by stimulating memories and significant feelings from the past. The melody may also be comforting and helpful in relaxing inhibitions to movement. Recorded music might also be necessary in one-to-one sessions or in group experiences where therapists and leaders must be directly involved in the movement process with others.

I lean toward the purist strain of staying away from recorded music in dance and movement therapy for many psychological and aesthetic reasons. I also find it more artistically challenging to make sounds together with movement. In my experience, the work tends to go deeper into the individual and group soul when we make contact with the archetypal continuities of moving to rhythmic vibrations being made in the moment. I am more apt to feel the trance-like effects of rhythm, to relax and be more perceptive of what others are doing and more totally present to the moment of expression, when I am making live rhythms in a group. Rhythm helps people relax the mind's inhibiting controls and to move from the whole of their bodies and from their contact with the ground.

I acknowledge that most people will continue to lean toward a reliance on recorded music in dance and movement therapy for purposes of convenience, a personal reluctance or inability to make live sounds, or simply an aesthetic preference for certain kinds of melodies or musical compositions. Technology has an important place in our lives and it can be a great asset to expressive arts therapy. The issues and methods that I am describing are also closely connected to our personal philosophies and styles of practice. My goal in this discussion of the relationship between sound and movement is to encourage expressive arts therapists to be sensitive to the way we use music when moving with others and to not just assume that dance happens in response to it.

POETRY AND CREATIVE WRITING

Although there are people who will always write spontaneously, and even out of necessity, most of us need support in beginning to create poetry. I avoid placing too much emphasis on the word "poetry" or "poem" when I begin to encourage people to express themselves creatively with language. These terms carry lots of expectations and for many people they are loaded with inhibitions.

As soon as people start to express themselves naturally, imaginatively, and forcefully with words, I might begin to describe the outcomes as poems, but at the start, I strive to reframe the poetic process as an aspect of everyday communication. Every person has a poem to create and communicate with others if inspired to become involved. In my experience, the most effective way of encouraging poetic expression is the creation of a predictable environment of support. The descriptions of my work with poetry closely connect to the preceding discussion of movement, sound, and voice and later reflections on improvisational drama and enactment.

Just as modern dancers, musicians, and visual artists perceive significant movement, sound, and visual configurations in daily life, I have tried to do the same thing with words and speech. The poem is about perception, hearing the words that are spoken in our environments, giving them a fresh emphasis, and making something from what already exists and which we might not otherwise see or appreciate. Creative work with language involves arranging and shaping words in new configurations. Life can be approached as a domain where people are talking poetically all of the time, but where few take the time to contemplate and record these expressions.

When I was teaching in the west of Ireland, a farmer said to me that his country was a land of poets because they simply describe what they see and feel when looking at the magnificent environments surrounding them. The same perspective can be applied to reflecting on the most ordinary and even disturbing situations. The poem is a response to what we sense and feel. Ezra Pound felt that poems are valued according to the way they arouse feelings with their ultimate significance depending on "only emotion" (Creeley, 1970, p. 95).

Poems respond to good and bad situations with human feelings ranging from outrage and fear to tenderness and longing. This expression of emotion can both release feelings and further sensibility. With respect to the latter, many of us tend to go through life somewhat anaesthetized to the feelings we have about experience, perhaps often as a necessity. These unacknowledged sensations can take a toll on our perceptual awareness and its relationship to emotional well-being. Aesthetic nerve endings have been deadened, numbed, and thoroughly disconnected from heart and mind. In this respect, poetry and the other expressive arts therapy media can take on an important public health role by helping people to cultivate life-enhancing emotional and aesthetic relationships with their environments.

Poems of Natural Experience

Rather than be limited by traditional notions of poetic form, I encourage people to let language emerge in response to their expressive needs and urges. Advocates of modernistic poetry make similar arguments for free expression in words. Emotion, breath, the transmission of energy, authentic voice, the perception of immediate things, the primacy of images, and structural liberty are characteristics of contemporary poetry that lend themselves to therapeutic application.

Psychotherapists conditioned to think of poetry only in terms of iambic pentameter and other conventional rules might familiarize themselves with free verse to more fully appreciate the writings of the people with whom they work. Formal structures of poetry—the shape of the verse, the length of the line, and punctuation—can correspond to the expressive needs and emotional energies of the person.

The modernist focus on experiencing the immediate presence of the poem and its expressive qualities was in sync with my overall goals when I began to work with the arts in therapy. As with contemplative disciplines, the focus on the present moment was energizing and enlivening.

When I was founding and developing the Lesley University graduate program in expressive arts therapy during the 1970s, I was influenced by the ideas of Charles Olson as conveyed in his essay *Projective Verse* (1966), a brief text originally published as a pamphlet in 1950. Olson strove to write in a way that reflected the *process* of how one perception "immediately and directly" leads to further perceptions. These innovations, or what may be perceived as a return to natural and innate poetic utterances, are especially significant for expressive arts therapy in that the goal of the projective poet is to create an expressive union between the poem and the person's experience of emotion. The poem is viewed by Olson as a "force" and as "energy" transmitted from one person to another. It is shaped by the most primary aspects of breath, bodily movement, and vocal sounds.

My poetry mentor Vincent Ferrini (1913–2007), the poet laureate of Gloucester, Massachusetts, was a close friend of Olson. Ferrini kept telling my expressive arts therapy students who came to him for advice, "The poem is in the air, in the atmosphere happening." He exhorted students and therapists to hear the poems they were living; to expand the making of poetry to action in the community, the creation of relationships, and the more comprehensive sanctity of living (1976, 2004).

The poet Elizabeth McKim became an early member of our Lesley faculty and she worked closely with Norma Canner in researching the movement basis of the poem and the role of bodily expression within the poetic experience. McKim also immersed herself in collaborations with Paolo Knill to expand her use of sound in poetry. The voice became a rhythmic and primal instrument of expression in addition to conveying ideas and feelings through the symbolic function of words. Thus the poem begins to operate on many different levels, both physical and mental. McKim explored the outer and inner limits of prosody, the total expression of the poem.

One of my most memorable experiences as a Lesley dean was conducting a group interview during the mid 1970s in the Cambridge house where our graduate program offices were located. McKim was upstairs leading a class on poetry, movement, and voice. As I listened to applicants describing their personal goals, the ceiling began to shake from the pounding of feet above and we were engulfed in rocking rhythms and free vocalization. McKim was leading a "warm-up" activity designed to help people use the whole of their bodily and sound expressions in making poems, and the students realized that working with us at Lesley would be very different from their previous school experiences.

The work that Elizabeth McKim and others were doing was not simply about primal release. A number of our faculty during the 1970s were interested in primal therapy, but their success as teachers was determined by their ability to connect therapeutic ideas and methods to the different arts disciplines. All of us were striving for a more open and complete integration of the senses and expressive faculties in each artistic modality.

McKim's poetry began to shift from reading to performance. She enacted her poems from memory in keeping with ancient traditions and made use of a wide spectrum of sounds and movements to deliver the words in the most expressive ways possible. The poem *Breath* (1988) grew from this work and conveys many of the essential principles of our expressive arts therapy discipline.

Breath

I kept you in
Wolf chewin' up the floorboards
Old woman with your toes cut off
Sullen child in a grey wool dress

Breath
I was doin' ok
Neat and leveled as a bonzai plant
I knew how to please
But breath
You had plans
You wanted to ride the freights
Play the drums
Do the love-boogie
Let a humming bird in
Make green uneven waves

Breath
I was plain scared
Who knows
Once you were out
You might trouble
My small upturned breasts
Wash me out
and away
Suck Suck

Breath
I wanted you so bad
I kept you tight
in the cramp of throat
in the high unrealized sound
But breath
You beat me
You came out
And you're good breath
You're *good you're good*
You're *good breath*
You're *good*

Through her art-based research, Elizabeth McKim lived the process she was teaching to others. Her exploration of relationships between poetry, movement, voice, and performance is ultimately oriented toward the most complete and natural expression of the spoken and written word. She writes: "The poet moves into the heart of the matter to name, to reveal (not explain) in language these fleeting and insistent messages that come spontaneously into our lives. These ideas are not general and abstract but specific, personal, and closely connected to our senses, our physical selves, our pulse and heartbeat, our humor, our outrage, our intimate and heard diction" (1999, pp. 211-212).

The poem grows from these organic sources and the most familiar and humble features of our experiences and environments, the rooms we inhabit, the streets we walk, and the things from nature that we touch and smell.

"A Responding Instrument"

There are many things that I do to help people get started with poetic expression. The most common method that I use, as described earlier with movement and sound, is the simple process of giving a response to another's artistic expression or to one's own. When people respond in a terse, image-based, and heartfelt manner to an experience that just occurred before them in paint, sound, movement, or some other medium, poetic speech emerges naturally as a response. The totality of expressive arts therapy thus coincides with Olson's definition of the poetic process of one perception leading to another.

It may be helpful to look at every perception as a creative act, as an opening of expression, and as the basis for a poetic response. William S. Burroughs in *Naked Lunch* says: "There is only one thing a writer can write about: *what is in front of his senses at the moment of writing.* . . . I am a responding instrument" (1959, p. 200). Every sensation can thus stimulate an imaginative response.

In my work with others, I have always approached poetry as a response to experience. This focus on making oneself "a responding instrument" eases the pressure that we often feel to be inventive and clever in our poetic expression. The emphasis shifts from drawing a poem out of myself to being totally present to another person, moment, or thing; to witness an occurrence or instant of life as completely as possible; and to then respond authentically with the goal of *giving something* to others.

When we see ourselves as responding to something that already exists, the whole process of writing is transformed. We take ourselves out of the role of "initiating" creative expression and just respond to things before us. The foundation of so many blocks to expression is the assumption that the creative act makes something from nothing. If we take this pressure off ourselves and look at the world as an ongoing process of creation that is grasped and appreciated through perception, then our expressive actions in any medium can be viewed as responsive acts that are part of a flow that is so much larger than our isolated selves. We are participants in a bigger stream of creation to which we contribute through individual expressions.

In my expressive arts therapy studios, I have found responsive writing to be the most effective way of helping every person express themselves in authentic poetic ways. When attention shifts from *making poetry* to being a *responding instrument*, we take on a completely different and perhaps more universally human role. We use words to convey our reaction to another person or an artwork. There is rarely a human situation where we do not have a response of some kind.

I urge people to convey how they feel about an expression; how it touches them or even upsets them; and to avoid judgments or intellectualized comments. "How does the expression act upon you?" I say. "What does it do to you? What does it arouse? What do you have to say about this? Talk back to the expression. Enter into dialogue with it. Respond to its imagination and feeling with yours. Do your best to respond immediately without too much thought. Don't worry about being incorrect because there is no one single and correct response to give."

Striving to express what we feel in reaction to an experience, rather than creating poetry or an artistic configuration of words, furthers the flow of our natural rhythms of speech and feelings. Everything is immediate and right in front of us and we "respond" instinctively.

I encourage people to write whatever enters their perceptions and thoughts when looking at an artwork that they have made or the creation of another person. The same thing can be done in response to an object from nature or something very ordinary in our environments. I ask people to concentrate on the flow of their perceptions and feelings and to avoid using too many words. I encourage the repetition of feelings or meaningful, even random, words and these patterns enhance rhythm which furthers fluidity and letting go. We encourage sensitivity to the sounds of words, the energy and tone of passages, as well as the meaning of a text.

These responsive expressions are immediate and totally tied to the emotions being experienced in the moment. They circumvent deliberations and other forms of inhibition. The emphasis is given to connecting words to whatever thoughts and feelings are passing through consciousness. Writing becomes a part of the more general movement of perceptions and emotion happening at a particular time.

In my group studios, as described earlier, we typically show our art and make brief individual rituals and performances while the group as whole watches and acts as witnesses. Rather than trying to talk about our reactions afterwards, I will often ask each individual member to write a terse, imagistic line or two about each performance after it occurs. At the conclusion of the eight to ten presentations, each person serving as a witness will have generated a ten to 20 line "poem" that not only gives an artistic response to each piece or performance, but invariably the separate reactions to each presentation blend together into a single poem that coheres, flows, and offers a transformative reaction to the sequence of individual presentations. The poetic response carries traces of the individual artworks being observed but makes them into yet another artistic moment that is complete within itself.

When we are witnessing another person's expression with the expectation of offering a creative response, our perceptions tend to be more vivid and attentive. Objects and events that might normally pass unnoticed evoke a passionate and imaginative response.

Writers describe how a single perception will set them off by releasing a series of emotional reactions as well as memories that connect to other experiences. A word can suggest further perceptions and feelings. One thing sparks another as the poetic process flows, and moves like a dancer making a movement in response to the gesture that went before it. Concentration on a particular thing, whether it is an image, feeling, person, or gesture results in a narrowing of perception that can paradoxically open a deep reservoir of personal expression. It as though the creation of a focal point, together with the need to respond, make a gateway or a channel through which expression can flow.

This kind of writing underscores how tightly designed structures can paradoxically liberate deep currents of expression. Perhaps even more essentially, these responsive writings experiences show how focusing on another person or an object together with the expectation of "giving to another person or thing" rather than "creating" may not only minimize self-consciousness but also catalyze expression.

The poem is organized around the experience and perceptions of the writer during a particular time of intense concentration on what other people are doing. The desire to support another person's expression and to give a heartfelt response intensifies attention and total involvement. In my experience, this activity reliably furthers the quality of poetic writing. People who usually find it difficult to write poetry or who tend to rely on clichés invariably discover new and more spontaneous ways of expressing themselves.

Instinctive Writing

Select any word that appears in your consciousness and write an instinctive response to it. Do not think about what you want to say and just record whatever images, words, sounds, or thoughts enter you mind—you can always edit latter. Focus now on the flow of words, perceptions, and feelings and do your best not to censor yourself in any way. Think of yourself as instinctively reacting to the word you select. Imagine the writing as an exercise, a game where you perceive and respond as automatically as possible, in the most peculiar and unrepressed ways.

When you have completed your flow of words, make a copy to keep and then feel free to edit another version into whatever emerges from the refinement process.

Don't be afraid if the text is strange. View weirdness as an expressive asset, a manifestation of the authentic self.

Spontaneous Repetitions

Take any word, the first one that comes to you and repeat it over and over again and let it connect spontaneously to other words. Try not to edit, judge, or censor yourself in any way. Just let the words emerge and try to feel them. As words appear, they elicit other words and images, all of which offer a foundation and physical structure that support the shaping of a poem.

Record your words and after three, four, or five minutes of improvisation, read what you have written.

On another sheet of paper select the words and passages that intrigue you most and either let them stand as is, or add more words and lines to make yet another creation. Something significant seems to happen when we are able to let go and allow the words and the process of expression carry us.

Witnessing Perceptions

Focus on different objects in your environment, or perceptions that you have when you look out a window. Randomly record whatever you see, the most fleeting and subtle glimpses.

This emphasis on recording the words and images that pass through your consciousness can minimize the pressure to create and make something from nothing. Perceptions are happening all of the time and the poetic process can be viewed as a responsive documentation of this ongoing flow of experience. Poetry can thus start by using words to try and express glimpses of what is already happening.

Concentrate only on the qualities of the thing you observe and let words emerge from this contemplative process. Allow the things of the world to express themselves through you in words and feelings and do your best not to hold anything back. The goal of this exercise is a relaxation of all censors and critics and allowing words to emanate as freely as possible. If you record everything that passes through you, there will always be time to go back later to edit and craft a composition.

As Charles Olson suggests, let one perception follow another in a purely natural way like breathing. Separate lines from one another in relation to breaths you take.

If you can surrender to the process of articulating perceptions, the quality of the words and passages might be superior to what you write in more consciously planned passages.

Word Improvisations and Weird Imaginings

Give yourself an entirely new and liberating basis for establishing value. Let your thoughts and words go wild, undomesticated. Try to believe that the more outlandish your expressions are, the better they will be.

Record the first word or phrase that enters your consciousness and then build upon it with the most unusual, weird, and outrageous imaginings.

The Primacy of Sound

The work described earlier with sound and vocal improvisation has a distinct poetic quality. When doing the exercises involving the repetition of words with sound variations and sound dialogues with another person, you can record these improvisations in written and audio modes and fashion them into a text.

Try to keep your emphasis on the sound qualities rather than on verbal meanings. Use this exercise to appreciate the vibrations and musical tones of poetry made by the voice. In shifting the orientation of the poem toward the felt and sensory cadences of vocal expression and away from the planning mind, we help correct an imbalance that many experience when writing. Paradoxically, these more sensory and physical approaches to expression can help to cultivate more original and imaginative poetic ideas and insights.

The Poem as Kinesis

Stand in silence and then begin to move with simple and natural gestures. As you make these movements, let yourself speak words in response to what you feel, see, or think. Let the words come directly from each movement as it follows another. Both words and movements emerge from the ones that go before and generate those that follow.

Try to envision the poem as a kinetic process rather than as a fixed entity. Do everything you can to relax the mind so that it controls the composition as little as possible. Editing and perfecting the words can happen later. Let the body lead and the words follow and then reverse the relationship.

Imagine the poem as a total expression, a prosody as described earlier, which is informed by your body movement, the sounds and energies of your voice, your breath, fantasies, and the overall drama of what you do.

Sustaining Movement

In my experience, the physical act of writing is always a precondition for creative discovery. I often resist becoming immersed in the process so I know firsthand how important it is to persist with the discipline of artistic activity. The best remedy for the reluctance to become involved with creative practice is to simply begin by concentrating on the manual aspects of writing.

Do your best to view the process of creating passages on a page as nothing but movement. Reflection and pauses are, of course, essential in the creative process, but in this warm-up exercise, try to keep your hands moving on a page or keyboard.

Write nonstop for a few minutes and focus more on sustaining the movement rather than thinking too much about what you are trying to say. Let your hands and fingers take the lead for awhile and trust their intelligence. Vary the pace of the process or try to move and write rhythmically.

These exercises activate the creative process and generate content that can be shaped, refined, and expanded in later phases of the work.

Word Play and Collage

Discover how new ways of imagining life can be created by putting words into new combinations.

Begin by selecting words in the most random way possible, either from your own expression or from a text. Arrange the words spontaneously and then begin to reflect on the combinations and compositions, building upon expressions that intrigue you or attract your attention.

Try to think about what you are doing as play rather than poetry. I predicate that the more completely you are able to play with the words and establish unplanned relations to other words and thoughts, the better and more satisfying the poetry will be.

This type of practice is intended to get you moving in different ways and responding to new things. The stimuli invariably help you access fresh streams of your own natural thought and expression.

Expression from the Basis of an Emotion, Dream, Inner Image

Use the most spontaneous flow of words to describe a feeling that you have. Do your best to connect to the emotion and let the words happen without thinking about what you want to say. Immerse yourself in the most personal feelings and allow the words come forward.

Once you feel that you have exhausted the flow of words, take a break and then go back to what you have recorded and see if you want to rearrange the words or expand upon them. Try to focus more on the expressions of the words, their uniqueness, and the total composition that you are making with them, rather than attempting a precise replication of the emotion you used as a stimulus. The poem will take on a life and structure of its own, a creation that grows from your emotion but which does not have to represent it in a literal way.

Do the same thing with dreams, memories, desires, and other inner images. Remember that you can never exactly make an external representation of something you feel or imagine inside. What you can do is use it as a source of expression and transform it into a new creation.

Place your emphasis on the expression of emotion, images, things that fascinate and provoke you. Try not to be overly concerned with specific structures and grammar. Concentrate more on the expressive qualities of words and passages—sounds, visions, imaginings. The purpose of the poem is to awaken, inspire, soothe, transform, startle, and arouse. Use whatever expressive tools further this purpose.

Voice, Words, and Enactment of the Poem

One of the most common problems encountered in sharing poetry is the insecurity that people experience when reading their work to others. Granted, poems have a special effect on people when they are read and experienced visually, but within the therapeutic process, there is a definite power to sharing the poem orally. When I notice that people are having a difficult time reading poems, I will often ask them to read a line or passage slowly, two or three times, until they feel comfortable. All of us need support in realizing that others really want to hear what we say and experience the cadence of our words.

Repetitious reading not only helps to overcome stage fright but also gives listeners the opportunity to more completely absorb the poetic imagery. Repetition tends to have a calming effect, and if the poem is a short one, repeated reading can evolve into a chant or mantra. In reading a poem, there is a great therapeutic value when the voice and inner emotion are in synchrony with the imagery and words being presented. When this feeling is achieved, the poem has an organic wholeness and flow that is in itself healing.

As described in the previous section, we practice freeing the voice and building self-confidence by concentrating on just a few words, a line, or brief poetic statement. Play and experimentation with sound, voice, and words always seems to have a liberating effect on people when they see how so much can be done with minimal creative material.

Teenagers and young adults smile and describe how at first they find it "weird" to read poems in this way, exercising a greater range of vocal expressions as contrasted to the literal reading to which they are accustomed. But as they grow more comfortable and the process becomes more effortless and organic, they find themselves realizing expressive powers that they never knew existed, or which they never dreamed of expressing to another person. They also discover how this expansion of verbal expression furthers the communication of the poem.

As people become more relaxed and confident expressing themselves naturally with voice, the range and quality of their poetic expression is enhanced. The poem flows from the body and the rhythms of its vocalization and movements. Words, images, and lines have a richer and more natural shape when they emerge from this expressive context which is so different from the more abstract and conceptual notion of the poem originating exclusively from the process of "thinking." The mind and, of course, the heart and soul have essential roles in the making of a poem but for most of us, these faculties do their best work when integrated with physical expressions. In addition to vocal play and experimentation, I encourage people to say words, phrases, and lines with their whole bodies, to move the poem in space, to experience and imagine words as expressions tied to a larger organic context of actions.

When I am trying to help a person relax and read in more natural and confident ways, I encourage pauses and periods of silence in keeping with the methods described for movement and sound. "Take a breath," I say and wait until you are comfortable and ready to read. As Longfellow said to the poet Whittier, "And speakest only when thy soul is stirred."

There is spaciousness in these moments of simple silence that focus attention and regenerate energies. They offer transitions between expressions and natural breaks. And as people welcome these moments as opportunities for reflection, they help to lower anxiety and expectations. "Let go of what just happened and how you feel about it," I say, "and get ready for what it is going to happen next. Practice moving between worlds, from one experience to the next, and try to discipline yourself to be totally immersed in the next expression that you will make or witness."

For most of us, silence has a history of a tension and even stress when associated with self-expression; it has sometimes been an impenetrable wall of intimidation that arouses fears of judgment or even ridicule. We also have a tendency to view silence as disinterest or an uncomfortable state that needs to be filled compulsively with chatter. When encouraging others to express themselves, I try to reverse our histories with silence and invoke its soothing and evocative qualities. Before and after someone reads a poem, we pause, reflect, and immerse ourselves in the qualities of the moment.

When silence is accepted and even enjoyed, the statements that emerge from it tend to have a greater fullness and significance. The contemplative pause takes on a purpose and value within the flow of expression.

In most life situations, especially when we are nervous, things happen too fast; we don't breathe in a conscious way; anxiety accelerates; and the combination of these and other factors can arouse panic and other conditions that can cause considerable damage.

Virtually every inexperienced person approaches the reading of a poem as a fast activity with few breaths and open spaces between the words, lines, and images. The person is typically uncomfortable and this condition together with the speed of the reading has a corresponding effect on the people who are witnessing the work. We need coaches who show us how to take it easy; slow everything down; try not to do too much; learn how to savor the words as we say them; hear ourselves speaking and feel the rhythms of our voices; and enjoy the process of speaking from the totality of our bodies and emotions.

I have discovered how important it is to have people stand, move into the center of a group or stage, and take time to feel comfortable so they can make use of their complete bodily presence and access the considerable energy that the setting offers to them when they read or repeat words and poetic lines. I encourage playfulness in exploring the space to lower the intimidation factor and I always suggest beginning with material that offers a certain degree of comfort and familiarity.

"We all have our areas of expertise in one area or another" I say. "Take a movement or way of speaking from an area where you feel confident and transfer it to moving and speaking in this space." Most of us have been conditioned to feel pressure when we speak before other people and the environment works against us as a suppressive force.

It is remarkable what a difference it can make when we stand up and begin to move naturally in a space with the voice becoming an integral part of the whole body's expression. This contrasts to the self-consciousness that typically accompanies the perception of the voice as a completely separate modality.

Personal Samples

Writing poetry helps me be more aware of passing moments and their beauty. The poem is a glimpse catcher, holding onto something that would be lost like a dream that is never told or recorded. Poems written in response to perceptions of things infuse me with their expressive energy. I take time to contemplate the world outside and step away from my preoccupations.

In keeping with the principles described in this section I try to express sensations automatically as I am having them and I go back afterwards with a critical eye to perfect the words, rhythms, and composition as best I can. I strive to extract the marrow from the experience of mixing perceptions and language and use as few words as possible. I long for things that I already have and dream with them in new ways through poetic reflection.

I wrote the following poem in response to an ordinary glance out of my house window.

Soulblast

man in bright blue tank top
and shorts on the neighbor's roof
April after snow
tanned beside the chimney with your brush

I cannot just look
and let you go
I need to keep

the random glimpse
you never saw
but for me like jumper cords
of invisible teeth locking onto
what flies from here
with hands changing hose washers
of another year

The writing process immerses me in a single perception that I had on an April morning when I saw a workman on a neighbor's roof in our New England village. April can still be cold so the warmth of the day and the man's appearance were distinctly new after months of winter.

There was suddenness to the experience that was in some ways startling. I wrote pages of lines and ultimately pared the poem down to the essential feeling of what I experienced. I kept the "jumper cords" and "hose washers" because they are unusual images that emerged from the reflections.

Writing poems can affirm the creative spirit after setbacks and losses. I wrote the following lines during a troubling time when I felt like I was losing control over things that mattered to me. Creative expression helped me embrace and even extol the difficulties, to harness the emotion of the failure and create with it.

We were not created to walk in straight lines
like ants in the sun
but to rise and fall, to dance wildly
to make our marks in the dust
and go on.

And when I felt empty and without direction and creative purpose, a poetic line takes the feeling and transforms it into an image of longing that continues to give me great pleasure.

Inspiration,
I dream of you walking through every door.

Here's one of my favorites, a passage written in my youth that expresses desire for something that cannot happen.

out of reach,
this love between the moon and me.

We can create poetry to hold childhood memories like sacred lockets. I wrote a poem about the vivid recollections of my mother, elegantly dressed and on her way out at night with my father. I gave the poem to my mother many years ago and I was stunned when my younger sisters selected it to be on the back cover of the program for her memorial service. Apparently my mother placed the poem with her special belonging before she was afflicted by Alzheimer's. The poem helped the family remember what my mother was before she lived for many years without any apparent awareness of herself and her surroundings.

Evening Ritual

a young boy
took delight in his mother's perfume & dress
on those nights when she got away
from the web of her eight

she kissed the little ones as
I waited for my taste of red lipstick
and honey breath
given generously before leaving

dazzling
and full of love
she was ready to go.

The poem suggests the immortality of memory. When a friend lost his mother I wrote:

The Empty Chair

It's final and never finished
forever here in a glance
as the shadow on her hand
vanishing
with headlines fleeting into nothing but the next
while she stays
in births of memory
flowing from the loss
in ravines of me
seeing vistas she never saw
before passing away, once again,
into what she gave.

I have four children, one son and three daughters, and they have taught me how to let go while at the same time keeping and savoring the most precious moments of life. I wrote this verse for the 16th birthday of my daughter.

> I cling to her hand at the bus stop past
> as she closes the door
> on our childhood rites
> and drops a seed
> to the spaciousness of tomorrow.

I write poems to mark important moments in the lives of friends. I wrote the following for the Golden Jubilee of Sister Kathleen Burke, the founder of the art therapy graduate program at Ursuline College in Ohio.

> your way of being
> what many profess
> and can never be
>
> a way
> where ego becomes nothing but breath
> like Job
> who utters
> I am dust.

After my first child was born I wrote to my parents.

> love comes
> from the first childhood touches
> and returns to them.

This poem to my parents can be likened to one of my favorite passages from *Ecclesiastes* that I read many years after writing the lines.

> All streams run into the sea,
> yet the sea never overflows;
> back to the place from which the streams ran
> they return to run again. (I:7)

All of our artistic expressions are parts of this stream that flows from a source and returns to it again and again to feed the ongoing force of creation.

READING LITERATURE AND SHAPING A LANGUAGE OF EXPRESSIVE ARTS THERAPY

Within the history of the arts in therapy there is an important tradition related to the reading of literature for healing purposes. Many of the principles involved with therapeutic reading can also be applied to listening to music, looking at visual art, watching films, and witnessing performing arts. However, I believe that reading is a uniquely active form of artistic participation that merits attention as an expressive arts therapy modality.

The early literature on poetry therapy was influenced by the medical approach of "prescribing a poem" in response to particular ailments (Leedy, 1969, 1973; Lerner, 1978; Morrison, 1987). This method can be viewed as part of the larger history of bibliotherapy that connects the reading of literature to emotional well-being and psychological insight (Mynes & Hynes-Berry, 1994; Rubin, 1978; Russell & Shrodes,1950; Shrodes, 1949). Poets and fiction writers have been insightful explorers of psychological dynamics well before the existence of psychology and they continue to offer discerning viewpoints on emotional experience.

Literature shows that we are not alone and singularly burdened with personal difficulties. Reading books, stories, and poetry in conjunction with psychotherapy is particularly helpful for adolescents and young people who are struggling with the creation of a personal identity. Characters in literature can be instructive and serve as role models for the young and people of all ages who need support and inspiration. As readers, we participate in literary scenarios and absorb their life giving energies.

The Principle of Correspondence

The psychological principle of isomorphism can help us understand how emotional states conveyed by poems, prose, and all forms of artistic expression have a corresponding effect on people who engage them. According to this approach, a hopeful poem will help to build the confidence of a depressed person and similar applications can be made in relation to other emotional states.

Poetry therapists will often catalog poems for use in relation to particular emotional disorders. They suggest one poem for a mildly depressed person and another for a person who is experiencing a more intense personal crisis. There are many who might discourage the reading of something like Yeats' great poem "The Second Coming" (1989) in the latter situation for fear that the already unstable and confused person might be overwhelmed by its intensities.

> Turning and turning in the widening gyre
> The falcon cannot hear the falconer;
> Things fall apart; the centre cannot hold;
> Mere anarchy is loosed upon the world.

My experience repeatedly shows that people suffering from strong emotional conflicts receive solace from poetry that corresponds to their conditions. Maybe the intensity of "The Second Coming" will be just the medicine that a person needs. I repeatedly see how people in crisis find support from strong poetry that helps them accept how there may be a purpose to how "Things fall apart." The current structure of existence might need to be broken apart in order for people to remake their lives. Strong and powerful medicines may be required to dissolve harmful patterns and habits.

I have learned to "trust the process" of a person's interactions with poetry and other forms of creative expression. The most effective ways of treating the emotions through the creative process cannot always be planned. Strategic "interventions" according to a therapist's assessment of a person's condition may sometimes result in superficial and manipulative techniques. Sometimes the soul will minister to itself in ways that defy logic and the best intentions of therapists. The most unlikely poem may be the one that helps a person in unexpected ways. The same applies to witnessing and perceiving other art forms.

Nevertheless, we can say with some general sense of predictability that certain forms of expression are likely to generate corresponding emotions in people. For example, Walt Whitman's "Song of Myself" (1926) is generally regarded as an uplifting and hopeful poem that helps people value their inner experience. When I read the following lines I experience a corresponding sensibility.

> I believe in you my soul, the other I am must not
> abase itself to you,
> And you must not be abased to the other.
> Loafe with me on the grass, loose the stop from your
> throat,
> Not words, not music or rhyme I want, not custom or
> lecture not even the best,
> Only the lull I like, the hum of your valved voice.

The poetry therapy practice of "prescribing poems" can be viewed as a contemporary manifestation of indigenous healing practices based upon the principle of correspondence, also known as the law of similarity. In my practice, I am not inclined to prescribe poetry, but I constantly observe how the person reading or listening to a poetic expression is likely to experience an inner reaction that corresponds to the emotional expression of the external form. Within native cultures in various parts of the world, words are used as healing charms that strive to activate conditions within the person that parallel the meaning of the utterance.

This principle of correspondence applies to healing with all of the other arts where certain kinds of physical features in visual images, sounds, movements, rituals, and dramatic enactments are likely to produce comparable reactions in the people who experience them. For example, we might work with stones to access their stability, water for fluidity, and so forth.

Indigenous healing practices throughout the world are based on the correspondence principle where difficulties might be transferred to an object which is carried off by a stream or burned in a ceremonial fire. In sweat lodge rituals, a malady is passed along to a stone and the heat of the fire takes it away. In all of these healing practices, the imagination makes use of symbols to stimulate corresponding conditions within the person. The same kind of thing can happen when we read poems or literary texts that act upon the imagination in suggestive ways, generating outcomes that are real and physical. The increasing appreciation of mind-body relationships within traditional medicine affirms how the creative imagination, in keeping with the history of charms, talismans, and healing rituals, has an important role to play in furthering mental and physical well-being.

People turn naturally to artistic expressions as sources of renewal because the arts express and embody the deepest realms of emotion in ways that are not accessible through conventional speech. Poetry and the other expressive arts sometimes treat the emotions in a homeopathic manner by introducing unsettling expressions, counter-irritants, which stimulate the healing forces of body, mind, and spirit. The upsetting qualities of the artistic expression activate our more comprehensive creative immune systems. The disturbing poem arouses depressed or dormant sensibilities which can further healing.

For example, people frequently turn to the darker poetic writings of Emily Dickinson as a source of healing (1924). What might be perceived as her negative ruminations turn out to be sources of strength and resilience. Dickinson's poem "I'm nobody! Who are you?" is often used by people as a source of emotional support and inspiration. I repeatedly see how the introduction of pathos stimulates an affirmation of experience and in some cases a sense of exhilaration.

> I'm nobody! Who are you?
> Are you nobody, too?
> Then there's a pair of us–don't tell!
> They'd banish us, you know!
>
> How dreary to be somebody!
> How public, like a frog
> To tell your name the livelong day
> To an admiring bog!

As C. G. Jung said, healing occurs when we realize that we are not alone in the pain that we are experiencing.

Dickinson's poetry is especially effective in helping people accept the conditions of their lives knowing that others have been afflicted by the same struggles. The poet fashions beauty and wisdom from suffering and offers inspirational soul medicine as we try to meet the ongoing challenges and setbacks of living.

> Life is but life, and death but death!
> Bliss is but bliss, and breath but breath!
> And if, indeed, I fail,
> At least to know the worst is sweet.
> Defeat means nothing but defeat,
> No drearier can prevail!

Emily Dickinson also helps people deal with the pressures of being different and how this can be threatening to others.

> Much madness is divinest sense
> To a discerning eye;
> Much sense the starkest madness.
> 'T is the majority
> In this, as all, prevails.
> Assent, and you are sane;
> Demur,–you 're straightway
> dangerous,
> And handled with a chain.

As we read and deeply contemplate these poems, they take us into the core of our troubled emotions and they show the way to healing through acceptance and understanding. The great poets do not fix or eradicate the problems of the soul and the dark places in our lives, but rather show us how to do something creative with them.

Theodore Roethke's writings evoke the deepest strains of the artistic tradition that finds meaning and even a sense of holiness in the difficulties of experience. In the tradition of Nietzsche and other artists of the soul, Roethke (1908–1963) shows us how to transform difficulties and think about them in different ways. His poem "In a Dark Time" (1966) emphasizes how "In a dark time, the eye begins to see." In another line of this intensely therapeutic poem he writes, "What's madness but nobility of soul? At odds with circumstance?"

Like Dickinson and Jung, Roethke affirms the solace that comes from knowing that we are not alone in our distress.

When I go mad,
I call my friends by phone:
I am afraid they might think
they're alone.

Poems like these might be read as a stimulus for discussion in groups or within individual therapeutic sessions. The poem's ability to clarify and express intense feelings serves as a catalyst, as yeast for the healing process.

When we read a text that captures what we feel, there is a sense of companionship that affirms our experience. As an adolescent just said to me, "For the first time in my life I felt that my ideas are well founded and in sync with someone else's." This young woman felt a "positive identification" as contrasted to the pattern of "always thinking that there is something wrong with me." This exchange helps me realize how reading literature enables the imagination to transcend the negative patterns and identifications that often characterize our daily lives.

Literature and poetry provide access to expressions that reach out to us as saviors and allies in times of difficulty. We see that others before us have not only experienced hardships and survived, but they have used setbacks as a basis for reaching out to others through creative expression. The text is a sanctum of imagination that enables us to penetrate, elevate, and transform, the conditions of our lives.

The Mind Is Shaped by the Company It Keeps

In her pioneering studies of bibliotherapy, Caroline Shrodes (1949, 1950) described how literature can be used in an educational way to consciously change behavior or to resolve difficulties by reading a text and applying it to our lives. Many people find comfort and inspiration by reading literary, psychological, spiritual, and religious texts in this way. Although people receive important assistance from the expansive self-help literature that exists in our society, Shrodes felt that deeper therapeutic transformations happen when people read fiction and literary writings with receptivity to the influences on their lives. She approached bibliotherapy as a discipline where there is a "dynamic interaction" between the reader and the text.

The literary work generates an emotional response from readers who might project themselves into situations within a text, feel empathy with characters and situations, experience emotional catharsis when reading, and gain a better understanding of their own lives and emotions. Reading a text can be transformative in and of itself or it might be used to further discussion within therapeutic relationships. Readers experiencing difficulties in life can gain strength by seeing how literary characters with similar afflictions respond. Oftentimes the failures and setbacks of characters can be as helpful to the reader as their triumphs.

When we are alone and open to influence, a poem or literary text often serves as an intimate companion that distinctly influences thought and behavior. The primary recommendation that I have with regard to the selection of readings has to do with the quality of writing. As in a conversation with another person, the imagination and language of a text will have a corresponding impact on the mind and sensibility of the reader. My experience as an educator has strongly reinforced how the mind is shaped by the company it keeps.

I have always leaned toward an open-ended way of working with literary materials. A complex and rich poem, story, or novel will always evoke reactions from readers that cannot be planned in advance. Like any other deep relationship, the nature of a person's interaction with a text will be infinitely variable and dependent on the changing conditions of life and the shifts of consciousness from moment to moment. Science affirms how change often happens in a random manner and without direction. Thus I strive to create situations where people are free to make their own connections to an artwork.

If I immerse myself in a text, it is likely to influence me in different ways with each engagement. Creative and transformative opportunities can be lost when those of us who strive to make these resources available to others, put all of our energy into strategically controlling the emotional reactions of readers. What matters most as a therapeutic outcome is encouraging others to become engrossed in the process of reading literature.

In 1950, Caroline Shrodes suggested that therapeutic transformations can happen to all readers. In an often cited passage, she says that bibliotherapy is a process "that lies within the province of every teacher of literature in working with every child in a group. It does not assume that the teacher must be a skilled therapist. . . . Rather, it conveys the idea that all teachers must be aware of the effects of reading upon children and must realize that, through literature, most children can be helped" (Russell & Shrodes, p. 335).

This is a provocative declaration for those of us who advocate the healing power of the arts. For many, the idea that a relationship with an artistic expression heals without the involvement of a trained therapist may threaten the identity of our profession. As I have mentioned earlier, healing through the arts happens inside and outside professional therapist-client relationships. By focusing exclusively on the important objective of advancing the professional and employment needs of expressive arts therapists, the field misses the larger need to make the process of artistic healing available to people everywhere.

A mentally challenged poet and painter in my community spoke of how creative expression relaxes and clears her mind when she returns from a day of work. She describes how she "learns a lot when it comes from the heart" and how creation generates the enjoyment of what becomes "her moment." These effects occur completely within the woman's private relationship with the creative process in reading and expressing herself.

Another person describes how reading helps to carry her beyond the tedium of her job and offers an imaginative adventure. Creative expression and reading become sanctuaries available to every person who makes a commitment to these processes.

I know from my own experience in reading poems and literature how my solitary relationships with the texts have helped me. In addition to Roethke's In a Dark Time, I have been greatly supported by the line, "I learn by going where I have to go;" from his poem The Waking. In addition to repeating this passage to myself in difficult times, I pass it on to students who resist challenging work or to people in my studios that are reluctant to take risks in their creative expression. Passages like this one can sometimes act upon us in ways that are more powerful and influential than direct contact with another person. The passages that move us also have a permanence and lasting power that contrasts to fleeting interactions with another person. We can keep and mark them as reminders, and return to them whenever we are in need.

When pursuing the reading of poetry and fiction with others, I encourage expressive arts therapists to explore the person's literary interests and build upon them. Discussions about memorable and personally meaningful readings can begin the process of using literature in expressive arts therapy. In my work with others, we will select pertinent passages and read them aloud in individual and group sessions, utilizing many of the vocalization methods described previously–repeating passages, varying the tone and pace of reading, and moving expressively while reading.

I also encourage therapists to introduce texts to sessions when they can be useful. In keeping with the classical principles of bibliotherapy, a reading might be selected that relates to a particular psychological or existential dynamic that is being manifested within the expressive therapy process. I have found that virtually any quality poem, story, or passage can arouse significant responses from readers and listeners. The text becomes an opening to psychological contemplation and a stimulus for expression, characteristically generating responses in keeping with the principle of correspondence as described above.

Although I emphasize and appreciate the importance of reading and reflection on texts as an end in itself, literary works can also be used to stimulate creative writing experiences where we respond to a passage, emotion, or situation conveyed by an author. And, of course, varied arts media can be used to respond to a text with movement, voice, pictorial imagery, dramatic enactment, and imaginal dialogue as described in this book. The writings of others can become participants in the expressive arts therapy studio as if the author were present, and we generate creative responses just as we do with the artworks of the people working with us in the present.

If we accept the premise that literature can help people everywhere to heal themselves, it follows that so much more can be done to advance this cause with the general public, especially with children. Expressive arts therapists need to follow the example of Caroline Shrodes and take the lead in researching and advocating for more high quality art experiences for people in all sectors of society from young children to the elderly. We have a responsibility and opportunity to promote the public health benefits gained from a more complete immersion in the arts. The nature of consciousness is determined by what we read and do not read. The soul needs challenging and inspirational language in order to experience corresponding conditions.

As a reader, I find that I am greatly influenced, often in a completely subliminal way, by the tone and speech patterns of materials that I read. This reality underlies the difficulties that people who do not read widely have in writing and expressing themselves. Reading has a profound effect on not only thought and expression, but also on the underlying nature of our psychic lives.

Cultivating Language that Feeds the Soul

James Hillman, who declares that "a field is its language" (1978, p. 203), has brought attention to the lifeless jargon that often characterizes psychotherapy and psychology. For example, I constantly hear therapists speak about the "populations" with whom they work and the "interventions" they make in their sessions. In response to statements like these, Hillman asks, what kind of myth are we living when we use language like this? Listen closely to the words you are using, he might say; you are making people into "populations" and approaching "interventions" like a military analyst.

We might ask whether the language of expressive arts therapy has beauty, aesthetic sensibility, and creative vitality? All of the arts therapy disciplines have tendencies to define themselves through the most conventional psychological and psychiatric language, a pattern suggesting an inclination to borrow and imitate rather than create. This derivative aspect can be attributed to the interdisciplinary basis of the arts in therapy where there is a mixing of artistic and psychological cultures with the language of the latter often dominating the relationship.

It seems clear that a primary objective of the creative arts therapies must be the cultivation of language that feeds the soul, furthers expression, and does everything it can to shape the mind in creative ways. We need imaginative communications that transmit rhythm, energy, confidence, and a deeper commitment to creativity within our discipline. Our language has to do more to inspire an ongoing process of creative expression and transformation within the context of expressive arts therapy practice.

In recent years, I have seen many positive changes taking hold in the creative arts therapies in terms of the professional discourse conveying a more soulful, artistic, and authentically expressive tenor. Within the American Art Therapy Association, Bruce Moon has led an effort to change the tone and language of the national conferences. His presentations, in keeping with the storytelling and poetic qualities of his books are delivered through rhythmic, compassionate, and soulful readings that are more like a poetry reading than the traditional academic slide presentations that have previously characterized art therapy professional presentations. The energy and style of Moon's ways of speaking, and often singing his message, may be having as much of an impact as the words themselves. Believing that therapists need to live what they are striving to bring to others and serve as examples of the healing process of art, he has always shown his own art in his books and has organized publications that allow other art therapists to present their art (Moon, 2001), poetry (Moon & Schoenholtz, 2004), and music.

In other important creative arts therapy publications Stephen Levine's *Poiesis: The Language of Psychology and the Speech of the Soul,* (1992), Cathy Malchiodi's *The Soul's Palette* (2002), Howard McConeghey's *Art and Soul* (2003), and Pat Allen's *Art Is a Spiritual Path: Engaging the Sacred through the Practice of Art and Writing* (2005) have made major contributions to changing the kind of language used to describe the work that they do with others.

In calling for a more sensory, poetic, and imaginative language in therapy and psychology, McConeghey says that the soul speaks through aesthetic perception and we should emulate children who tend to see more deeply than we do when looking at the world and perceive "the golden luster of essential reality" (2003, p. 7). Pat Allen believes that language in therapy should "extend the creative act" (2005, p. 66); Cathy Malchiodi wants to let artworks "speak their truths" (2002, p.105); and Stephen Levine affirms how "imagination is the healer" (1992, p. 92) in expressive arts therapy where we need to use language that corresponds to the whole complex of the soul's depths, memories, sensibilities, wounds, darkness, chaos, illuminations, longings, and gifts of beauty.

These writings by Moon, Allen, Levine, Malchiodi, and McConeghey have acted as a subliminal form of bibliotherapy for their readers. Individuals and the entire context of the creative arts therapies are being transformed through engagements with a new kind of literature that exemplifies how art and psychology can be fully and dynamically integrated.

I do not want to dismiss the need to interact with others within universally accepted language formats that join our small discipline of expressive arts therapy with larger health, education, and arts communities. But at the same time, I encourage expanding the boundaries of language, writing in ways that correspond to the work we do, and creating a literature that inspires and helps to shape minds and souls in more creative ways.

THE VISUAL ARTS

All of the previous practice suggestions, especially the movement related activities, relate in various ways to what I do with the visual arts in my studios. In the most elemental sense, I view painting, drawing, and sculptural construction as a process of "moving" together with diverse art materials. Conversely, the movement, sound, and poetic methods that I describe have emerged from my experimentation with painting and drawing. My appreciation of the significance of essential gestures, repetition, and the progressive variation and unfolding of expression is grounded in my practice and research of the visual art experience.

The visual arts involve the making of images and objects and so I am as concerned with what we do with these creations once they arrive as I am with the process of making them. The bifurcation of process and product, a popular dualism in art therapy and with others striving to further creative expression, is for me a physical and artistic impossibility, an artificial mental construct, since these qualities are totally complementary and necessary elements in making a work of art. What we need to do is encourage more creative and less judgmental ways of embracing the art object as a partner in expression.

Because the visual arts have played such an important role in shaping my more comprehensive approach to expressive arts therapy, there will be some inevitable overlap between this section and other parts of the book. I give my attention here to drawing, painting, and the various three-dimensional materials that I use in my studios, realizing that potential visual arts media are vast and coverage of the full spectrum of possibilities is beyond the limits of this section. I have always made considerable use of collage, elemental printmaking together, various kinds of photography, and new digital media, and my studios strive to be as receptive as possible to a person's particular interests in the visual arts and other artistic disciplines. Hopefully, this review of essential visual art activities and their integration with other art forms can be applied to a broader range of media.

Making and Repeating Marks

As a painter involved with the expressive arts therapy process for four decades, I have increasingly simplified my methods of practice. As described in the earlier discussion about the interplay between structure and freedom in the expressive arts therapy studio, limits and clear directions can often further discovery. However, in keeping with my previous statements, I have moved away from leader-introduced themes unless people need this type of structure.

I concentrate on painting and drawing as kinetic as well as visual expressions. I say to people, "If you keep moving with art materials and continuously make marks with a sense of purpose, whatever needs to emerge from your creative expression will appear."

In this respect, art making can be likened to free association in psychoanalysis and contemplative practices, with Michael Franklin (1999, 2001) and Laury Rappaport (2008) making important contributions to integrating the latter with art therapy. We respond to whatever presents itself in the moment.

Images that appear from spontaneous gestures are in my experience more therapeutically and artistically significant that those that are made in response to themes introduced by therapists. The processes of art making and the compositions that emerge from a person's natural artistic movements are permeated with psychological and personal significance. And as I have described earlier, the resistances and challenges that may arise when getting started can ultimately inform the creative process and generate important expressions.

Approaching painting and drawing as movement expressions helps people to reframe the art-making experience in a way that side-steps the usual inhibitions and expectations.

Rather than starting with an image in your mind that you then transmit through your arm and hand to the surface, begin by making spontaneous marks and gestures with the art materials. Just move, I say, and keep moving. Repeat your gestures over and over again and trust that a composition will start to develop. Try to stay with the most essential gestures and let them build upon one another.

I describe how a painting and drawing can grow from the repetition of simple marks on a paper or canvas and by moving paint and textures on a surface. This is a universally accessible way of approaching painting and drawing and I am always impressed by the aesthetic quality of artworks that emerge from these movements. In my own art, I keep rediscovering how preconceived compositions tend to lack spontaneity, expressive power, and imagination. Often I will do my best work when I become annoyed with what I am doing and aggressively move the paint without a plan of any kind.

The gestures suggest more creative and original forms and combinations of colors. It is almost magical how these characteristics emerge and the artistic discipline becomes a process of keeping, eliminating, and building upon the spontaneous arrivals.

The discipline, I say, is one of staying with the gestures and letting them construct a composition. Where archetypal psychology says "stick to the image," I emphasize sticking to the movements of expression from which artistic images emerge. My orientation toward painting within the expressive therapy studio favors maximum spontaneity. As Vincent Van Gogh said in a letter to the young painter Émile Bernard, dated April 12,1888–"I follow no system of brushwork at all, I hit the canvas with irregular strokes, which I leave as they are, impastos, uncovered spots of canvas–corners here and there left inevitably unfinished–re-workings, roughness" (LuBow, 2006, p. 67).

I repeatedly observe how people start off with expressive and powerful graphic strokes and marks and then think too much, lose confidence in the process, and shift to making more stereotypic, consciously controlled, and schematic images. I do everything I can to help them stay with natural gestures and let the process of making basic marks change and develop organically.

Painting from the Whole Body

Although I appreciate the different qualities of painting and drawing on varied surface sizes, I will always begin my studio groups by giving people the opportunity to work large. An expansive painting surface welcomes expression and helps people move from their whole bodies as contrasted to more conventional notions of painting and drawing on smaller surfaces.

"Paint from your thighs, your feet, and your lower body," I say. "Try and relax mental controls and expectations." As I described earlier, I will make percussive rhythms in studio sessions to support letting go.

This emphasis on making visual expressions from the whole body infuses the artistic image with movement and energy. It also helps people to get beyond the inhibiting notion that paintings and drawings involve the representation of preconceived mental images.

I encourage people to use these bodily gestures as a way of establishing the more general compositional structure of a picture which can be further developed with smaller gestures and brush strokes. I also feel that this bodily approach to painting encourages a more complete expression of energy within the art-making process.

Artworks made in this way are reliably expressive and they offer people a universally accessible and aesthetically stimulating way of beginning the painting and drawing process. As I have mentioned previously, the main deterrent to actualizing this expressive potential is personal doubt, debilitating self-criticism, and the inability to sustain the making of gestures with a belief that significant imagery will result from the most basic movements.

Sequential Images and Creating a Series

As with creative movement and sound improvisation, one painting and drawing will emerge from another and carry the overall process of expression in a purposeful direction. Making a series of pictures gives us the opportunity to continuously explore a feeling or an idea in different ways. The sequence of images is a palpable affirmation of how we change and alter interpretations of life situations even when feeling stuck or fixated on a particular perspective on a problem.

Changes in attitudes and psychological states occur in correspondence to what is taking place within the process of making art and the contemplation of images that manifest different conditions of life. In this sense, the process of art and the pictures that we make are sometimes a step or two ahead of the reflecting mind.

Often with a series of pictures, we need the fifth, sixth, or seventh image to more completely understand what begins to emerge in the earlier paintings or drawings. In this kind of sequence, the process of expression is incremental and the images further a more complete communication by building upon one another.

Conversely, we might also discover through an extended series of images that the first painting or drawing conveyed a full representation of a particular feeling or condition that we could not at first appreciate.

The series of pictures affirms how expression is a process, a sequence of events that build upon and relate to one another with each particular instance being understood more completely when viewed within the larger context. The succession of images also helps us realize how an individual artwork is an accumulation of many different phases of emanation, building upon pictures within pictures, with each segment of materialization playing an important part in the whole process of expression.

Objects and Materials from Nature

Within my group studios the two-dimensional constants of painting and drawing are accompanied by the equally regular process of making objects and constructions with materials gathered from nature. Years of practice have brought me to these two primary and complementary domains of visual art making. The object-making activities introduce the important discipline of sculpture and construction with physical materials.

I always include modeling and the making of objects with clay in my studios. Like painting and drawing, this earthen medium has endless artistic potential and everything that I say above with regard to painting and drawing can be applied to clay—working with the whole body, building from repetitions of simple marks and shapes, working sequentially and enabling the process of change within the medium and the emergence of new forms and discoveries to suggest corresponding inner states within the person. In addition to its sculptural and image-making qualities, clay also introduces an important tactile sensibility into the expressive arts therapy studio which accounts for its appeal to many people. Occasionally, some participants will have difficulty getting their hands dirty and immersing themselves in the physicality and sensuousness of this medium, but these tensions can also hold the sources for psychological inquiry and new learning. Michelle Rhodes describes how the different physical conditions of clay from moist and supple to hard, dry, and "cooked" can be analogized to different emotional states (2008, p. 35).

The power and significance of clay lies largely in its simplicity, its ancient presence in the world, and it ability to provide opportunities for a vast range of constructions from the most elemental coils, orbs, and slabs to highly refined objects and environments. The medium is perhaps the most amenable of all visual art materials to being shaped in response to touch.

Where clay requires shaping by the artist, constructions made with sticks, grasses, shells, pine cones, stones and other natural materials give us the opportunity to bind pre-existing things together into new forms and relationships. In my studios, we make these sculptural objects by fastening materials together with twin, wire, or natural substances. Working with materials from nature tends to infuse the studio with a shamanic and sacred atmosphere. The natural things carry and convey spirits associated with memories of their places of origin together with a sense of the life forces that brought them into being.

We will use these materials to make hand-held objects that become partners in creative movement, drama, and ritual. Individuals and groups will also create stationery constructions and sculptural environments within the studio and on-site in nature with stones, wood, found objects, and things gathered from the site.

Shrine Making and Creating Environments

Some of the most personal and deeply moving work that I have observed in expressive arts therapy has been focused on creative interactions with objects and photographs that connect to other people, memories, and desires.

Judy Weiser (1993) and Jerry Fryrear and Irene Corbit (1992) have written about the psychological and artistic significance of family photographs and the process of taking photos of personally significant places and things. Photography is an art form that can in and of itself generate a lifetime of expressive arts therapy practice (Krauss & Fryrear, 1983).

In my book *Earth Angels: Engaging the Sacred in Everyday Things* (1995), I describe the universal and often spontaneous way in which people construct personal shrines in their homes and work spaces. In the expressive arts therapy studio, we will similarly gather together objects, talismans, photographs, small artworks, and other things and arrange them within boxes and other enclosures.

The process of selecting and organizing these things within a particular space invariably generates fascinating and aesthetically stimulating configurations. However, what distinguishes this work from other visual art activities is the way in which the pre-existing objects, and especially those with personal histories, evoke emotions and memories of loss, happiness, and significant moments in a person's life. Within the expressive arts therapy studio, these personal objects, photos, and shrines are reliable sources of inspiration for stories and ritual enactments.

PERFORMANCE, DRAMA, STORYTELLING, AND IMAGINAL DIALOGUE

Performance art, dream enactment, storytelling, imaginal dialogue, and other forms of dramatic improvisation have become primary dimensions of practice within my expressive arts therapy studios. My experience supports C. G. Jung's observation that the inner life of the psyche in both dreams and imagination is essentially dramatic. Similarly, whenever we attempt to describe or relive the events of our lives, or envision ourselves living in new and different ways, dramatic enactment is the medium that is uniquely capable of holding these varied elements.

From the first days of my practice at Danvers State Hospital, dramatic improvisation played an integral role within our studio practice, and especially as described earlier when we introduced video technology. In the early 1980s, I began to give performance art a primary place within the studio and soon after we expanded the dramatic and imaginative work to include dream enactment and imaginal dialogue.

As I have repeated throughout this section, I am focusing on individual artistic media for the purpose of explicating their particular and distinct qualities whereas in practice, we will generally integrate the different arts. I am describing my work with drama last in this chapter since it is a discipline that most completely integrates all of the other arts as well as everything I have previously said about movement, sound/voice, poetry, literature, and the visual arts. And as suggested in *The Arts and Psychotherapy* (1981), the process of enactment is a common thread to all forms of artistic expression.

Performance Art

My practice of performance art began with the process of individuals enacting a situation, feeling, character, or a figure in a painting, drawing, or dream. We interpreted the images with our bodies and actions and gave them the opportunity to further their expression and connections to the artist through performance. The method has taken on a primary place in my work since it generates exceptional artistic and psychological depth via the most essential and universally accessible means of expression.

In keeping with everything that has been said in this chapter, I have continuously concentrated on simplicity in performance art, discovering that an uncomplicated orientation and economy of expression enhance a sense of presence for both performers and witnesses. Our performance art pieces occur within a designated time frame generally ranging from five to 12 minutes depending on the context and the time that is available.

The approach that I take to performance is closely connected to the visual art tradition whereby the artist becomes a part of the artwork, usually immersed in ritualistic acts of some kind. The performance will sometimes enact the most ordinary actions of daily life—sitting, brushing hair, pouring water or sand, cutting paper, ironing clothes while humming, constructing and deconstructing objects, dropping pebbles into a container or onto the floor. Within the theater tradition, this approach can be likened to experimental, minimalist, and psychological explorations of Artaud, Brecht, Beckett, Grotowski, Gregory, and others.

As stated earlier in relation to dance, we do not use recorded music of any kind and the performance utilizes only natural sounds. Extended dialogue and traditional dramatic scripting and planning are also discouraged. Rather we try to present authentic and primary existential gestures and actions that take on aesthetic and emotional significance through the process of enactment in the presence of others.

I ask people to merely begin with a sense of something that they might do and then allow the piece to develop organically. Performers generally plan the things that they will have with them, the arrangement of the space, and how they will present their bodies, while everything else is left to the process of emergence during the piece. However, in some cases, a performer may prefer to let every possible element of the piece emerge without plans. People are always surprised and even stunned by how the performance unfolds naturally and effortlessly when they establish a sense of complete presence and a total commitment to what they are doing.

If there is a figure or element in an artwork or dream that a person wants to know more completely, the performance might embody some aspect of the situation and typically the artist is able to gain a new understanding and empathy as a result of the enactment. Taking on the role of a dreaded figure can help us understand it more completely. As I have emphasized previously, we approach this form of artistic expression with a belief that even the most disturbing, frightening, and perplexing figures in our dreams and art are ultimately intimates of our psyches who we can engage as helpers and guides.

This particular form of deeply attentive performance art is a method that I have developed in my studios with a range of people from various sectors of life and it is a discipline that requires a relatively intact psyche, the ability to tolerate and ultimately embrace uncertainty, and the capacity to sustain attention and concentrated activity in the presence of others for an extended period of time. The commitment that a person brings to the work and the degree of immersion in whatever is being enacted, will always affect the power and impact of the performance.

Most highly functional people in society find it demanding to do this type of performance work and we have found that the challenge of the experience is a major factor in mobilizing creative and psychic resources and ultimately furthering concentration and a deep sense of presence during the enactment.

My work with performance and every method of practice described in this book has been explored in settings that range from groups of severely impaired psychiatric patients to studio sessions with experienced artists and therapists. I have found that the various forms of performance art that I use can be adapted to the needs of various situations and what the individual person is capable of doing. I never approach groups of human beings as generic "populations" nor with preexisting ideas about what a person or group can and cannot do.

Witnesses, as described earlier in this book, play a key role in creating the overall performance space. Through silent and complete focus they establish a safe and accepting environment which has an energizing effect. Performers are asked to stay within the space designated for the enactment and not directly engage witnesses with physical actions which tend to interrupt the concentration of the performance experience and confuse the distinct and complementary roles of performers and witnesses.

In my studios, we take a silent pause after each performance and the artist then listens to responses from witnesses and audience members without speaking. Witnesses express what touched them during a presentation or what they felt. I request that they do not to ask questions since this draws the performer into conversation and breaks the atmosphere of listening in a way that sustains the focus of the original performance. After five or seven witnesses respond, we take another pause and then the performers speak about the experience.

My first performance art experiences dealt exclusively with individual enactments. Since I was working with groups where many people might like to work and where time was often a factor, I began to experiment with group performances of two, three, and four people. What started as an attempt to deal with a practical problem generated a new and distinct form of group performance where up to four people work together at the same time.

Group artistic expression benefits from clear rules where each performer stays within a designated space and does not directly interact with other performers. These interactions are fine as a form of improvisation and play within other dramatic situations, but they break the concentration and distinctly individuated enactments that occur within performance art.

The performances can be likened to a form of surreal theater which entails what I call a "performance reality," which is different from the realities of daily life and often generates a certain degree of creative tension since the performers are engaged with intensely concentrated actions and they do not directly interact with one another. This suspension of typical reality creates a dreamlike setting which is fascinating to observe.

I refer to this process of people working together as the "principle of simultaneity" within performance art. The performers do completely separate things, yet they are totally united on stage, working as a team in making a whole that constitutes the different elements.

The work generates a creative space that can be likened to the theater explorations of Antonin Artaud who was similarlycommitted to essential gestures, feelings, bodily postures, and sounds that fill the performance space without any reliance on conventional language and talking. The actions of performers have an immediacy which directly impacts viewers without narrative explanations. The actions take on symbolic meaning and suggest sacred rites. The performance often becomes what Artaud called a "magical ceremony" (Schumacher, 2004, p. 83).

Individual performers describe how they are energized by the collaboration with others even though they are so focused on what they are doing that they cannot observe the expressions of partners. I refer to this dimension of group performance as the "sacrifice" that performers make for the overall sake of the work and its impact on witnesses in the audience.

In preparing what they will doing on stage, the performers are asked to be sensitive to sound since the auditory aspect will move beyond the individual performance spaces and generally be heard by everyone. Sometimes these sounds can enhance the whole performance and the different qualities can contribute to a meaningful whole, so I do not discourage the making of sounds. I ask that performers be sensitive to the effects of sound and perhaps not make loud, crashing sounds if partners are exploring tranquility.

Yet I have found that all artistic rules can sometimes be broken or stretched in ways that further discovery and add meaning within expressive arts therapy. In a certain situation, an intense conflict between different dimensions of sound might generate a state of discomfort which can be transformative. I have observed both positive and negative outcomes in relation to these conflicting sound expressions and in my role I try to make performers aware in advance of this dimension of expression and responsible for whatever they chose to do.

Acceptance of these guiding principles generally gives participants greater freedom of expression. Although chaos can often have a formative role within artistic inquiry as emphasized throughout this book, there are situations such as group performance where it can undermine cohesion and safety if it becomes a characteristic of the overall milieu. Performers need support and predictability in the studio environment if they are to risk embracing the unknown and personal confusion within their enactments.

As described earlier, the performances and the participation of witnesses establish a creative space that is characterized by an unusual sense of concentration and presence. Within this context the simplest gestures and actions take on aesthetic and emotional meaning and significance. This heightened awareness and the more general atmosphere of the performance space become primary vehicles for the healing that occurs through a deepened appreciation of the aesthetic and transformative qualities of everyday life that are readily accessible to us, but not usually recognized and savored.

Dramatic Responses to Dreams

Dramatic enactment has become my preferred modes of responding creatively to dreams. There is such a strong tendency in most people to try and conceptually figure-out and explain dreams that we tend to miss the opportunity to engage their mystery and imagination.

Jung's methods of active imagination offer many different ways of engaging dream images (Chodorow, 1997). In my studios, I will typically begin by having a person describe a dream and we will select a particular scene, image, action, or feeling that we enact in an extended and focused way. Words have an important role, but I find that dreams are interpreted and relived more creatively and completely through our bodies, movements, and dramatic gestures.

Before beginning a dramatic enactment, the dreamer is encouraged to tell and retell the dream in as much detail as possible, a process that helps us all become aware of things that are not at first apparent. I and other group members try to withhold judgments and psychological explanations as part of an overall effort to reveal the expressive nature of figures, scenes, and things that appear within the dream. We discover how this kind of ongoing description of elements, actions, and feelings helps us establish a much deeper sense of the dream whereas facile psychological and conceptual interpretations tend to cut off the dream's ability to continuously act upon our sensibilities and thoughts.

Narrative and verbal descriptions can then be greatly enhanced by imaginative engagements which enable the dreamer and witnesses to establish a more comprehensive relationship to the dream and the psychic realm from which it originates. As my Jesuit mentor used to say to me, reason is a wonderful instrument, but it has its limits. When we use all of our senses in cooperation with the mind, we penetrate realms that cannot be accessed through verbal analysis alone.

The core premise of my work with dreams and all other forms of artistic imagery is that we want to get to know them better rather than try and determine what they "mean." The dream can be likened to a person, a place, or circumstance that we come to understand through experience and extended contact.

The discipline of enacting a dream is one of immersing ourselves in a situation or a feeling as completely as possible. We strive to keep the relationship alive and experience it in varied ways, with different senses, and from multiple perspectives. All of these methods are concerned with holding onto the dream image and allowing it to work on us. We are interested in appreciating the dream's complexity and depth and do our best to resist the inclination to reduce it to a single meaning. As I say in my studios, we also want to infuse the psychic sense of the dream into our artistic expressions and our daily lives.

Where some perceive dreams as nonsensical discharges of physical energy, I approach them with a sense of wonder and admiration for their intelligence. I repeatedly discover how dream experiences gather together events and concerns from my day life and organize them into dramatic enactments that are sometimes wondrous and at other times disturbing. As emphasized in every aspect of my expressive arts therapy practice, the unsettling dreams help us pay attention to things that we overlook or deny during the day.

Since the dream operates with an intelligence that transcends rational and linear thinking, it then lends itself to ways of knowing and expression like dramatic enactment that correspond more closely to its essential nature. For example, rather than trying to explain a paradoxical situation in a dream, we enact it. We might find that allowing ourselves to be carried away by a torrential stream will result in being taken to a place where we need to go. We might fight furiously against the surging water in the dream and repeat these gestures in a dramatic enactment only to discover that when we tire of the effort, we are overcome with a sense of relaxation and flow.

When we stop talking about dream scenarios and enact them through our bodies, we accept and understand them in a more complete way. The bodily enactment generates a comprehensive integration of the dream and day worlds and creates a new experiential basis for conceptual insight.

By dramatizing the frightening figure that chases us, we find that it might be trying to get our attention. Enacting the pounding gestures in a dream might give us some insight into our needs to take it easy and not try too hard to exert our will on a situation, or perhaps the aggressive gestures are also encouraging us to become more assertive and utilize our power.

We might also speak to these figures, ask them to tell us about themselves, establish empathy and take them seriously, with all of these drama methods giving us the opportunity to get outside our usual perspectives on things. The creative imagination enlarges our vantage points on life and provides a more complete sense of reality.

Experience has taught me that the deepest and most complete sense of transformation happens when we are able to stay connected to the dream and keep its mystery and imagination alive in our lives. As a leader of an expressive arts therapy studio, my primary task is always one of helping people to trust that if they can relax the explaining mind and maintain creative contact with dreams, their lives and expression will be enriched.

Dreams and other forms of creative expression are modes of symbolic communication that will convey insights and expand our awareness of life. They are expressive vehicles that give form to aspects of experience that otherwise exist in non-conscious realms. But rather than simply acting as messengers that serve the conscious mind, I experience dreams and other forms of imaginative expression as companions and helpers that show us how to hold everything together in an ongoing process of experience that integrates all of our creative and life affirming resources.

Empathetic Storytelling

Within expressive arts therapy, we are constantly telling and listening to stories. As we let the figures in paintings, photographs, dreams, and other artistic media tell stories about themselves and their perceptions, I am continuously taken aback at how this process enables people to express themselves in more imaginative and insightful ways. Perhaps this results from having the opportunity to augment their usual ways of perceiving and speaking. I think it may also have something to do with the fact that characters in creative expressions really do have important things to tell us.

Although people in my studios will often tell stories about their personal experiences, I am more apt to focus the storytelling process on speaking from the perspective of figures, characters, and situations in dreams and artistic expressions. When we establish empathy with these things outside of ourselves, we paradoxically find that they take us closer to our personal feelings and life conditions. "They" generally do a better job revealing our emotional landscapes when speaking through us than we do when we speak in more self-conscious ways about ourselves.

When I encourage the dog in my painting to say something about himself or the trees to speak about their lives next to the water and rocks, I access points of view and creative insights that I do not articulate when I describe what I think is happening in a picture from "my" perspective. We can learn a great deal from things in nature and animals about how to be more effective in the world.

I continually witness how most people respond favorably to the suggestion that the painting, object, photo, figure, movement, or any other expression of imagination might have something to say about itself, its situation, its feelings. The idea of the story is in this respect a gateway to imagination which incites creative expression in a surprisingly universal way. I sense that people experience a relief of some kind when they are asked to speak for someone or something other than themselves.

Empathy with the figures in a painting, photograph, or dream enables people to access emotions and sensibilities that lie outside the realm of how we usually think about our lives and experiences. Perhaps we express our deepest humanity and sensitivity and even show ourselves most transparently and completely when we think we are speaking for another figure. The creative process of dramatic empathy is thus a therapeutic and healing condition in itself.

In a session with a group of young adults, I suggested that they approach their artistic images as oracles and ask them questions about personal concerns or areas in their lives where they felt the need for direction and guidance. This way of imagining artworks activated unexpected powers of expression and insight within the participants. When we would "ask the oracle" for help with an issue, a shift of consciousness occurred that enabled people to step away from their usual modes of thought and expression. Even within our most personal musings this sense of the other is invaluable in expanding perspectives and creative discovery.

Dialoguing with Images and Things

The various forms of dramatic enactment that I am describing here are manifestations of an improvisational theater of the imagination. Everything that we do in expressive arts therapy can be viewed as parts of this larger artistic and dramatic context.

The process of imaginal dialogue has assumed a major place in my expressive arts therapy practice over the past three decades because it expands the range of perceptions, viewpoints, and possibilities for exploring experience through words. The descriptions that I have given of the principles of dream enactment and storytelling apply to the process of dialoguing with images and artworks where particular expressive qualities are encouraged to speak for themselves.

As I emphasize in *Art as Medicine* (1992), imaginal dialogue involves a shift from speaking *about* the figures of imagination to talking *with* them. The tone of talking tends to become intimate and psychologically penetrating when we are given the opportunity to converse outside the usual realms of habitual speech and access more poetic and imaginative ways of viewing experience. Through dialogue, the range of "persons" is expanded and we are not limited to the first person singular, the habitual "I" position of regular conversation. Imaginal dialogue offers access to the plural voices and perspectives in a conversation and within us.

Most people find it difficult at first to speak in this way since it goes against the grain of our most accustomed ways of conversing and viewing reality. There is a certain loss of control involved that can feel strange at the start. When people feel that the process is a bit crazy, I underscore how it can be viewed as poetic and creative speech. "Poets," I say, "speak to rocks and trees all of the time and these elements in turn speak through poets and writers."

I lean toward modes of expressions that challenge our habitual judgments about the nature of reality and find great value in maintaining a certain creative tension by operating close to the edges of assumptions about what we can and cannot do. Discomfort is certainly not introduced for its own sake but as described throughout this book, it frequently accompanies expressions that take us into unfamiliar realms.

When people start to dialogue with images, they will often begin with questions–"Who are you? What are you doing here? What are you trying to tell me?" I discourage questions of this kind and taking on the role of interrogators.

The easiest way to begin an imaginal dialogue is by making simple statements "to" the image. We thus talk from our usual vantage points but address what we say to an imaginal other. Speaking "as" an image is harder for many people since it takes them out of their habitual reality. However, young children generally speak both "to" and "as" imaginal figures with a natural ease.

I try to help people pay as much attention to the tone of voice as to the contents of their speech. How we speak is often more expressive than what we say. We might state and restate an expression with a variety of tones to explore the range of emotions evoked by a particular situation.

These repetitions help us to speak in ways that feel right which is important since the manner of speech will often influence the impact of the dialogue as much as the content. The overall process is distinguished by the dynamic of interaction, give and take, and reciprocity. We enter into an "I-thou" and compassionate relationship with the images and artworks that function as partners.

As stated above, it is generally easier for people to start these interactions by speaking as themselves. I suggest beginning by just telling an image what we see when we look at it, how we feel about its qualities, what intrigues us. This way of speaking guarantees that we will have something to say. If we are able to feel compassion and express our sensibilities toward an image, the statements can quickly become intimate and emotionally moving.

I have also found that moving in response to an image for a few minutes in ways described earlier can help prepare people for more spontaneous dialogue. The movement tends to reliably activate verbal expression perhaps because it minimizes feelings of distance between the person and the image and makes use of the whole body as a conduit.

People are encouraged to take their time when dialoguing; to ease the pressure that we inflict on ourselves to say something deep and significant; to be comfortable with modest and terse statements; to take pauses and opportunities to reflect; and to generally try and let expressions emerge from what they see and feel. As mentioned in an earlier section, moments of silence are encouraged and I keep emphasizing that less is more and discourage the kind of compulsive speech that we often use just to fill empty space.

After speaking to an image in this way, we might ask it to respond; to tell us how it felt about what we said; to say something that it would like us to know about itself, something that might be very different from what we described; or to talk about how it views us.

When people are able to personify an image or object and see it as a living thing, as an intimate other, they have generally entered the realm of poetic and dramatic dialogue. The primary obstacle to this kind of speech is the literal mind that guards against fluid passages amongst different realms of reality. The core premise for using imaginal dialogue within expressive arts therapy is its ability to expand our resources for expression and understanding.

Perhaps because it most thoroughly challenges the limits of conventional reality, image dialogue calls attention to the wisdom and transformative powers of the creative imagination. When joined with all of the other expressive arts therapy media and resources described in this chapter, dialogical inter-action with the objects of expression provides opportunities to perceive and shape our lives in ways that are informed by a creative intelligence that can do so much to heal and enhance the world.

THE WORK AHEAD

My overwhelming sense as I complete this book which strives to document four decades of expressive arts therapy practice is that the work is forever beginning. As I keep emphasizing, the expressive arts therapy process is constantly being discovered for the first time by people throughout the world.

It is so wonderfully paradoxical how one of the earth's most ancient phenomena, healing through creative expression, is revealed with a freshness and novelty that continuously invites people to become involved. Everything about art and healing, from its way of entering the world to how it works, is grounded in a process of renewal.

There is a spaciousness characterizing the arts and healing that provides ample opportunity for newcomers from a vast spectrum of places. My hope is that this breadth of participation will keep expanding in the years to come and immunize the expressive arts therapy discipline from the narrow specialization that predictably snuffs out imagination. Creative vitality thrives when boundaries are crossed and widely different participants and interests come together to make something new and different.

I trust that our expressive arts therapy community is committed to being shaped by each new engagement, doing our best to model openness to what we do not know and to the process of discovery which is the essence of art. We find our deepest renewal in the energy and vision of new participants, and hopefully this book can play a part in sustaining these core values of expressive arts therapy.

BIBLIOGRAPHY

Adamson, E. (1990). *Art as healing.* London and Boston: Coventure.

Akenside, M. (1744). *The pleasures of imagination.* (No other citation information available.)

Allen, P. (1992). Artist-in-residence: An alternative to "clinification" for art therapists. *Art Therapy: Journal of the American Art Therapy Association, 9* (1), 22–29.

Allen, P. (1995). *Art is a way of knowing.* Boston: Shambhala.

Allen, P. (2005). *Art is a spiritual path: Engaging the sacred through the practice of art and writing.* Boston: Shambhala.

Anderson, W. (Ed.). (1977). *Therapy and the arts: Tools of consciousness.* New York: Harper and Row.

Arnheim, R. (1954). *Art and visual perception: A psychology of the creative eye.* Berkeley and Los Angeles: University of California Press.

Arnheim, R. (1971). *Visual thinking.* Berkeley and Los Angeles: University of California Press.

Arnheim, R. (1971). *Entropy and art: An essay or disorder and order.* Berkeley and Los Angeles: University of California Press.

Arnheim, R. (1972). *Toward a psychology of art: Collected essays.* Berkeley and Los Angeles: University of California Press.

Arnheim, R. (1989). *Parables of sun and light: Observations on psychology, the arts, and the rest.* Berkeley and Los Angeles: University of California Press.

Atkins, S. (2002). *Expressive arts therapy: Creative process in art and life.* Boone, NC: Parkway.

Atkins, S. (2005). Artists in community: The Black Mountain College and the white mountain graduate school. *POIESIS: A Journal of the Arts and Communication, 7,* 108–124.

Berry, P. (1974). An approach to the dream. *Spring,* 58–79.

Betensky, M. (1973). *Self-discovery through self-expression: Use of art in psychotherapy with children and adolescents.* Springfield, IL: Charles C Thomas.

Bloomgarden, A., & Mennuti, R. (Eds.). (2008). *Psychotherapist revealed: Therapists speak about self-disclosure.* New York: Routledge.

Burroughs, W. S. (1959). *Naked lunch.* New York: Grove Press.

Campo, R. (1993). *The poetry of healing: A doctor's education in empathy, identity and desire.* New York: Norton.

Campo, R. (2003). *The healing art: A doctor's black bag of poetry.* New York: Norton.

Chavis G., & Weisberger, L. (Eds.). (2003). *The healing fountain: Poetry therapy for life's journey.* St. Cloud, MN: North Star Press of St. Cloud.

Chodorow, J. (Ed.). (1997). *Jung on active imagination.* Princeton, NJ: Princeton University Press.

Cobb, E. (1992). *The ecology of imagination in childhood.* Dallas, TX: Spring.

Coleridge, S. (1907). *Biographia literaria,* 1817 (J. Shawcross, Ed.). London: Oxford University Press.

Condon, W. S., & Ogston, W. D. (1966). Sound and film analysis of normal and pathological behavior patterns. *The Journal of Nervous and Mental Disease, 143* (4).

Creeley, R. (1970). *A quick graph: Collected notes & essays* (D. Allen, Ed.). San Francisco: Four Seasons Foundation.

DeSalvo, L. (1999). *Writing as a way of healing: How telling our stories transforms our lives.* Boston: Beacon Press.

Dickinson, E. (1924). *The complete poems of Emily Dickinson.* Boston: Little, Brown, and Company.

Eliade, M. (1964). *Shamanism: Archaic techniques of ecstasy.* New York: Pantheon.

Estrella, K. (2005). Expressive therapy: An integrated arts approach. In C. Malchiodi (Ed.), *Expressive therapies* (183–209). New York: Guilford.

Feder, E., & Feder, B. (1981). *The expressive arts therapies.* Englewood Cliffs, NJ: Prentice-Hall.

Felstiner, M. L. (1994). *To paint her life: Charlotte Salomon in the Nazi era.* New York: Harper Collins.

Ferrini, V. (1976). *Selected poems.* (G. Butterick, Ed.). Storrs, CT: The University of Connecticut Library.

Ferrini, V. (2004). *The whole song: Selected poems* (K. Warren & F. Whitehead, Eds.). Urbana and Chicago: University of Illinois Press.

Fish, B. (2005). *Image-based narrative inquiry of response art in art therapy.* Doctoral dissertation, Union Institute and University.

Fleshman, B., & Fryrear, J. (1981). *The arts in therapy.* Chicago: Nelson Hall.

Fox, J. (1995). *Finding what you didn't lose: Expressing your truth and creativity through poem-making.* New York: Jeremy P. Tarcher/Putnam.

Fox, J. (1997). *Poetic medicine: The healing art of poem-making.* New York: Tarcher.

Franklin, M. (1990). Aesthetics and empathy: A point of convergence. *American Journal of Art Therapy, 29* (2), 42–47.

Franklin, M. (1999). Art practice/psychotherapy practice/meditation practice: Sitting on the dove's tail. *Guidance and Counseling, 15*(3), 18–22.

Franklin, M. (1999). Becoming a student of oneself: Activating the witness in meditation and super-vision. *American Journal of Art Therapy, 38*(1), 2–13.

Franklin, M., Farrelly-Hanson, M., Marek, B., Swan-Foster, N., & Wallingford, S. (2000). Transpersonal art therapy education. *Art Therapy: Journal of the American Art Therapy Association, 17*(2), 101–110.

Franklin, M. (2001). The yoga of art and the creative process: Listening to the divine. In M. Farrelly-Hanson (Ed.), *Spirituality and art therapy: Living the connection* (pp. 97–114). London: Jessica Kingsley.

Fryrear, J., & Corbit, I. (1992). *Photo art therapy: A Jungian perspective.* Springfield, IL: Charles C Thomas.

Fuchs, M. (1999). Between imagination and belief: Poetry as therapeutic intervention. In S. Levine & E. Levine (Eds.), *Foundations of expressive arts therapy: Theoretical and clinical perspectives* (pp. 195–210). London: Jessica Kingsley.

Fuchs-Knill, M. (2004). *To day: Poems and poetics.* Toronto: EGS Press.

Gallas, K. (1994). *The languages of learning: How children talk, write, dance, draw, and sing their understanding of the world.* New York: Teachers College Press.

Goren-Bar, A. (1997). The "creation-axis" in expressive therapies. *The Arts in Psychotherapy, 24* (5), 411–418.

Gottlieb-Tanaka, D. (2006). *Creative expression, dementia and the therapeutic environment.* Doctoral Dissertation, University of British Columbia, Vancouver.

Grenadier, S. (1995). The place where the truth lies. *The Arts in Psychotherapy, 22* (5), 393–402.

Heifetz, R., & Linsky, M. (2002). *Leadership on the line: Staying alive through the dangers of leading.* Boston: Harvard Business School Press.

Hillman, J. (1975). *Loose ends: Primary papers in archetypal psychology.* Dallas, TX: Spring.

Hillman, J. (1975). *Re-visioning psychology.* New York: Harper and Row.

Hillman, J. (1977). An inquiry into image. *Spring,* 62–88.

Hillman, J. (1978). Further notes on images. *Spring,* 152–182.

Hillman, J. (1978). *The myth of analysis: Three essays in archetypal psychology.* New York: Harper and Row.

Hillman, J. (1979). Image sense. *Spring,* 130–143.

Hillman, J. (1979). *The dream and the underworld.* New York: Harper and Row.

Hillman, J. (1983). *Healing fiction.* Barrytown, NY: Station Hill Press.

Hillman, J. (1983). *Archetypal psychology: A brief account.* Dallas, TX: Spring.

Hillman, J. (1983). *Inter views: Conversations with Laura Pozzo on psychotherapy, biography, love, soul, dreams, work, imagination, and the state of the culture.* New York: Harper and Row.

Hillman, J. (1989). *A blue fire: Selected writings of James Hillman* (T. Moore, Ed.). New York: Harper and Row.

Hillman, J., & Ventura, M. (1993). *We've had a hundred years of psychotherapy—and the world is getting worse.* San Francisco: Harper.

Hillman, J. (2004). *A terrible love of war.* New York: Penguin

Holt, J. (2005). Creativity as the immune system of the mind and the source of the mythic. In C. Clarke (Ed.), *Ways of knowing: Science and mysticism today.* Exeter, England.

Johnson, D. R. (1984). Establishing the creative arts therapies as an independent profession. *The Arts in Psychotherapy, 11* (3), 209–212.

Johnson, D. R. (1985). Envisioning the link amongst the creative arts therapies. *The Arts in Psychotherapy, 12* (4), 233–238.

Johnson, D. R. (1999). *Essays on the creative arts therapies: Imaging the birth of a profession.* Springfield, IL: Charles C Thomas.

Jones, D. (1983). An art therapist's personal record. *Art Therapy: Journal of the American Art Therapy Association, 1* (1), 22–25.

Jones, M. (1968). *Beyond the therapeutic community: Social learning and social psychiatry.* New Haven, CT: Yale University Press.

Jones, M. (1982). *The process of change.* Boston: Routledge & Kegan Paul.

Kandinsky, W. (1970). *Concerning the spiritual in art.* New York: George Wittenborn. (Original work published 1912, *Über das geistige in der kunst*).

Kapitan, L. (2003). *Re-enchanting art therapy: Transformational practices for restoring creative vitality.* Springfield, IL: Charles C Thomas.

Knill, P. (1978). *Intermodal learning in education and therapy.* Cambridge, MA: Author.

Knill, P. (1979). *Ausdruckstherapie.* Lilienthal, Germany: ERES.

Knill, P. (1983). *Medien in therapie und ausbildung.* Suderburg, Germany: Ohlsen-Verlag.

Knill, P., Barba, H., & Fuchs, M. (1995). *Minstrels of soul: Intermodal expressive therapy.* Toronto: Palmerston Press.

Knill, P., Levine, E., & Levine, S. (2005). *Principles and practice of expressive arts therapy: Toward a therapeutic aesthetics.* London: Jessica Kingsley.

Köhler, W. (1970). *Gestalt psychology.* New York: Liveright.

Kossak, M. (2007). *Attunement: Embodied transcendent experience explored through sound and rhythmic improvisation.* Doctoral dissertation, Union Institute and University.

Kramer, E. (1958). *Art therapy in a children's community: A study of the function of art therapy in the treatment program of Wiltwyck School for Boys.* Springfield, IL: Charles C Thomas.

Kramer, E. (1971). *Art as therapy with children.* New York: Schocken Books.

Kramer, E. (1979). *Childhood and art therapy: Notes on theory and application.* New York: Schocken Books.

Kramer, E. (2001). *Art as therapy: Collected papers.* London: Jessica Kingsley.

Krauss, D., & Fryrear, J. (1983). *Phototherapy in mental health.* Springfield, IL: Charles C Thomas.

Landgarten, H. (1981). *Clinical art therapy: A comprehensive guide.* New York: Brunner/Mazel.

Landgarten, H., & Lubbers, D. (1991). *Adult art psychotherapy.* New York: Brunner/Mazel..

Langer, S. (1951). *Philosophy in a new key: A study in the symbolism of reason, rite, and art.* New York: Mentor Books.

Langer, S. (1953). *Feeling and form: A theory of art.* New York: Charles Scribner.

Langer, S. (1967). *Mind: An essay on human feeling* (Vol. 1). Baltimore: John Hopkins University Press.

Larsen, S. (1976). *The shaman's doorway: Opening the mythic imagination to contemporary consciousness.* New York: Harper and Row.

Leedy, J. (Ed.). (1969). *Poetry therapy.* Philadelphia: Lippincott.

Leedy, J. (Ed.). (1973). *Poetry the healer.* Philadelphia: Lippincott.

Lepore, S., & Smyth, J. (Ed.). (2002). *The writing cure: How expressive writing promotes health and emotional well-being.* Washington, DC: American Psychological Association.

Lerner, A. (Ed.). (1978). *Poetry in the therapeutic experience.* New York: Pergamon Press.

Levick, M. (1983). *They could not talk and so they drew: Children's styles of coping and thinking.* Springfield, IL: Charles C Thomas.

Levine, E. (1995). *Tending the fire: Studies in art, therapy and creativity.* Toronto: Palmerston Press.

Levine, S. (1992). *Poiesis: The language of psychology and the speech of the soul.* Toronto: Palmerston Press.

Levine, S., & Levine, E. (Eds.). (1999). *Foundations of expressive arts therapy: Theoretical and clinical perspectives.* London: Jessica Kingsley.

Levine, S. (Ed.). (2002). *Crossing boundaries: Explorations in therapy and the arts.* Toronto: EGS Press.

Levine, S. (2002). Therapy, trauma and the arts: Towards a Dionysian poiesis. In Stephen Levine (Ed.), *Crossing boundaries: Explorations in therapy and the art, A festschrift for Paolo Knill* (pp. 79–107). Toronto: EGS Press.

LuBow, A. (2006). Letters from Vincent. *Smithsonian,* (38) 10, 64–71.

Malchiodi, C. (1998). *The art therapy sourcebook.* Los Angeles: Lowell House.

Malchiodi, C. (1998). *Understanding children's drawings.* New York: Guilford Press.

Malchiodi, C. (Ed.). (2000). Special section: Is art therapy a profession or an idea? *Art Therapy: Journal of the American Art Therapy Association, 17* (4), 247–254.

Malchiodi, C. (2000). Alliances, partnerships, and collaborations: Maintaining and sustaining an art therapy community. *Art Therapy: Journal of the American Art Therapy Association, 17* (4), 242–244.

Malchiodi, C. (2002). *The soul's palette: Drawing on art's transformative powers for health and well-being.* Boston: Shambhala.

Malchiodi, C. (Ed.). (2005). *Expressive therapies.* New York: Guilford.

Marcow Speiser, V., & Speiser, P. (2007). An arts approach to working with cross cultural conflict. *The Journal of Humanistic Psychology, 47* (3), 361–366.

Marcow Speiser, V., & Speiser, P. (2007). The use of the arts in working with fear and stress in the Israeli context. In I. Serlin (Ed.), *Whole person healthcare, Volume 3* (249–258). Westport, CT: Praeger.

Marcow Speiser, V., & Speiser, P. (2005). A theoretical approach to working with conflict through the arts. In V. Marcow Speiser & M.C. Powell (Eds.), *The Arts, Education and Social Change* (101–112). New York: Peter Lang.

Mazza, N. (1999). *Poetry therapy: The interface of the arts and psychology.* Boca Raton, FL: CRC Press.

Mazza, N. (2003). *Poetry therapy: Theory and practice.* New York: Brunner-Routledge.

McCarthy, D. (2007). *"If you turned into a monster": Transformation through play: A body-centered approach to play therapy.* London: Jessica Kingsley.

McCarthy, D. (Ed.). (2008). *Speaking about the unspeakable: Non-verbal methods and experiences in therapy with children.* London: Jessica Kingsle.

McConeghey, H. (1994). Arnheim and art therapy. *The Arts in Psychotherapy, 21* (4), 287–293.

McConeghey, H. (2003). *Art and soul.* Dallas, TX: Spring.

McKim, E., (1988). *Boat of the dream.* West Roxbury, MA.: Troubadour Press.

McKim, E. (1999). Poetry in the oral tradition: Serious play with words. In S. Levine & E. Levine (Eds.), *Foundations of expressive arts therapy: Theoretical and clinical perspectives* (pp. 211–222). London: Jessica Kingsley.

McNiff, S. (1973). A new perspective in group art therapy. *Art Psychotherapy, 1* (3-4), 243–245.

McNiff, S. (1974). Organizing visual perception through art. *Academic Therapy Quarterly, 9* (6), 407–410.

McNiff, S. (1974). *Art therapy at Danvers.* Andover, MA: Addison Gallery of American Art.

McNiff, S. (1975). Strategies for unification. *New Ways, 1* (4), 2 & 15.

McNiff, S. (1975). On art therapy: A conversation with Rudolf Arnheim. *Art Psychotherapy, 2* (3-4), 195-202.

McNiff, S., & Cook, C. (1975). Video art therapy. *Art Psychotherapy, 2* (1), 55–63.

McNiff, S., & Knill, P. (1975). Art and music therapy for the learning disabled. *New Ways, 1* (2), 5–6.

McNiff, S. (1976). Art activities for evaluating visual memory. *Academic Therapy Quarterly, 11* (3), 283–296.

McNiff, S., & McNiff, K. (1976). Art therapy in the classroom. *Art Teacher, 6* (2), 10–12.

McNiff, S. (1976). Art, artists and psychotherapy: A conversation with Robert Coles. *Art Psychotherapy, 3* (3-4), 115–133.

McNiff, S. (1979). From shamanism to art therapy. *Art Psychotherapy, 6* (3), 155–161.

McNiff, S. (1981). *The arts and psychotherapy.* Springfield, IL: Charles C Thomas.

McNiff, S. (1984). Cross-cultural psychotherapy and art. *Art Therapy: Journal of the American Art Therapy Association, 1* (3), 125–131.

McNiff, S. (1986). *Educating the creative arts therapist.* Springfield, IL: Charles C Thomas.

McNiff, S. (1987). Pantheon of creative arts therapies: An integrative perspective (with commentaries by Thomas Moore and Irene Corbit). *Journal of Integrative and Eclectic Psychotherapy, 6* (3), 259–290.

McNiff, S. (1987). Clinical breadth and the arts: Interdisciplinary training in the creative arts therapies. In K. Bruscia & C. Dileo Maranto (Eds.), *Music therapy education* (pp. 177–185). Philadelphia: Temple University Press.

McNiff, S. (1988). The shaman within. *The Arts and Psychotherapy, 15* (4), 285–291.

McNiff, S. (1988). *Fundamentals of art therapy.* Springfield, IL: Charles C Thomas.

McNiff, S. (1989). *Depth psychology of art.* Springfield, IL: Charles C Thomas.

McNiff, S. (1989). The shaman as archetypal figure. *Common Boundary, 7* (5), 22–24.

McNiff, S. (1990). The artist as shaman. *Common Boundary, 8* (6), 11–12.

McNiff, S. (1991). Ethics and the autonomy of images. *The Arts in Psychotherapy, 18* (4), 277–283.

McNiff, S. (1992). *Art as medicine: Creating a therapy of the imagination.* Boston: Shambhala.

McNiff, S. (1994). Rudolf Arnheim: A clinician of images. *The Arts in Psychotherapy, 21* (4), 249–259.

McNiff, S. (1995). Keeping the studio. *Art Therapy: Journal of the American Art Therapy Association, 12* (3), 179–183.

McNiff, S. (1995). *Earth angels: Engaging the sacred in everyday things.* Boston: Shambhala.

McNiff, S. (1997). Art therapy: A spectrum of partnerships. *The Arts in Psychotherapy, 24* (1), 37–44.

McNiff, S. (1998). *Trust the process: An artist's guide to letting go.* Boston: Shambhala.

McNiff, S. (1998). *Art-based research.* London: Jessica Kingsley.

McNiff, S. (2000). Art therapy is a big idea. *Art Therapy: Journal of the American Art Therapy Association, 17* (4), 252–254.

McNiff, S. (2001). Pandora's gifts: The use of imagination and all of the arts in therapy. In J. Rubin (Ed.), *Approaches to art therapy: Theory and technique* (2nd ed.) (pp. 318–325). Philadelphia: Brunner- Routledge.

McNiff, S. (2002). The discipline of total expression: An abiding conversation. In S. Levine (Ed.), *Crossing boundaries: Explorations in therapy and the arts* (pp. 7–19). Toronto: EGS Press.

McNiff, S. (2003). *Creating with others: The practice of imagination in art, life and the workplace.* Boston: Shambhala.

McNiff, S. (2004). *Art heals: How creativity cures the soul.* Boston: Shambhala.

McNiff, S. (2006). The terrifying beauty of creating anew. *POIESIS: A Journal of the Arts and Communication, 8,* 100–103.

McNiff, S. (2007). Knowing Rudolf Arnheim (1904–2007). *Art Therapy: Journal of the American Art Therapy Association, 24* (3), 138–142.

McNiff, S. (2008). Creating with the shadow: Reflections on Stephen K. Levine's contributions to expressive arts therapy. In P. Antze & E. Levine (Eds.), *In praise of poiesis: The arts and human existence* (pp. 20–31). Toronto: EGS Press.

McNiff, S. (2008). Creative expression in service of others: Reflections on transparency in art therapy practice. In A. Bloomgarden & R. Mennuti (Eds.), *Psychotherapist revealed: Therapists speak about self-disclosure.* (pp. 219–235). New York: Routledge.

Mettler, B. (1960). *Materials of dance as a creative art activity.* Tucson, AZ: Mettler Studios.

Mirriam-Goldberg, C. (Ed.). (2007). *The power of words: A transformative language arts reader,* Keene, NH: Transformative Language Arts Press.

Moon, B. (1990). *Existential art therapy: The canvas mirror.* Springfield, IL: Charles C Thomas.

Moon, B. (1992). *Essentials of art therapy training and practice.* Springfield, IL: Charles C Thomas.

Moon, B. (1994). *Introduction to art therapy: Faith in the product.* Springfield, IL: Charles C Thomas.

Moon, B. (1997). *Art and soul.* Springfield, IL: Charles C Thomas.

Moon, B. (1998). *The dynamics of art as therapy with adolescents.* Springfield, IL: Charles C Thomas.

Moon, B. (2000). *Ethical issues in art therapy.* Springfield, IL: Charles C Thomas.

Moon, B. (2001). *Working with images: The art of art therapists.* Springfield, IL: Charles C Thomas.

Moon, B., & Schoenholtz, R. (2004). *Word pictures: The poetry and art of art therapists.* Springfield, IL: Charles C Thomas.

Moon, B. (2007). *The role of metaphor in art therapy: Theory, method and experience.* Springfield, IL: Charles C Thomas.

Moon, C. (2001). *Studio art therapy: Cultivating the artist identity in the art therapist.* London: Jessica Kingsley.

Moore, T. (Ed.). (1989). *A blue fire: The selected writings of James Hillman.* New York: Harper and Row.

Moore, T. (1990). *Dark Eros: The imagination of sadism.* Dallas, TX: Spring.

Moore, T. (1992). *Care of the soul: A guide for cultivating depth and sacredness in everyday life.* New York: Harper and Row.

Moreno, J. L. (1973). *The theatre of spontaneity*. Beacon, NY: Beacon House.

Morrison, M. (Ed.). 1987). *Poetry as therapy*. New York: Human Sciences Press.

Mynes, A. M., & Hynes-Berry, M. (1994). *Biblio/poetry therapy: The interactive process*. St. Cloud, MN: North Star Press of St. Cloud.

Naumburg, M. (1928). *The child and the world: Dialogues in modern education*. New York: Harcourt, Brace.

Naumburg, M. (1947). *Studies of the free expression of behavior problem children and adolescents*. New York: Grune and Stratton.

Naumburg, M. (1950). *Schizophrenic art: Its meaning in psychotherapy*. New York: Grune and Stratton.

Naumburg, M. (1953). *Psychoneurotic art: Its function in psychotherapy*. New York: Grune and Stratton.

Naumburg, M. (1966). *Dynamically oriented art therapy: Its principles and practice*. New York: Grune and Stratton.

Naumburg, M. (1973). *An introduction to art therapy: Studies of the "free" art expression of behavior problem children and adolescents as a means of diagnosis and therapy*. New York: Teachers College Press.

Newham, P. (1993). *The singing cure: An introduction to voice movement therapy*. London: Rider.

Newham, P. (1998). *Therapeutic voicework: Principles and practice for the use of singing as a therapy*. London: Jessica Kingsley.

Newsome, B., & Silver, A. (Eds.). (1977). The Addison Gallery of American Art: Video for special audiences. In *The art museum as educator: A collection of studies as guides to practice and policy*, prepared by the Council on Museums and Education in the Visual Arts (pp. 170–176). Berkeley and Los Angeles: University of California Press.

Nietzsche, F. (1967). *The birth of tragedy and the case of Wagner* (W. Kaufmann, Trans.). New York: Vintage.

Olson, C. (1966). *Selected writings of Charles Olson* (R. Creeley, Ed.). New York: New Directions.

Pfister, O. (1923). *Some applications of psychoanalysis*. London: George Allen and Unwin.

Prinzhorn, H. (1972). *Artistry of the mentally ill*. New York: Springer-Verlag.

Rank, O. (1968). *Art and artists*. New York: Agathon.

Rappaport, L. (2008). *Focusing-oriented art therapy: Accessing the body's wisdom and creative intelligence*. London: Jessica Kingsley.

Reich, W. (1973). *Selected writings: An introduction to orgonomy*. New York: Farrar, Straus & Giroux.

Rhodes, M. (2008). Getting the inside out: Speaking with clay. In D. McCarthy (Ed.), *Speaking about the unspeakable: Non-verbal methods and experiences in therapy with children* (27–44). London: Jessica Kingsley.

Richter, J. P. (1973). *School for aesthetics* (M. R Hale, Trans.). Detroit: Wayne State University Press. (Original work published as *Vorschule der Aesthetik* in 1804).

Rilke, R. M. (1984). *Letters to a young poet* (S. Mitchell, Trans.). New York: Random House.

Robbins, A., & Sibley, L. B. (1976). *Creative art therapy*. New York: Brunner/Mazel.

Robbins, A. (1980). *Expressive therapy: A creative arts approach to depth oriented treatment*. New York: Human Sciences Press.

Robbins, A. (1987). *The artist as therapist*. New York: Human Sciences Press.

Roethke, T. (1966). *Collected poems*. Garden City, NY: Doubleday.

Rogers, N. (1993). *The creativity connection: Expressive arts as healing*. Palo Alto, CA: Science and Behavior Books.

Rubin, J. (1978). *Child art therapy*. New York: Van Nostrand, Rheinhold.

Rubin, J. (1984). *The art of art therapy*. New York: Brunner/Mazel.

Rubin, R. (1978). *Bibliotherapy sourcebook.* Phoenix, AZ: Oryx.

Rubin, R. (1978). *Using bibliotherapy: A guide to theory and practice.* Phoenix, AZ: Oryx.

Russell, D., & Shrodes, C. (1950). Contributions of research in bibliotherapy to the language arts program. *The School Review, 58,* 335–342, 411–420.

Salomon, C. (1981). *Charlotte: Life or theater? An autobiographical play by Charlotte Salomon* (L. Vennewitz, Trans.). New York: Viking.

Schumacher, C. (Ed.). (2004). *Artaud on theatre.* Chicago: Ivan R. Dee.

Serlin, I. (Ed.). (2007). *Whole person healthcare.* Westport, CT: Praeger.

Serlin, I. (2007). The arts therapies: Whole person integrative approaches to healthcare. *The California Psychologist* (40), 6–9.

Shrodes, C. (1949). *Bibliotherapy: A theoretical and clinical-experimental study.* Unpublished Ph.D. dissertation. Berkeley, CA: University of California.

Speiser, P. (1996). *The development of an expressive arts therapist as a paradigm for the development of a field.* Doctoral dissertation, Union Institute and University.

Stanislavski, C. (1971). *Creating a role* (E. R. Hapgood, Trans.). New York: Theatre Arts Books.

Stanislavski, C. (1976). *An actor prepares* (E. R. Hapgood, Trans.). New York: Theatre Arts Books.

Suzuki, S. (1989). *Zen mind: Beginner's mind.* New York: Weatherhill.

Temin, C. (1991). A little museum with a mission. *Boston Globe,* January 2.

Tøjner, P. E. (2003). *Munch: In his own words.* Munich, Prestel Verlag.

Valéry, P. (1965). *Idée fixe* (D. Paul, Trans.). New York: Pantheon.

Wadeson, H. (1980). *Art psychotherapy.* New York: John Wiley & Sons.

Watkins, M. (1983). The characters speak because they want to speak. *Spring,* 13–33.

Webb, P. (1989). *Portrait of David Hockney.* New York: Dutton.

Watkins, M. (1986). *Invisible guests: The development of imaginal dialogue.* Hillsdale, NJ: Analytic Press.

Weiner, R. (2007). *Contemplating improvisation.* Masters project video, Lesley University.

Weiser, J. (1993). *Phototherapy techniques.* San Francisco: Jossey Bass.

White, H. (1978). *Tropics of discourse: Essays in cultural criticism.* Baltimore: The Johns Hopkins University Press.

Whitman, W. (1926). *Leaves of grass.* New York: Doubleday.

Winnicott, D. W. (1969). The use of an object. *International Journal of Psycho-Analysis,* (50), 711–716.

Winnicott, D.W. (1971). *Playing and reality.* New York: Routledge.

Yeats, W.B. (1989). *The collected poems of W. B. Yeats.* New York: Scribner.

CHRONOLOGY

Key Dates

March 1970. Shaun McNiff is hired as the art therapist at Danvers State Hospital, Danvers, Massachusetts and begins to work with all of the arts within the hospital studio.

1972. William Goldman, MD, the Commissioner of Mental Health for the Commonwealth of Massachusetts, introduces the term "expressive therapy" to designate all of the arts in therapy and appoints Shaun McNiff to represent this integrated discipline on an advisory committee promoting multidisciplinary training in the Commonwealth.

1972. The exhibit Art Therapy at Danvers is presented at the Addison Gallery of American Art, Phillips Academy, Andover, Massachusetts. A grant from the Massachusetts Council for Arts and Humanities enables the Addison Gallery to publish *Art Therapy at Danvers* (1974) and have the exhibit tour museums and universities galleries throughout the Northeast.

1972, Christopher Cook, Director of the Addison Gallery begins to work with Shaun McNiff and introduces video technology to the hospital studio which naturally elicits and integrates all of the arts.

January 1973. Shaun McNiff teaches the first art therapy graduate class at Lesley University.

March 1974. Shaun McNiff founds the Institute for the Arts and Human Development at Lesley University and develops the first multidisciplinary expressive arts therapy masters program as well as an integrated arts program for teachers. The Massachusetts Department of Mental Health awards McNiff and Lesley a grant to pursue multidisciplinary training in all of the arts together with psychiatry, psychology, social work, nursing, and other disciplines.

1974–1978, Shaun McNiff collaborates with Christopher Cook in running an expressive arts therapy program focused on the use of video as an integrating medium at the Addison Gallery of American Art.

1974, Paolo Knill teaches a music course in the new Lesley program and joins the Lesley faculty full time in 1976 and focuses his teaching on arts integration.

1979, Shaun McNiff works together with Vivien Marcow Speiser, a 1977 Lesley graduate, and others to establish The Arts Institute Project in Israel and Marcow Speiser becomes the founding Director.

1980, Paolo Knill in cooperation with Hans Helmut Decker-Vogt in Germany arranges a Lesley affiliation with the latter's Institut für Medien und Ausdruckstherapie. A new organization in both Germany and Switzerland is called the Lesley Institut für Medien und Ausdruckstherapie (The Lesley Institute for Media and Expressive Therapy, LIMA) and it becomes a Lesley affiliate program. In 1985 LIMA changes its name to ISIS, the International School for Interdisciplinary Studies.

1980, Phillip Speiser, a 1978 Lesley graduate, founds the Scandinaviska Institutet for Uttrykande Konst (Scandinavian Institute for Expressive Arts) in Gothenburg, Sweden and the program becomes affiliated with Lesley University in 1981. The first annual Nordic Conference on Expressive Arts takes place in 1982.

1983, Jack S. Weller develops expressive arts therapy courses in the Arts and Consciousness program at John F. Kennedy University in California.

1984, Natalie Rogers establishes the Person-Centered Expressive Therapy Institute, Santa Rosa, California.

1984–1988, Suzanne Lovell organizes an annual Creative Arts Therapies Conference at Sonoma State University in California and in 1990 formalizes the M.A. Psychology program to include 6 semesters of creative arts imaginal practices. In 1993 she originated the creative arts component of the Institute of Imaginal Studies, Petaluma, CA.

1985–1986, Stephen K. Levine, on sabbatical from York University in Canada, serves as a post-doctoral fellow at Lesley University and enters the expressive arts therapy community.

1986, Jane Goldberg establishes the Expressive Arts Training Institute in Newport Beach, California, offering a two year Expressive Arts Certification Programs with sessions held throughout the United States and internationally.

1988, Jack Weller establishes the second graduate training program in expressive arts therapy at the California Institute of Integral Studies in San Francisco, first as a certificate and then with a team of faculty adding an M.A. in 1996.

1990, Stephen Levine establishes *CREATE: Journal of the Creative and Expressive Arts Therapy Exchange* in Toronto.

1990, Phillip Speiser, Stephen Levine, Jack Weller, and Shaun McNiff discuss calling the integrated arts professional discipline "expressive arts therapy" rather than expressive therapy.

1991, Stephen Levine and Ellen Levine establish ISIS Canada, a graduate level training program affiliated with ISIS Switzerland and Lesley University.

1994, IEATA is established.

1994, Paolo Knill leaves Lesley to co-found the European Graduate School in Switzerland which is incorporated in 1996.

1995, Shaun McNiff leaves Lesley University to serve as Provost and Dean of Endicott College in Beverly, Massachusetts, and continues teaching and lecturing throughout the United States, serves on the Advisory Board of European Graduate School, and returns to Lesley in 2002 to become the first University Professor.

1999, *POIESIS: A Journal of the Arts and Communication* is established by Stephen Levine in place of CREATE.

1999, Sally Atkins establishes a specialization in Expressive Arts Therapy within the Master of Arts degree in Community Counseling at Appalachian State University in Boone, North Carolina. Atkins and colleagues began offering expressive arts therapy courses at the university in the mid 1980s.

2002, Cappi Lang Comba founds the Expressive Arts Therapy concentration within the Counseling Psychology masters program at Prescott College in Arizona and initiates the first Summer Institute in 2003.

2007, 7th International Conference of IEATA held at Appalachian State Universitydraws full capacityattendance and affirms the growth of expressive arts therapy.

2009, Paolo Knill, joins with Shaun McNiff, Vivien Marcow Speiser and others to celebrate three decades of expressive arts therapy in Isreal at an international conference sponsored by Lesley University and the Israeli Association of Creative and Expressive Therapies. Later in the year, the 8th International Conference of IEATA is held at Lesley University where the discipline of expressive arts therapy was first established.

INDEX

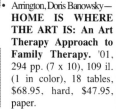
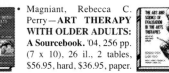
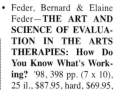